COLLECTORS' GUIDE TO
Nineteenth-Century
Photographs

WILLIAM WELLING

COLLIER BOOKS

A Division of Macmillan Publishing Co., Inc.

New York

COLLIER MACMILLAN PUBLISHERS

London

Macmillan Publishing Co., Inc.
866 Third Avenue, New York, N.Y. 10022
Collier Macmillan Canada, Ltd.

Library of Congress Cataloging in Publication Data

Welling, William B
Collectors' guide to nineteenth-century photographs.

Bibliography: p.
Includes index.
1.   Photographs—Collectors and collecting.   I.   Title.
[TR6.5.W44   1975b]   770'.75   75-22002
ISBN 0-02-000960-7

Also published in a hardcover edition
by Macmillan Publishing Co., Inc.

First Collier Books Edition 1976

Designed by Jack Meserole

PRINTED IN THE UNITED STATES OF AMERICA

CONTENTS

Illustrations / vii

Acknowledgments / ix

Preface / xi

Cased Photographs

Tintypes

Stereographs

Card Photographs

Photographic Prints

Photographic Literature

Photographic Miscellany

Photographer Listings

Photographic Archives

Photographic Societies

Appendix

ILLUSTRATIONS

ACKNOWLEDGMENTS

In 1972, when George R. Rinhart sold a collection of over 500 daguerreotypes to Arnold H. Crane, the transaction was described by *The Antique Trader* as "the biggest antique photographic sale—in terms of quantity, quality and price—in the entire history of the trade." This addition to the Crane collection also made it one of the world's most renowned collections of antique photographs in private hands. Fifteen choice daguerreotypes from the Crane collection are reproduced in these pages from negatives made by Mr. Crane, a prominent Chicago lawyer and onetime commercial photographer. For these I am more than grateful. Over 125 rare specimens from the Rinhart collection (principally card stereographs) are also reproduced in these pages. No greater motivating force exists in the field of collecting and preserving vintage photographs and photographic literature than George Rinhart; and one might search in vain to find a curator who could match his technical expertise or the wellspring of relevant historical information he seems always to have at his fingertips. I wish to pay particular tribute to Katerina Czarnecki, without whom this project might never have been successfully launched. Hers has been the role of principal moral support, as well as of unceasingly constructive advice and help in approaching the corridors of the publishing world. I am also indebted to Richard W. Strehle for his material help in preparing the manuscript, to Harvey S. Zucker for that extra dimension of interest and involvement in preparing most of the photographic reproductions, and to Jack Meserole for his tasteful book design.

Sources of Illustrations

COLLECTION OF GEORGE R. RINHART Pages 6; 24; 32; 36 (Figs. 2, 3); 38; 40–49; 50 (Figs. 1, 2); 52; 56; 58–59; 61; 62; 64; 68 (Figs. 1, 2, 3, 5); 69 (Figs. 6, 7, 10); 80; 86 (Fig. 1); 90 (Figs. 1, 4); 98 (Fig. 3); 102 (Fig. 1); 106; 110 (Fig. 1).

COLLECTION OF ARNOLD H. CRANE Pages 8; 10–12; 14–16; 36 (Fig. 1); 90 (Fig. 2); 98 (Fig. 1).

THE FLOYD AND MARION RINHART COLLECTION AT THE OHIO STATE UNIVERSITY DEPARTMENT OF PHOTOGRAPHY AND CINEMA Pages 18; 20 (Figs. 1–6, 8); 22.

COLLECTION OF HARVEY S. ZUCKER Pages 50 (Fig. 3); 82 (Fig. 3); 90 (Fig. 3); 98 (Figs. 2, 4); 102 (Fig. 2); 110 (Fig. 2); 112 (Fig. 4).

KODAK MUSEUM, Kodak, Ltd. Page 74

GERNSHEIM COLLECTION, HUMANITIES RESEARCH CENTER OF THE UNIVERSITY OF TEXAS Page 20 (Fig. 7).

COLLECTION OF WILLIAM KALAND Page 84 (Fig. 1).

COLLECTION OF THE AUTHOR Pages 2; 4; 26; 30; 33; 60; 63; 66–67; 68 (Fig. 4); 69 (Figs. 8, 9); 70; 76; 78; 82 (Figs. 1, 2); 84 (Figs. 2, 3); 86 (Fig. 2); 88–89; 92; 104; 110 (Fig. 3); 112 (Figs. 1, 2, 3).

PREFACE

The year 1839 is the generally accepted birth date of photography. But for ten years thereafter, no one published a single journal, manual, or book covering what was, or had been, happening in photography. Even men of science in the 1840s disdainfully alluded to it as "ingenious," or "pretty," but undeserving of serious attention.[1] For most of the world, photography continued to be known for a long time as "the new art."

Today exhibits of fine art photographs in museums, institutions, and galleries draw large crowds, but not until 1893 was such an exhibit held at a major museum—the Kunsthalle in Hamburg. Today no photographic works in the world are more renowned than those taken in the 1840s by D. O. Hill and Robert Adamson, using one of photography's first processes, the calotype. Yet they were little noted at the time and remained buried in Edinburgh until their "rediscovery" and first public exhibition in the 1890s.

Over the years, there have been few collectors in the field of photography to match those in the world of art. Among the earliest and largest collections was that of Gabriel Cromer, which was assembled over a period of many years in Paris before being acquired by the Eastman Kodak Company in 1939. Eastman paid half a million francs for the collection (equivalent to $12,000 in American money in 1939) and shipped it to Rochester, New York, in fifty-six packing cases "on the last freighter out of England at the start of World War II," according to Dr. Walter Clark, the retired head of the company's research laboratories.[2] Another famous collection is that of the British photo historian Helmut Gernsheim, described as "the largest set of photographic antiquities in private hands" when it was acquired by the University of Texas in 1964. The first major American collector appears to have been a Chicago perfume manufacturer, Alden Scott Boyer (1887–1953), whose collection of some 3,000 books, periodicals, and photographic albums was considered "the most important private collection of historical photographic material in America" when it was donated by Boyer in 1951 to the International Museum of Photography at Rochester (to which the Cromer collection had also been transferred).[3]

The first major U.S. auction of nineteenth-century photographs and photographic literature occurred in 1952, and the first auction of this type at the Sotheby Parke-Bernet Galleries in New York took place only as recently as 1970. Three years later, Sotheby's found that its business volume in vintage photography and photographic literature had reached the point in London where a special department was needed for it.

Since 1966 photographic historical societies have been organized in many U.S. and European cities. In 1974 a national U.S. society was founded, the Photographic Historical Society of America, to which local societies can become affiliated. A computer center has even been established to list all known photographic collections of interest to collectors and institutions.

In 1972 the first American professorship of the history of photography (funded by an endowment of $1 million) was established at Princeton University.[4] Pennsylvania State University followed suit a year later. There are now a myriad of newsletters and journals emanating from the new collecting societies. Recently one such newsletter circulating among camera collectors went out of business, evidently unable to compete with the explosive events in the field; in the final issue, the editor noted that the value of items had risen so sharply that collectors were becoming hesitant to sell, and that "antiques shops and others only too happy to list items in the newsletter found that they could sell whatever was on-shelf in days, without awaiting the issue of a newsletter in three months." He noted too that "collectors had found it easier to find each other as the first national directory [of camera collectors] was issued; as new groups formed in cities in every region of the country; as local groups found they could sponsor semi-annual trade fairs—at which new collectors could find each other; and as collectors became businessmen—traders issuing monthly or quarterly newsletters with lists that permitted instant telephone or mail buys."[5]

The display of photographs in museums, libraries, and private galleries is also finally coming on par with the display of noted works of art. In 1951, as part of the great Festival of Britain, the Arts Council exhibited masterpieces from the Gernsheim collection at the Victoria and Albert Museum. The council presented an even larger display from other collections in 1972. The previous year, *The New Yorker* had observed that "there has been a growing (and long overdue) interest in the works of the masters of photography as objects of acquisition, and within the last few years a number of galleries have opened where distinguished prints may be bought for sums that, as art prices go, are fairly modest."[6] Not everyone today would agree with that statement, as still more new galleries have opened and even long-established art galleries have begun scheduling photographic exhibits. "Prices of 19th and early 20th century photographs have risen sharply in the last two years, exerting an upward pull on contemporary photographs as well," commented the *Wall Street Journal* in October 1974.[7] Somewhat unheralded, the Smithsonian Institution opened that year a new Hall of Photography, followed by the more publicized opening eight months later of the International Center of Photography, New York's first museum of its kind.

Many people still question the logic of collecting photographs as one would collect works of art. To such people, it seems that because photographs can be made in any quantity from negatives, there is little point in attaching undue value to any particular print. But what they fail to appreciate is that many, if not most, nineteenth-century photographs in private hands—or still to be found—are separated from their negatives, and that the vast majority of these negatives were destroyed or have long since disappeared. As for nineteenth-century images in miniature cases (daguerreotypes and ambrotypes), no negative was ever involved in their production; each is a one-of-a-kind item, unless a particular specimen (for example, the image of a celebrity) was copied later by a negative

photographic process. But then, as with any noted work of art, who would value a later copy, however finely executed, on a par with the original? Many copy photographs exist of the few daguerreotypes made in the 1840s of Edgar Allan Poe, yet one of the originals brought $9,000 at a Chicago auction in 1973.

Materials and techniques used in printing photographs change with time, and the use of an original negative (if one exists) or copy negative to duplicate an item will never produce an image similar in character to the original specimen, no matter how much care is taken in printing or in toning the copy so as to mirror the color or effect to be found only in a vintage photograph. Many people fail to realize, too, that photographers in actual practice rarely make vast numbers of original prints from their negatives, and that prints by recognized masters of the medium, however old or new, are, and will always remain, collectors' items.

Make no mistake about it, the treasure hunt is still on. Today discoveries of nineteenth-century photographic treasures—as well as the intended disposal of known treasures—attract far greater notice, particularly in the press. When the earliest known photographs of the White House and U.S. Capitol (a collection of daguerreotypes) turned up at a California flea market in 1972, newspapers across the country carried the story. That same year, when the Royal Academy of Art in London decided to sell its priceless bound volumes of calotype photographs taken by the Scottish photographers David Octavius Hill and Robert Adamson (and presented to the society by Hill in 1848), there was such a public outcry that the society was forced to withdraw the collection from the planned Sotheby's auction. In the course of the outcry, the society was reminded that the Gernsheim collection had been passed up in England at the time of its original availability for a fifth the price reportedly paid for it later by the University of Texas.

Today history would probably not repeat itself in the haphazard way in which Congress, after the Civil War, appropriated funds to purchase some, but by no means all, of Mathew Brady's negatives and photographs. Vast numbers of Brady's prints and negatives found their way to the Library of Congress only after

World War II. Brady's grandnieces donated more than 3,000 negatives in 1954, six years after a duplicate set of 4,500 negatives had been donated by the son of Gen. Albert Ordway, who with Col. Arnold Rand of Boston had acquired the set in the 1890s. In 1970, Colonel Rand's own personal albums of Brady photographs turned up at a New York antiques fair (and have since been acquired by the International Museum of Photography in Rochester).

Then, too, there is the amusing story of how some of the best photographs of the 1896 Klondike gold rush managed to survive and end up in the University of Washington Library. It seems that the photographer, Eric Hogg, found the glass negatives too bulky to carry around with him, so he stored them at various places along the way to or from the Klondike area. Many years later, the occupant of a house in Dawson City found a group of the negatives stored in the walls of his newly purchased home. He was then planning to build a greenhouse, so he carefully dug them out to use in the structure. He tried, but could not manage, to remove the "gray stuff" he found on the glass; and just as well he couldn't, for the gray stuff was a negative image, and once this was recognized, the negatives ultimately found their way to safekeeping.[8]

Proper recognition of the importance of nineteenth-century glass negatives, however bulky, remains even now a matter of great concern to historians and collectors. Because they are bulky and it is costly to make modern prints from them, many such negatives remain unidentified or are simply discarded. For years people systematically removed the images from old glass negatives in order to use the glass again for new negatives or, as in the case of "Mr. Bender's Sad Story" (see box), to apply the glass to other usage. Another tragic case was the fate of many glass negatives made by Edward S. Curtis (1868–1952) of all of the principal Indian tribes in North America at the turn of the century. Photogravure prints (produced by a photomechanical printing process) were made from these negatives and published in a celebrated publishing venture backed by J. P. Morgan early in this century. But during World War II many of the original negatives, which had remained housed in the basement of the Pierpont Morgan Library in New York, were sold as junk.[9]

Only when one delves deeply into nineteenth-century photographic literature does it become apparent how many major works or even entire galleries of prominent photographers were destroyed by fires and other calamities. Perhaps the most noted U.S. example was the destruction by fire in 1852 of a New York gallery that housed the National Daguerreotype Gallery, comprised of all of the first daguerreotype portraits of American statesmen and other celebrities taken in 1842–43 by Edward Anthony and several partners. Only one daguerreotype of John Quincy Adams was recovered from the rubble of this catastrophe, which also consumed a collection (and perhaps the major portion) of calotypes and other early examples of photographs on glass and ivory belonging to Frederick and William Langenheim, the holders of American rights to W. H. Fox Talbot's calotype process (the Langenheims operated the gallery for several years prior to its destruction).[10] In 1867, just a month before his death, Antoine Claudet, Britain's most celebrated daguerreotype photographer, lost all of his daguerreotypes, negatives, pictures, and papers in a fire in his studio on Regent Street. Presumably this loss included the negative for a carte de visite of France's Queen Marie Amélie (see pages 57, 71), who with her husband, the deposed King Louis Philippe, spent her last years in exile in England and posed for Claudet at some point prior to her death in 1866.[11] C. D. Fredericks, for twenty years operator of New York's largest photographic gallery, was burned out in 1886.[12] The largest collection of negatives of Chicago taken before the great fire of 1871 was lost in an earlier fire, which occurred in 1870.[13] Charles W. Seely, publisher of the *American Journal of Photography*, twice lost his books and papers in fires (in 1874 and 1882), prompting a competitor journal to comment in 1896: "Perhaps to this double calamity is due the fact that of his *American Journal of Photography*, there is no complete file known to the writer."[14] In a report entitled "Great Fires of 1876," a New York insurance journal counted 9,301 fires that year, listing the following as "special hazards": hotels (318); planing saw mills (263); drug stores (145); churches (66);

MR. BENDER'S SAD STORY

[NOTE The following statement was supplied to Mr. R. W. G. Vail, Director of the New-York Historical Society by Mr. Charles Bender, and was called to our attention by Miss Alice Lee Parker of the Library of Congress. It is here transcribed, virtually verbatim, with the kind permission of Mr. Vail, Miss Parker and Mr. Bender. We believe that such reminiscences should be given currency, as they both focus attention on a certain regrettable lack of foresight, still not wholly overcome, and lay a foundation for further precision of the details. That wholesale destruction took place, there is little doubt. But the precise content of any lot about to be scrapped does not undergo the scrutiny afforded a lot of material about to be preserved, and these circumstances are subject to a certain amount of hearsay.

Mr. Bender states that he was born in 1880 and, in a letter, says that when he "bought the Brady negatives from Brady's nephew who worked for Mr. Rice," he was about 18 years old. Brady died in 1896. The main sequences of original negatives produced by the field photographers under Brady's administration and by the Brady Studio are at the Library of Congress, the National Archives and Records Service and the Handy Studio, all in Washington, with scattered lots of plates in various collections. But it is entirely possible that a certain quantity of Brady plates, not necessarily originals, found their way into Rice's stock.

Mr. Bender's letter further states that he now thinks he purchased the Panama Canal negatives from some photographer in Philadelphia, but not from Rau. And he says that "there were some cases of Brady negs. Missing Short on delivery in Phila., Pa."]

—P.V.

New York, Sept. 14, 1953

About 45 years ago I was in business with my father buying up old negative glass at Pennsylvania Avenue near the Capitol in Washington, D.C. There was a photographer there whose name was Orville Johnson, and I bought some old negatives from him. During my conversation with him, he referred me to a photographer by the name of Rice on F. Street, Washington, D.C. A famous photographer whose name was Brady worked with Rice as assistant photographer and left all his negatives of the Civil War (1861–65). Mr. Rice took me over to Ford's theatre where Lincoln was shot and there I purchased all the original wet plate negatives made by Brady. There were about 90,000 of these negatives stored there. There were a lot of original negatives made by Brady of Abraham Lincoln, General Grant and all the officials and celebrities, the entire collection gathered by

FROM *Eye to Eye*, vol. 3, no. 9, New York, December 1953.

Brady. I offered to sell the original negatives of Lincoln and other celebrities of the time to the Philadelphia Inquirer *and the* Philadelphia Public Ledger *and* The Bulletin *but they told me they already had negatives of Lincoln and although their negatives were not originals, they were not interested.*

So, my Dad said to me that if the negatives had any value, Brady and Mr. Rice would not have sold the collection to us, and so we went to work and salvaged the negatives by removing the emulsion and retaining the silver, and we sold this glass to photographers, and gas meter manufacturers, etc. We did not receive more than $1,000. to $1,500. for all this glass. Some of the glass was sold to one of the first manufacturers of dry plates, Corbet [i.e. Carbutt] (Dry Plate Company).

Then I bought a lot of negatives from Gutekunst, and a collection of old negatives from Bachrach's in Baltimore; also a collection from Foster in Richmond, Virginia. I bought a collection of old negatives in Montgomery,

Alabama about Jefferson and the Confederates of the South, and a collection from Moses on Canal Street (New Orleans). I remember buying Anderson's collection in Union Square, New York City. My father bought a collection of negatives from Tipton, Gettysburg, Pennsylvania. We used to buy all over the United States. We used to buy a million negatives a year, and a lot of the negatives contained the early American history of the different cities. I used to visit cities, populations of 25,000 and over, Pittsburgh, Cincinnati and all over the country and bought all the negatives for the value of the glass and silver. The thing that I had in mind was that the value of reclaiming the glass and silver was nothing compared to what those negatives would have been worth today had they been saved. If the public could appreciate the value to future generations lost when the negatives of the building of the Panama Canal by Count De Lesseps were destroyed. I bought those negatives from a photographic firm on Otis Street, Philadelphia opposite the old Post Office building there. I bought negatives from Rau, who was the official photographer of The Pennsylvania Railroad and from The Baldwin Locomotive Works in Baltimore.

From Bachrach I bought the original negatives of the hanging of Mrs. Surratt. I also got the negatives of those guilty in the assassination of President McKinley. Mr. Bachrach sold me these negatives in Baltimore, Md.

The reason that I have never given out this history about the Brady negatives was that I felt people would ridicule me for destroying the negatives of the Civil War.

I was a partner of my father and came to Philadelphia. My father had his place of business at 142 Race Street, Philadelphia. He was one of the pioneers in that field of buying up old photographic plates and reclaiming the glass and the silver.

When the publisher of the Reviews of Reviews of The Civil War [i.e. Photographic History of the Civil War, ed. by F. T. Miller, 1911] found that we had destroyed all those negatives he jumped three feet off the floor and hit the ceiling.

My present address is 1316 N. Venetian Way, San Marco Beach, Miami Bay, Florida. I was born in Philadelphia March 7, 1880.

This information has been kept quiet by me all these years on account of the ridicule.

What brought me up here was to see Mr. Vail about some information on the early history of Wilbur J. Florence, who was one of the founders of the Arabic Order of The Mystic Shrine, and decided to discuss the long kept secret because it would be of interest to the members of the New-York Historical Society and others interested in the preservation of things historically important.

I was present the night they brought up the miners in the Fairmont, West Virginia (1907) disaster. I was on the Chesapeake & Ohio railroad on my way to Charleston, West Virginia and it was snowing.

I also bought the negatives of the Englishman who was a partner of Brady. [i.e. Alexander Gardner] These negatives were stored in the warehouse of the Eagle Company, in Brooklyn. I bought negatives of the activities when they built the Capitol in Washington, D.C. (one thousand 18 x 22). I bought them from the heirs of the English photographer, partner of Brady. The heirs names were Armstrong.

I bought negatives of the Southern Confederacy from Foster in Richmond, Virginia and from Moses in Canal Street, New Orleans. I bought these negatives at the following prices: 5 x 7 $1.50 per 1,000, 8 x 10, $10.00 per 1,000, 6½ x 8½ $5.00 to $6.00 per 1,000, 10 x 12 $15.00 per 1,000, 11 x 14 $20.00 per 1,000, 14 x 17 $30.00 per 1,000, 16 x 20 $50.00 per 1,000, 18 x 22 10¢ apiece, 20 x 24 $200.00 per 1,000. We bought 100,000 plates a month or a million plates a year.

Most of the glass used for the indestructible eye pieces for gas masks in the first world war were from rejected plates sold to us by the Eastern [i.e. Eastman] Kodak Company of New York.

For the entire 90,000 negatives, after we removed the emulsion and sold them for glass, the entire value did not amount to more than $1,500. It took over a month's work to remove the emulsion and the silver. One of the Lincoln negatives today would bring about $5,000. There were a few dozen Lincoln negatives in that collection.

* * * * *

machine shops (53), and photographic galleries (37).[15]

While this book concerns itself with photographs made in the nineteenth century, there is evidence that photographic negatives and images made in the present century have not fared much better than their earlier counterparts. Undoubtedly there have been fewer losses by fires since 1900, but the destruction and discarding of photographic negatives and prints has otherwise continued. The question remains as to how extensively the revival of interest in nineteenth-century items will beneficially affect the concern for and preservation of negatives and prints secured in more recent years. Perhaps an even more basic question is, How firm are the roots of the new collecting phenomenon itself? According to one major news magazine, "the collectible photograph is suddenly a hot item," by which is meant photographs of *any* vintage.[16] But to another observer (the proprietor of one of the largest photographic galleries in New York), this has meant that "people who know nothing about photographs have begun to buy for status or an investment."[17]

Despite these sentiments, it appears that people today generally exhibit a better appreciation of photographs than ever before, whether they are viewed as works of art, or as irreplaceable images of particular moments in time, or as recordings of fashions, styles of architecture, or a cultural heritage worth remembering and perhaps emulating or reviving. Museums and institutions continue to evidence an interest in acquiring and exhibiting photographic treasures; photography courses at colleges and universities continue to proliferate; and the spread of new photographic literature, coupled with the reprinting of out-of-print works, continues unabated. Just as our vocabulary once assimilated such terms as *Americana* (the collection and study of things American) and *philately* (the collection and study of postage stamps), so now a new term, *photographica*, has made its appearance. In 1974 the editor of *Popular Photography* said the term "is struggling—successfully, I think, but struggling nonetheless—to creep into the vocabulary of photography." He described the new term in these words: "Photographica seem to define themselves as those components of the art, science and craft that are worthy of being collected, studied, discussed, researched, bought, sold, restored, and otherwise enjoyed for themselves rather than as tools, or for the utilitarian functions they normally perform."[18]

Perhaps a major reason why the movement for collecting and preserving vintage photographs has been so tardy in coming to life is because the parameters—particularly the nineteenth-century parameters—have never been clearly defined for the layman. If this book has any purpose, it is to accomplish this single, all-important task.

WILLIAM WELLING

New York, April, 1975

Cased
Photographs

The Elements of a Daguerreotype Made in the 1840s

1 The positive image is secured (reversed) on a silvered copper plate exposed in camera. No negative is involved.
2 A sheet-brass mat, typical of the style in the 1840s, is placed over the daguerreotype plate to give a protective border.
3 A sheet of clear glass cut to same size as mat is placed over mat. Plate or window glass was used.   **4** Completed daguerreotype is assembled and placed in right-hand section of a miniature case. Cases manufactured in the 1840s were made of wood and were lined inside with narrow strips of velvet-covered cardboard. This held the image snugly in the right-hand section and provided a border for an embossed velvet pad, normally glued in the left-hand section opposite the image.

DAGUERREOTYPES

The name *daguerreotype* applies to the form of photograph invented by Louis Jacques Mandé Daguerre (1787–1851), who introduced the process in 1839. With notable exceptions, daguerreotype portraits or views were not taken successfully on any large scale until after the introduction of methods for lessening camera exposure time from minutes to seconds (in 1841) and the adoption of the first true camera portrait lens (available in 1841 but not used widely until 1843). The first major display of some 1,000 daguerreotypes took place at an industrial exposition in Paris in 1844.[19] A French technical journal reported sales of 2,000 daguerreotype cameras and over half a million camera plates in 1847.[20] Horace Greeley's New York *Tribune* estimated that by 1853, "there cannot be less than 3 million daguerreotypes taken annually in the United States."[21]

A daguerreotype (see illustration, left) is a photograph that has been secured on the silver-coated surface of a copper metal plate. The metal plate, whose silvered surface was sensitized by the fumes of iodine, was placed in a camera and exposed. No negative was involved, and the image produced on the plate was the reverse of the image the camera saw (a situation that is overcome when a negative photographic process is used).

A daguerreotype image should be considered a delicate item; it cannot be cleaned or polished, but it can be restored if the image has become tarnished. Methods of daguerreotype restoration are discussed on page 27.

Daguerreotypes were made in many sizes, some as large as 13½ x 16½ inches at the Southworth and Hawes gallery in Boston.[22] But the standard sizes found today (and referred to by this nomenclature in photographic literature) follow.

Daguerreotype images were placed in miniature cases. These included leather-bound cases, wooden cases with embossed paper or papier-

Ninth plate	1½ × 1¾ inches
Sixth plate	2 × 2½ inches
Quarter plate	2¾ × 3¼ inches
Half plate	4½ × 5½ inches
Whole plate	6½ × 8½ inches
Double whole plate	8½ × 13 inches

mâché coverings, and plastic cases, sometimes mistakenly referred to as gutta-percha cases (no gutta-percha is known to have been used in their manufacture). Today the name *daguerreotype* is frequently applied to every form of old photograph in a miniature case, but as we shall see, this is also incorrect.

Methods of coloring daguerreotypes were introduced in 1842, but some doubt was cast on the widespread success of various coloring methods used in the 1840s when the applicant for an 1852 coloring patent stated in his application that many photographers had abandoned coloring because a large proportion of images so treated were clouded and spoiled.[23] Today, a finely colored, well-preserved daguerreotype has high value, but the vast majority of images with coloring applied to clothing or jewelry worn by the sitter have no greater value than daguerreotypes without such coloring.

The collecting of daguerreotypes did not begin on any sizeable scale until well into the present century. A collection exhibited in New York and Washington, D.C., in the winter of 1933–34 was considered at the time to be the most extensive collection ever assembled in private hands.[24] At one time, daguerreotypes were so common that metal dealers found it profitable to buy and melt them for the infinitesimal film of gold to be extracted from the mats and preservers.[25] Many antique dealers used to throw away the images in plastic cases in order to sell the cases as cigarette boxes.

The Elements of an Ambrotype Made in the 1850s

1 The ambrotype's positive image on glass **2** Resembled a glass negative, but it could not be used as a negative to produce positive prints on paper or other format. It required either a blackened varnish on the back side of the glass or a black backing **3** To provide the appearance of a positive picture. **4** Picture was then given a sheet-brass mat, **5** Sometimes a metal support, **6** And a gold-plated protector **7** To wrap and secure all elements tightly before the completed ambrotype was placed in right-hand portion of case. **8** Completely assembled ambrotype is shown separately.

AMBROTYPES

Ambrotypes resemble daguerreotypes and are frequently referred to as "daguerreotypes on glass," but they differ in that the image of an ambrotype has been secured on a piece of glass as opposed to a piece of silvered copper plate used for a daguerreotype. The best way to tell the difference between the two is to hold one in each hand and turn your hands slightly to the right and to the left. The ambrotype does not exhibit the mirror effect that the daguerreotype does.

Ambrotypes were first introduced in England in 1852 by the sculptor and amateur photographer Frederick Scott Archer (1813–57), who the previous year had invented the glass negative photography process. They were given the name *ambrotype* after the process took hold in the United States in 1854. If you remove an ambrotype image from its miniature case and strip it of its backing, it resembles a glass negative. But an ambrotype image is actually a positive image, as opposed to a negative image (which is used to make positive images). The sensitizer (collodion) was prepared and applied differently in each case; in the case of the ambrotype, a weaker solution was used, with the result that after the image was exposed on the sensitized glass plate in the camera, the plate could not be used as a negative to make positive prints on paper or some other format.[26] The ambrotype image remains a one-of-a-kind image on its glass plate, just as the daguerreotype remains a one-of-a-kind image on the silvered surface of a copper plate.

When an ambrotype glass image is given a backing of black varnish or paint (or black paper or black cardboard), it no longer looks like a negative, but achieves instead the appearance of a positive photograph (see illustration, left). During its lifetime (the mid-1850s to the mid-1860s), the ambrotype proved popular as a mode of securing a good likeness in the same type of miniature case that a daguerreotype had, but at considerably less expense. The result was that ambrotypes proved popular with the cheaper portrait galleries both in England and the United States but were not even made by some of the more fashionable establishments. A few ambrotypes of a beardless Abraham Lincoln survive, but these were taken in his rustic years. An ambrotype portrait by Mathew Brady is today a prized collector's item. In 1858 the New York police department adopted the process to establish the first police "rogues' gallery" containing filed images of wanted criminals and arrested persons.[27]

Because of an unpopular U.S. patent issued for a specific mode of making ambrotypes, photographers in the 1850s produced them by varying means, which causes some confusion today. The method patented in 1854 called for coating the image side of the glass with balsam of fir and then hermetically sealing a second piece of glass of the same size to the coated side of the image glass. This provided a secure specimen, and many ambrotypes found today have two pieces of glass sealed together in this manner.[28] But many ambrotypes were made with only one piece of glass. On some the image is secured on the back side of the glass plate and is covered with a protective coating of varnish, which may or may not require an additional black backing to render the image positive. On others, the image is secured on the glass plate without any suitable protective coating, and it can be wiped off the glass with a finger or a cloth. The way an ambrotype was made does not normally affect its value today, unless the image is improperly protected or is damaged. The principal means of determining an ambrotype's value are first, by the quality of the specimen as a photographic achievement, and second, by the subject matter or identification of the photographer if known.

UNIDENTIFIED FOREBEARS

"Millions of daguerreotypes were made, but of the surviving specimens, aside from well-known public characters, not one in a thousand can be identified." So wrote the editor of a photographic annual in 1949.[29] His comment applies equally well to ambrotypes. Few people made records in their miniature cases as to who or what was the subject of the image recorded. The next two or three generations, who knew the subjects, have long since passed on. Many cased images were thrown away; others lay for decades in attics or were sold to second-hand stores or antique dealers.

Daguerreotypes and ambrotypes that survive today do not all have the same relative value. Some are sharp and clear, with faces that are attractive by any standard or that portray unusual character; other images are dull, lifeless, or lacking in appeal. The miniature case may be in fine condition, or damaged, or lacking a cover. Just because it is a daguerreotype or ambrotype does not mean that one should attach great value to it, particularly if the image is a poor one of the countless thousands that must remain forever unidentified. If a daguerreotype exhibits lines or scratch marks on its silvered image, it is likely that someone tried to clean it with a cloth or rag, thereby substantially reducing its interest and value. Many ambrotypes found today exhibit cracks in their original varnish backing, and this, too, diminishes their value.

There are several ways to determine the value of an average, unidentified daguerreotype or ambrotype portrait. First, specimens bearing a photographer's imprint either on the matting or on a printed card contained in the case behind the image are of particular value to collectors. Secondly, valued images are sharp and clear and exhibit a pose that is natural and not tense (or wide-eyed, as is sometimes the case). The sitter in a quality daguerreotype or ambrotype is normally well dressed, and he or she may be holding a book or other object that provides a note of interest. The best American, English, and European specimens exhibit an appreciation for, and careful attention to, the dictates of traditional portraiture—interesting lighting and posing and facial expressions. Particularly in the United States, many people from all walks of life gravitated to the daguerreotype business in the 1840s, and the vast majority of them were untrained for a vocation requiring real artistic skill and talent. During the 1840s, too, the chemicals used in daguerreotype work were not uniform; exposures were a critical matter and failures were frequent. This was true even for the best photographers of this early period, such as Antoine Claudet, Britain's most celebrated daguerreotypist, who stated in an American scientific journal in 1845: "The great number of elements acting in the daguerreotype process, of which we are ignorant concerning all their properties, and the influence of various unknown causes, which undoubtedly perform a part in the operation, render the process very difficult and uncertain. So many conditions are requisite to a successful operation, that, indeed, it might be said that failure is the rule, and success the exception."[30]

A blackened or dull daguerreotype image found today may also originate from a later period (after 1853), when the so-called "cheap" galleries made their appearance in many cities. The editor of a photographic journal of the period described the specimens produced by such "25-cent galleries" as "perfect abortions in all points."[31] Little time was spent in posing sitters in these galleries; as soon as they were seated, an exposure was made and they were sent to an adjoining room, where the developed plate was soon ready. If they had any complaints, they could pay another quarter and go through the process a second time.

Franklin Pierce. This sixth-plate daguerreotype (several times enlarged) of the 14th U.S. President was probably taken in 1842, the last year of the one term he served in the U.S. Senate. The photographer was Pierce's New Hampshire neighbor, H. H. Long (later active in St. Louis). Pierce probably sat motionless for 30 seconds or more for this earliest known likeness.

CASED IMAGES OF "NAME" PEOPLE

"Oh, I'll bet that was *somebody*," most of us have said or thought to ourselves at one time or another about some figure we have seen passing by. Even if we didn't know who the person was, there was something about his or her looks or bearing that caused us to take particular notice. Time and again, collectors of cased images have experienced this feeling in examining specimens that they are considering buying or that they may already possess but cannot identify. Increasing value is being attached to daguerreotypes or ambrotypes of identified "name" people and to some extent even of suspected "name" people even though they remain unidentified. Unusually fine daguerreotype portraits of unidentified sitters brought $25 to $50 apiece at a New York auction of nineteenth-century photographs in 1971. A year later, a set of equally fine unidentified images by the noted American and British photographer John J. E. Mayall (1810–1901) brought the equivalent of $100 apiece at a Sotheby's auction in London.

Images of suspected "name" people should be set apart from other specimens and carefully studied or shown to persons knowledgeable in history who are familiar with the names and faces of people prominent in the last century. Quite a number of daguerreotypes of American presidents have been found among lots of otherwise unidentified specimens in antique stores and flea markets. One such item, a daguerreotype of John Quincy Adams, was purchased for fifty cents at an antique store in 1970. Clearly, it would have been well worth the time of the original owner of the Adams image to consult even the most readily available history books or picture books covering people, places, and events of the nineteenth century. The more earnest researcher will find "portrait gallery" books and illustrated biographical dictionaries in most major libraries; if they were published after 1850, they frequently contain engravings or lithographs made from daguerreotypes. A handy modern reference for those wishing to examine the faces of prominent Americans of the nineteenth century is the *Dictionary of American Portraits* edited by Hayward and Blanche Cirker (Dover Publications, 1967), which contains over 4,000 portraits dating from the beginning of the Republic to the twentieth century.

The value of the most coveted daguerreotype or ambrotype images of "name" people remains, and probably will continue to remain, elusive (as, indeed, the works of famous artists have known varying scales of value in the course of changing interests and tastes). The relative fame or public esteem achieved by the subjects clearly has much to do with the value of their likenesses. For example, a tiny ninth-plate daguerreotype image of Henry Thoreau brought $2,000 at a public auction in 1972, while a slightly larger sixth-plate image of British Prime Minister Benjamin Disraeli brought only $45 at another U.S. auction the same year. Considerable publicity was given to the sale of a half-plate daguerreotype image of Edgar Allan Poe a year later for a whopping $9,000 (at that time the largest price ever paid for a single photograph).

It is important to keep in mind that a daguerreotype or ambrotype portrait is a one-of-a-kind photograph. Copy daguerreotypes or copy ambrotypes were made from original plates, but this was never done on a large scale, so the likelihood of copies of an original image turning up is extremely small. After 1860, daguerreotypes and ambrotypes of many "name" people taken earlier in the century were copied in card photograph form (carte de visite or cabinet card) or as photographic prints, but while valuable as nineteenth-century specimens, these will never be valued as highly as the originals.

A Gallery of Rare Daguerreotype Portraits

1 Nathaniel Currier (1813–1888), the lithographer and founder of the firm of Currier and Ives, shown in his uniform as a member of the New York State Militia.　　2 James Merritt Ives (1824–1895), partner in the Currier and Ives firm, shown in his attire as a Brooklyn, N.Y., volunteer fireman. Ives's interest in volunteer fire work was expressed in the firm's many prints depicting firemen and fires.　　3 Dennison Olmstead (1791–1859), noted U.S. physicist and astronomer. He was professor of natural philosophy and astronomy at Yale from 1836 until his death.　　4 Sam-

5

6

7

uel F. Du Pont (1803–1865), Civil War admiral and leader of Union naval forces that successfully captured two forts at Port Royal in 1861 but failed to subdue Fort Sumter in 1865. Du Pont Circle in Washington, D.C., now bears his name.   **5** Wendell Phillips (1811–1884), the abolitionist leader and president of the American Anti-Slavery Society, shown with members of his family. Phillips was also a champion of the rights of the American Indian and of the early American labor movement.   **6** John Plumbe (1809–1857), proprietor of the first U.S. chain of photographic galleries in the 1840s and first to advocate a railroad connecting the East with the West. His various business ventures failed, and he died by his own hand.   **7** Edgar Allan Poe (1809–1849), poet, journalist, and short story writer. This sixth-plate daguerreotype brought $9,000 at public auction in 1973.

1

2

1 Military band, circa 1850s   2 Elephant and pinto horse, circa 1850s, possibly in Central Park, New York City

CASED IMAGE COLLECTORS' ITEMS

In addition to celebrities and scenic views, numerous types of daguerreotypes and ambrotypes may be considered collectors' items, including:

People clothed in their occupational garb or holding or displaying the tools of their trade
Military personnel
Groups of people
Animals or people with animals
Nudes
Images by identified photographers
Death portraits
Blacks and Indians
Persons wearing glasses
Side-view portraits

Many cased images can be classed as unusual for other reasons. For example, the sitter may be holding a particular item of significance —a sign, a book whose title can be read, or the cased image of a loved one—or the pose or facial expression may be unusually striking; or there may be something of significance in the background or foreground of the image. Images of American soldiers that can be verified as having been taken in the 1840s or 1850s should be studied carefully; the United States maintained only a nominal standing army prior to the Civil War, so a soldier who incurred the expense of having a daguerreotype or ambrotype likeness made prior to the war was very likely someone who intended to make the service a career and who subsequently rose to a position of command.

Death portraits were a peculiarly American phenomenon in the daguerrean era, and some photographers specialized in taking such portraits. Photographic houses even provided special framing mats in black, as well as cases of sentimental design, which are now quite rare.

Small daguerreotype and ambrotype images will be found set in lockets, breast brooches, and pins, as well as in bracelets, rings, and even the heads of canes. Such images, which will occasionally be found in a jewelry store or pawnshop, were made as early as 1840, when the miniature oil portrait was still a popular item. The first American-made camera, patented both in the United States and England, took images no larger than an inch square, and these lent themselves quite readily to encasement in jewelry. In addition, a number of early daguerreotypists—Mathew Brady and Jeremiah Gurney among them—were jewelers by trade before taking up photography.

The quality of an unidentified daguerreotype or ambrotype specimen has much to do with its value, too. Many ambrotypes were of poor quality because they were made cheaply and because the exposure was slow (from a few seconds up to twenty seconds), resulting not infrequently in an inferior pose or a bad facial expression. The English photographer and photo historian John Werge found the "low tone" of most ambrotype specimens "very objectionable."[32] But high-quality ambrotype images, clear and sharp in every detail, *were* made by the better photographers, and even Werge exhibited an ambrotype of his own making at an 1885 exhibition, thirty-two years after it was made.

Care should be taken to examine the matting or other elements of a cased image of unusual interest. Occasionally this will reveal a finely printed name, symbol, or other form of information to add to the specimen's interest and value.

A Gallery of Cased Image Collector's Items

1 A Southern man with daughters and their mammy, a quarter-plate image made by Thomas Easterly, the early St. Louis photographer.   **2** Two metalworkers with the tools of their trade.   **3** Jewelry salesman displaying a carrying case with earrings, brooches, watches, lockets, etc. Image was made by Robert Vance in his "premium" daguerrean gallery in San Francisco in 1854.   **4** Enlarged reproduction of a sixth-plate daguerreotype of a nude.

4

Imperial plate daguerreotype view of the interior of the Crystal Palace in London, made by John J. E. Mayall at the time of the 1851 exhibition of "The Industry of All Nations."

DAGUERREOTYPE AND AMBROTYPE VIEWS

Cased image views are among the most sought-after daguerreotype and ambrotype specimens. None is known to exist of New York City, where many of the foremost American photographers of the 1840s and 1850s operated, and there is an equal dearth of views made in England. Among the earliest surviving daguerreotype views are those of the city hall in Toulouse, France (taken on February 27, 1840), and a series made of buildings and scenery in New Hampshire and Boston by a Boston dentist in April 1840.[33] In a few cases, daguerreotype cameras were used to record panoramic views. This was first done in 1844 by Frederick and William Langenheim of Philadelphia, who took separate views of Niagara Falls from the same vantage point, then pieced the plates together, made copies, and sent the copies to the principal crowned heads of Europe. In 1845 a German photographer residing in Paris made panoramic views of that city by inserting a curved plate in his camera and moving the lens horizontally through an angle of more than 150 degrees during the exposure.[34] Panoramic daguerreotype views were also made of Cincinnati and San Francisco in 1846 and 1851 respectively.

Samuel F. B. Morse exhibited a daguerreotype of New York's City Hall in February 1840, but this image as well as others Morse is known to have taken has disappeared.[35] So, too, have daguerreotype views made in New York that were copied by engravers to illustrate an article on New York in the February and April 1853 issues of *Putnam's* magazine.

Occasionally major "finds" turn up. In 1972, the earliest known daguerreotypes of the White House, the Capitol, and other buildings and monuments in Washington, D.C., and Baltimore, taken in 1846, were found at a flea market in California. They were immediately purchased by the Library of Congress at a price reported to be $2,000 a specimen.[36]

In general, the value of most daguerreotype or ambrotype views may now be placed in the realm of three figures, with those of particular note commanding four figures or more. For example, a half-plate ambrotype view of a building and store with a large group of men standing in front of it taken circa 1857 brought $80 at a New York auction in 1971. In 1975 a fine half-plate ambrotype view of a western hotel with a stagecoach and a small cluster of people in front of it taken in the late 1850s brought $650 at auction in New York.

Today collectors keep a watchful eye out for celebrated items known to have existed at one time, but which are now lost. These include daguerreotype views made on at least three government expeditions to the American West in the 1850s; daguerreotypes taken by a photographer who accompanied Matthew Perry to Japan; and more than three hundred whole-plate views made in California by Robert Vance in 1849 and 1850 (see page 117).

Few "candid" photographs were attempted in the daguerrean era. In the nineteenth century these were termed "instantaneous" views. Cameras in the 1840s and 1850s, unless in the most expert hands, were incapable of stopping action during an exposure. But "instantaneous" daguerreotypes are known to have been taken, as for example those reportedly made in Le Havre in 1851 by Hippolyte Macaire of a trotting horse, a moving carriage, seascapes with waves, a man walking, and a steamship with smoke coming out of its funnel. Macaire's feats were reported in the October 8, 1851, issue of *La Lumière*, which indicated that the photographer could command 100 francs each for such photographs. In 1858 the *American Journal of Photography* marveled at instantaneous views made in New York by James Cady, but these, too, are not known to be extant.

Examples of Popular Embossed-Paper Designs on Wooden Cases

1 Lovebirds   2 Hummingbird   3 Scroll and leaf   4 Birds and flower vase   5 Octagon   6 Grapes
7 Lilies   8 Morning glory   9 Thistle   10 Lyre   11 Roses   12 Spear and rod   13 Flag   14 Eagle
15 Cross patee   16 Loving cup

WOOD AND LEATHER MINIATURE CASES

The first daguerreotype exhibited in New York, in September 1839, was contained in an expensive morocco case of the type used previously to house miniature paintings. While many of the first specimens made in England were placed in pinchbeck cases or in black papier-mâché frames similar to those used for silhouettes, quickly the custom grew, both in the United States and England, of adopting the morocco case for the silvered images of the new daguerrean "art." Then in 1843 a Boston case maker, William Shew, conceived the idea of producing cheaper, wooden cases that could be covered with embossed paper. This marked the beginning of a sizeable new industry, which turned out millions of cases manufactured in a variety of materials and shapes.

The most prevalent cases found today are those made of wood, and the number of different embossed designs on these cases has been estimated at between 500 and 600.[37] Less prevalent today are cases made of papier-mâché, papier-mâché inlaid with mother-of-pearl, tortoiseshell, and silk. The vast majority of these, as well as the plastic ones discussed later in this book, were made in New York, Philadelphia, Boston, and Connecticut communities including Waterbury, Watertown, New Haven, Derby, Bristol, and Southampton. Presumably the reason for such a proliferation of manufacturers lies in the fact that neither Shew nor the largest manufacturer (the Scovill Manufacturing Company in Waterbury) bothered to obtain patents for their designs.

Wooden cases were manufactured of shaped pieces of wood fitted together and glued to form two joined rectangular or square frames. The image is normally fitted into the right-hand frame, and a cloth-covered pad is usually found in the left-hand frame opposite the image. Pads consist of cotton batting covered with embossed velvet or plain silk in solid colors—red, blue, purple, green, etc. Occasionally a photographer's name will be found embossed in the pad covering, which gives the specimen greater value. Cases of cheap construction have a single hook for closing; those of more expensive design have two hooks. Thick, book-style cases made of papier-mâché (introduced in the late 1840s) were given more formidable, hinge-clasp closures, which were also adopted for use on expensive leather cases sold after 1850.

During the period 1827–38, John J. Audubon published his monumental *Birds of America*, which contained a thousand life-size figures of some 500 different feathered species. The volume created a widespread artistic interest in nature, which was carried through to the designs applied to miniature daguerreotype and ambrotype cases. Nature motifs are among the most prevalent on specimens found today.

Following is a list of the most popular design motifs on embossed paper, leather, and papier-mâché cases manufactured in the daguerrean era:

Birds
Flowers (particularly roses, depicted in thirty or more variants)
Fruit (particularly grapes)
Hexagon and octagon motifs
Lyres (reflecting an influence of Greek literature and architecture)
Loving cups
Spears and bows and arrows
Ornate circle and oval motifs
Religious crosses (popular in the United States during the Civil War)
The American flag and eagle (also popular in the Civil War)
Scroll and leaf motif

1 Book-style case   2 Tiny golden rose   3 Scenic inlaid mother-of-pearl   4 Animal design (deer at rest)
5 Typical inlaid mother-of-pearl   6 Washington Monument (early design)   7 Kilburn folding pocket case
8 Mascher folding pocket case

RARE EMBOSSED CASE DESIGNS

The most sought-after collectors' items among daguerreotype and ambrotype case designs today are those manufactured after 1850, when the cases took on greater varieties of shape, design, and construction. Among the most prized are the papier-mâché specimens containing mother-of-pearl designs. These were constructed usually with white pearls or more brilliantly colored "Aurora" pearls laid on a soft black japan varnish coating the surface of the papier-mâché board. The papier-mâché substrate was manufactured by heat-pressing glued sheets of ordinary paper. Even rarer are papier-mâché cases with hand-painted landscape scenes bordered by inlaid mother-of-pearl. Still another variation is the mother-of-pearl design on a tortoiseshell case.[38]

Thicker image cases made to resemble books first appeared in the 1840s, but did not gain popularity until the following decade. These are frequently fitted with two images, which face one another when the case is open. The edges of this type of case are frequently gilt-painted to resemble the pages of a closed book.

In 1852 a Philadelphian, John F. Mascher, placed on the market a daguerreotype case containing two images side by side on one side of the case and on the other a folding eyepiece with two lenses for viewing the daguerreotype images stereoscopically. A year later in London, Antoine Claudet and W. E. Kilburn introduced folding pocket stereoscopes of somewhat similar design in which the opened flaps containing the pair of lenses transformed the morocco case into a box stereoscope. All of these folding cases are now quite rare, although they were manufactured in quantity prior to the introduction of more formal box stereoscopes and later, hand-held devices for stereoscopic viewing.

Also extremely rare today are case designs depicting rural scenes or persons or animals in a scenic setting with a country house (or a particular homestead, such as Washington Irving's on the Hudson). A leather case exists with the intended (but later amended) design for the Washington Monument in Washington, D.C., on it, and plastic cases were produced with several versions of the Washington Monument in Richmond, Va. No case design is known to exist of the first Washington Monument erected in Baltimore in 1825, however, and such an item, if found, would be of exceedingly high value.

Only a few examples are known to be extant of leather cases with animal design motifs. Equally rare are cases with a silk covering. Leather cases bearing a tiny gold rose in the center are also extremely rare, due to the fact that in the 1840s a golden rose was a symbol of high position and honor and therefore not often used in case design.[39]

Although case designs of flower arrangements in baskets are not uncommon, designs of flower or fruit arrangements in vases, urns, or goblets are.

Examples of Rare Plastic "Union" Case Designs

1 Indian profile   2 Angel carrying babies   3 The Lord's Prayer   4 Union Forever   5 Egyptian women and baby   6 Landing of Columbus   7 Dog holding basket   8 Highland hunter   9 Scroll, Constitution and laws   10 Church window   11 Sailboat   12 Holy Family   13 Horse race   14 Civil War camp scene   15 Sailor with telescope

PLASTIC "UNION" CASES

Except for those wooden or leather cases bearing unique embossed design motifs, plastic cases for housing daguerreotypes and ambrotypes constitute today the principal collector's items in the miniature case field. These "union" cases (so named because the word *union* appeared in the patent) made their appearance in 1854. Union cases are frequently but mistakenly referred to as gutta-percha cases, owing to a common misconception that they were made from the rubberlike vegetable substance called gutta-percha, which is obtained by extracting and drying the sap of certain trees found in the East Indies, Malaya, and other equatorial areas. Instead, union cases were made of a plastic material consisting of shellac, black or brown coloring, and excelsior, ground wood, or sawdust pressed in dies or molds of exquisite and detailed design. Their manufacture actually marked the beginning of thermoplastic molding, although the feat went unheralded at the time. Despite the fact that union cases resemble hard rubber, they do not possess the sturdy characteristics of hard rubber, and are actually somewhat fragile and susceptible to chipping.

Approximately eight hundred design motifs on plastic cases are known to exist.[40] The designs for many of the beautifully detailed covers were derived from classical paintings and etchings and reflect popular interest in the areas of nature, history, patriotism, and religion.

NATURE SCENES   Among the most prevalent of union case designs are those with birds, flowers, urns, bowls, vases, goblets, and baskets of flowers or fruits. Cases also come in a wide variety of floral patterns and related motifs.

HISTORICAL SCENES   Although the dies were reported still to be in existence several decades ago, the two historical scenes of Washington crossing the Delaware and Columbus landing in America are among the most prized plastic case items. Equally sought after are sculptured profiles of Washington and the American Indian. A case with a profile of Washington, for example, brought $140 at a New York auction in February 1975.

PATRIOTIC MOTIFS   Case designs with patriotic motifs began to appear just before the Civil War. These included designs of the American eagle, constitutional scroll and emblem patterns, weapons, and camp scenes. A case bearing the sculptured image of the Union ironclad vessel, the *Monitor* (with a fort in the background), brought $110 at the aforementioned auction.

RELIGION   Religious motifs on plastic cases take the form of prayer books, angels, crosses, church windows, and scenes depicting the Holy Family. While some of these were made in large quantity, most are now scarce collectors' items.

PARTICULAR MOTIFS   There are a vast number of particular design motifs that are quite uncommon. These include Cupid; firemen; children (frequently with animals); horses racing; people in groups (musicians, chess players, family gatherings, a country dance, etc.); and hunting scenes. Also scarce are motifs of gems (cameos, precious stones, jewels, star sapphires, etc.) and circle and quatrefoil designs.[41]

Evolution of Mat Styles

1 Early to mid-1840s   2 Late 1840s to early 1850s   3 Mid-1850s to early 1860s

DATING CASED PHOTOGRAPHS

It is important to recognize that many daguerreotypes or ambrotypes handed down over several generations have been removed from their original cases and placed in different cases of the same size, either because an owner wished to enhance the appearance of a particular image or because the original case had been damaged or lost. In either event, this makes it difficult to date many images unless it can be verified that they are contained in their original cases. Only a few people—experts on the fashions of the daguerrean era or those able by scientific means to determine the age of a daguerreotype copper plate—can date precisely the silvered image on a particular daguerreotype plate if the plate has been separated from its original case.

The mat styles used in cases (see examples, left) evolved from simple designs to rather ornate specimens during the daguerrean era, and these are most helpful in dating. During the 1840s, thin brass mats of oval, octagonal, or other plain design patterns were used. These were placed over the image and covered with a piece of glass of the same size. The three elements (image plate, mat, and glass cover) were placed in the right-hand section of a miniature case and secured by a thin rim of velvet-covered cardboard which surrounded the inner borders of the case. After 1850, a fourth item was added. This was the preserver, a thin, pliable, and gilded brass margin, ornate in decor, which surrounds the three elements and tightly holds them together; flaps on the preserver bend around the back portion of the image plate on all four sides. Daguerreotypes and ambrotypes will frequently be found today separated from their miniature cases, but contained in these flexible preservers.

Sometimes the layman can readily discern whether an image is in its original case. For example, the image of a Civil War soldier, if found in a case with an octagonal or other plain mat design of the 1840s, is clearly not in its original case, since the more ornate mat designs had become prevalent in the Civil War period. An ambrotype, if found in a case with the type of plain mat design prevalent in the 1840s, can also be construed as out of character, since the ambrotype was not invented until 1852. Similarly, the image of an identified person known to have been dead prior to 1850 should not be in a case with a mat design of the style prevalent in the 1850s or 1860s.

Cased daguerreotype images with some coloring on them date from as early as 1842, when the first U.S. patent for such coloring was awarded. Images in book-style, nonplastic cases were probably made in the period 1849–54, although it is possible that some were made later. Embossed paper and leather cases with nature designs were most prevalent in the 1840s, so images in such cases probably date from this period. Plastic cases date from 1854. Those bearing patriotic designs (the American flag or eagle, scroll or constitutional motifs, etc.) or war motifs (crossed cannons, camp scenes, etc.) were made after 1860.

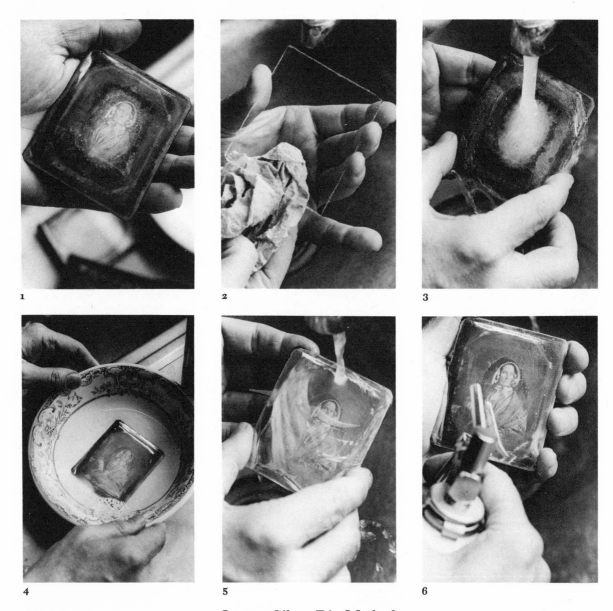

Instant Silver Dip Method

1 Remove silvered copper plate image from its case.　　**2** Clean glass cover.　　**3** Rinse image plate under cool running water.　　**4** Rock plate for 30 seconds in dish or pan containing instant silver dip. Remove when image discoloration disappears.　　**5** Again rinse plate thoroughly for 30 seconds.　　**6** Immediately spray-dry image with aerosol spray.

RESTORING DAGUERREOTYPES

There is no universally adopted practice for restoring daguerreotypes that have become tarnished with age. Indeed, experts at the International Museum of Photography at George Eastman House in Rochester, New York, take the position that cleaning should not be undertaken as a matter of course, because experience has indicated that tarnishing occurs more rapidly after a specimen has been cleaned.[42]

Images cleaned by any method may develop a case of "measles," according to a symposium on daguerreotype restoration held by the Photographic Historical Society of New York in 1972. "Measles" are tiny black spots that appear after cleaning—defects which microscopic analyses indicate are related to bits of polishing rouge left on the image plate at the time the exposure was originally made.

No daguerreotype plate should be cleaned with a cloth or silver polish. This will simply scratch and destroy the image. Late in the nineteenth century, and for many years into the present century, experts recommended cleaning daguerreotypes by immersing them in distilled water with a small amount of potassium cyanide. But this is no longer recommended, because potassium cyanide is an extremely dangerous chemical to be used by the layman.

Two methods of daguerreotype restoration widely used today are the formula devised by the Missouri Historical Society and an instant silver dip method used by many collectors where images of no particular historical significance are involved.

Missouri Historical Society Method[43]

(1) Remove image from its case and wash it in distilled water for several minutes to remove surface dirt.

(2) Immerse plate in a chemical solution consisting of:

Distilled water	1500 cubic centimeters
Thiourea	70 grams
Phosphoric acid (85%)	80 cubic centimeters
Non-ionic wetting agent	2 cubic centimeters

(The plate can be left in this solution virtually indefinitely, but it is ready to be removed when discoloration of the image is removed.)

(3) Remove plate from the chemical bath, hold it under running water for approximately one minute, then place it in mildly soapy water and agitate briefly.

(4) Rinse plate again under running water, then wash it in distilled water.

(5) Immerse plate in 95% grain alcohol (one minute).

(6) Remove plate and hold it high over a small flame until dry.

Plates cleaned in the above manner will retain their mirrorlike quality, according to the society. Specimens cleaned with potassium cyanide, however, have been found to lose their original lustre.

Instant Silver Dip Method

(1) Remove image from its case and rinse both sides in cool running water, using fingers to aid cleaning of the back side.

(2) Place plate in a dish or pan containing instant silver dip solution; rock container for about half a minute, or until discoloration of the image disappears.

(3) Remove plate from cleaning solution and immediately rinse both sides again in cool running water (about half a minute).

(4) Shake water off plate and immediately spray-dry the image side with an aerosol spray container. Spray in a regular pattern, left-to-right, top-to-bottom.

Tintypes

The tintype was photography's first medium to attract people of modest means to pose for husband-and-wife and boyfriend-and-girlfriend portraits.

TINTYPES

Invented in 1856 by an Ohio professor of chemistry and physics, the tintype was an off-shoot of the daguerreotype and the ambrotype. As with the daguerreotype, the image of a tintype was secured on a metal plate exposed in the camera, but the metal was iron instead of copper and it was lacquered with a black japan varnish instead of being coated with silver. As with the glass plate of an ambrotype, the metal plate of a tintype was sensitized with collodion before the camera exposure.

When multilens cameras and mechanisms for moving the negative plate inside a camera came into vogue after 1860 (see page 57), it became possible to expose four images of roughly 2½ × 3½ inches on a single sensitized tintype plate placed in the camera, or from twelve to thirty-six smaller images on special plates. All the photographer had to do was sensitize one plate, make one exposure, put the plate through one development process and one fixing operation (hypo), and then cut apart the individual pictures secured on the plate with a pair of tinshears.[44] Prices for tintypes made in this fashion after 1860 were as low as twenty-five cents for four pictures from a single exposure, or fifty cents for a dozen of the smaller images. The smallest tintype images (those produced in quantities as high as thirty-six on a single plate) are known as tintype "gems."

Having originated away from the centers of photographic "action" in the 1850s, the tintype's popularity did not really begin until the Civil War. Then the photographers' stock proved more durable for field use, and there were no negatives to contend with at campsites. Tintypes could also better withstand the vicissitudes of the U.S. Army mail service than any other form of photograph. After the war, however, the tintype failed to achieve "social status" and was made principally in the United States by special tintype, as opposed to regular photographic, galleries. "These hideous, cheap-looking pictures," as historian Helmut Gernsheim referred to them, "failed to establish themselves in England, France and other countries of the Continent until the late seventies, when they were introduced as 'an American novelty' by beach and street photographers."[45] Nevertheless, the tintype was a distinct American success. More soldiers posed during the Civil War, and more husbands and wives and boy friends and girl friends posed after the war, for tintype portraits than for any other form of photograph. An entire class of photographers emerged whose specialty was taking tintype portraits. The images were frequently colored by hand, as were daguerreotypes and ambrotypes. Like the images of daguerreotypes and ambrotypes (where no negative is involved), a tintype image is also reversed.

Outdoor scenes and images of identified persons of note are prime tintype collectors' items today—particularly "name" portraits, since the process was virtually never used in taking portraits of celebrities. One major exception was the presidential election of 1860, when small medals containing tintype portraits of Lincoln, Douglas, and other candidates were prepared in large quantity. But these, too, are now major collectors' items. Other sought-after items: people clothed in their occupational garb or holding or displaying the tools of their trade; portraits of blacks, Indians, animals, and people with animals. Because tintypes were ill suited for stereoviewing, tintype stereoviews are also rare items.

Examples of Tintype Collector's Items

1 Humorous studio group pose   **2** Horse and carriage   **3** Man with pistol   **4** Barn scene   **5** Horse and buggy   **6** Drummer   **7** Ready for the horse show   **8** Fireman   **9** Stereoview   **10** Man with banjo   **11** Man with bicycle   **12** Men in jail garb   **13** Regular Army officer and family (circa 1870s)   **14** Civil War soldier (a tintype cased to resemble the more expensive ambrotype)

9

10

11

12

13

14

Stereographs

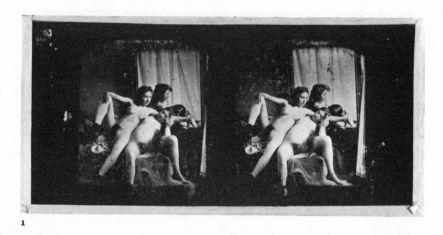

1

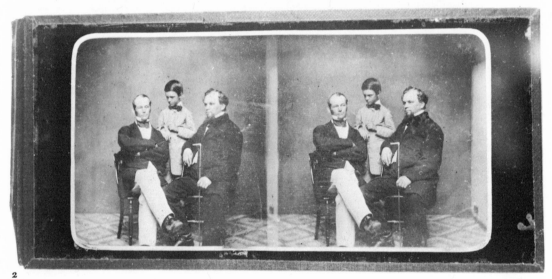

2

3

1 Daguerreotype stereograph   **2** Ambrotype stereograph   **3** Glass stereograph (Moscow, circa 1865)

The early forms of photography (the daguerreotype, ambrotype, and calotype processes) were all used—beginning in 1851 with the daguerreotype process—to make stereographs, or stereoviews, as they are perhaps more frequently called today. These are paired photographs of the same image, which were first taken with two cameras side by side (in the early 1850s) and later with binocular cameras having dual lenses (which provided dual images of the subject being photographed on a single negative plate). When the paired images were developed and viewed stereoscopically, the viewer could see a single image in three dimensions.

The British daguerreotypist Antoine Claudet is considered the pioneer experimenter in daguerreotype stereographs; however, the British firm of Negretti and Zambra produced specimens taken of the London Crystal Palace at the time of the great 1851 exhibition which were among the first to gain widespread note. Presumably calotype stereographs also made their appearance at this time, but this cannot be accurately documented. Paired daguerreotypes were also sold in miniature cases having folding eyepieces for viewing the images stereoscopically (see page 20). These were marketed in the United States beginning in 1852 and in London beginning in 1853. Evidently no attempt at large-scale production of daguerreotype stereographs was made in the United States, and the vast number of calotype stereographs now extant are European, since the calotype process was not practiced in America to the extent it was in Europe (see page 75). This means that American-made daguerreotype or calotype stereographs are very valuable today.

Glass stereographs made their appearance in Europe and America as early as 1852 but were not promoted commercially in the United States before 1855, the year Frederick and William Langenheim of Philadelphia undertook to make the first series of labeled "American Stereoscopic Views" of scenery between Philadelphia and Niagara Falls. No complete set of these Langenheim glass views is known to exist, but collectors continue to keep a watchful eye out for specimens from the series. Perhaps the largest early U.S. venture in glass views was that begun in 1861 by the San Francisco photographer C. E. Watkins, who issued a series of views of tourist meccas in the West, including Yosemite, big trees, Indian groups, and the Sierra Nevadas.[46] European photographers made many more glass views after 1860 than U.S. photographers. Those made in France by Ferrier and Lamy are said to number more than 30,000.[47]

Following are representative prices realized for early stereographs at several New York and London auctions. The high figure for the 1975 item by an unknown photographer suggests that the value of early stereographs may be rising:

ITEM	PLACE OF AUCTION	DATE	SALE PRICE
Daguerreotype stereograph still life (photographer unknown)	New York	1975	$ 275
Daguerreotype stereograph by P. H. Delamotte of Napoleon III, Empress Eugénie, Queen Victoria, and gathering at London Crystal Palace April 20, 1855	London	1972	300
Daguerreotype stereograph by Antoine Claudet of a couple, July 9, 1856 (glass cracked; case flap missing)	London	1972	150
Glass stereograph by Frederick Langenheim of Niagara Falls, after 1856	New York	1972	50
Glass stereograph by Frederick Langenheim of Gen. Winfield Scott seated in front of doorway in West Point (circa 1865)	New York	1972	150
Glass stereograph by Frederick Langenheim of Genesee Falls, N.Y., 1856	New York	1971	110

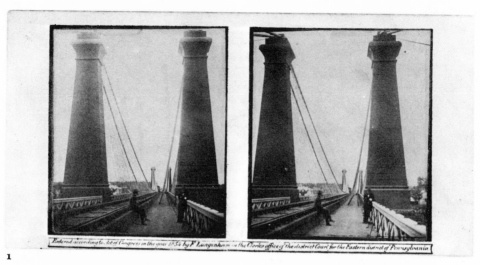

Early Card Stereographs

1 Railroad suspension bridge over the Niagara River, 1854   2 The Crystal Palace, reerected at Sydenham, circa 1858   3 Early French card with initials *J.M.* on back side

CARD STEREOGRAPHS

The first card stereographs (introduced circa 1850–51) were of the calotype variety. After 1851, card stereographs were produced principally from collodion glass negatives—initially on plain paper, but subsequently on albumen paper (after 1854 in England; after 1860 in the United States). Volume was not large until after 1854, when W. H. Fox Talbot lost his battle in the British courts to extend his calotype patent to collodion photography.

No other form of photograph provides such a complete record of a world shedding its agrarian heritage and opting for a new industrial and urban way of life. Beginning about 1858 stereo cameras photographed everything in the way of people, places, and events, near at hand and far away. By 1862 the London Stereoscopic Company (with Ferrier of Paris close behind) was selling a million card views annually.[48] In New York, Edward Anthony that same year had more modest sales of "several hundred thousand" cards.[49] Soon nearly every parlor had its stereoscope for home viewing, much as every living room today has its television set.

The earliest card stereographs are extremely thin, and many of those made in France carry the photographer's initials only. The first American card series was issued by Frederick and William Langenheim, in 1854 (see example, left) and again in 1858 (the series called "American Stereoscopic Views"). In 1859 the Langenheims began importing foreign-made card views. The same year, the London Stereoscopic Company began distributing its own series, "America in the Stereoscope," with views taken in the United States by the English photographer William England.[50] During the period 1858–65, the dominant publishers of U.S. views were Anthony, the Langenheims, George Stacey, and D. Appleton and Co. For several decades after the Civil War, Anthony, the American Stereoscopic Company (successor to the Langenheims after the war), and

the Kilburn Brothers of Littleton, New Hampshire, dominated the U.S. market until the 1890s, when door-to-door sales were initiated by such large firms as Underwood and Underwood, Keystone View Company, Griffith and Griffith, and the H. C. White Company.[51]

Subjects of interest to card collectors are legion, but several categories are covered in the pages that follow. During the early period (1860s), certain U.S. photographers issued views separately from the larger publishers, and among the more important of these are series made by the following: John Soule and DeLoss Barnum in Boston; J. A. Williams in Providence; Bierstadt Brothers in New Bedford, Massachusetts; Jeremiah Gurney in New York; James Cremer and John Moran (brother of the celebrated painter) in Philadelphia; William Chase in Baltimore; John Carbutt in Chicago; A. A. Hart in Sacramento. In England, Francis Bedford made several thousand views (issued in regional series) of cities and communities throughout Britain and Wales. European photographers who made noteworthy card series in the 1860s were: the house of Lamy in France; Christian Konig, Franz Richard, C. Schmidt, the Creifelds, and S. P. Christman in Germany; Sommer and Behles, Adolphe Godard, Carlo Ponti, and Carlo Naya in Italy; and Adolphe Braun in Switzerland.[52]

Card stereographs were made of all major U.S. cities, but few are to be found today of Pittsburgh, Cincinnati, Detroit, or Denver. Card stereograph portraits are rare items, particularly those of American presidents Lincoln, Johnson, Grant, Garfield, Benjamin Harrison, Hayes, and Cleveland. The growth of large metropolitan newspapers and the popularity of illustrated weeklies (*Harper's Weekly*, the *Illustrated London News*, etc.) stimulated a market for card views of major news events and happenings, particularly disasters. These, too, are avidly sought by collectors.

Celebrities

1 Samuel F. B. Morse, photography pioneer and inventor of the telegraph   **2** Sir David Brewster, with lenticular stereoscope invention on table   **3** William E. Gladstone, before becoming prime minister of England

1

3

2

Unusual Specimens

1 Tissue paper card, colored on back, is seen in color with rear lighting.   **2** Doll stereo view. These were rarely made and are prime collector's items.   **3** This card gives illusion of movement if eyes are blinked in stereo viewing.

1

2

3

Wartime Views

1 Gunboat *Masessoit* on James River; officers' barge waits at Aikens House wharf.   **2** Confederate prisoners after surrender at Battle of Gettysburg.   **3** French soldiers, probably at time of the Crimean War.

1

2

3

Blacks

1 "Melody." Few cards depicting blacks were posed.   2 Georgia plantation scene: "They go to the barn to grind the ax."   3 "Oh, let me live in Freedom's Land, or die if still a slave."

1

2

3

The Early American West

1 View down Black Canyon from Mirror Bar, by T. H. O'Sullivan   2 Railroad construction site at Rollins Mills, South Boulder, Colorado Territory   3 "The Grizzled Giant," 80 feet in diameter, probably by T. C. Roche, 1870–71

1

2

An Indian Home, near Soda Springs, Idaho.

3

The American Indian

1 Sioux leader, Red Cloud. He signed a peace treaty in 1868.   **2** An Indian view by C. R. Savage. Many of his negatives were lost in an 1883 fire.   **3** Indian guard confined in Fort Marion at St. Augustine, Fla., circa 1865.

2

1

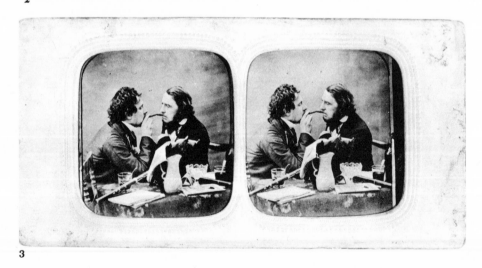

3

Genre

1 "The Babes in the Wood," typical of London Stereoscopic Co. humorous cards   2 An 1871 card by John P. Soule of Boston, an early American specimen   3 A tissue card by J. Elliott, exhibiting coloring when back-lighted

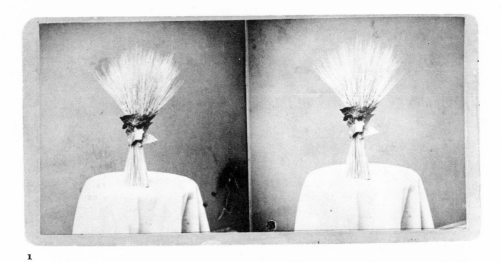

1

2

3

Still Lifes

1 Sheaf of Wheat. Still lifes are rarities among card stereograph pictures.   **2** Untitled. No collecting category for still lifes has previously been noted.   **3** Untitled. Note two butterflies on side and top of flower arrangement.

1

2

3

Disasters

1 View from the Court House steps after the 1871 Chicago fire (G. N. Barnard photo). **2** Johnstown flood in Pennsylvania in 1889 was the worst in U.S. history. **3** Mislabeled card is view of Leeds, Mass., after 1874 flood in Mill River Valley.

Photography Themes

1 Wagon of W. B. Gardner, Sherborn, Mass., one of countless unknown photographers.　　**2** Floating darkroom. In 1850s, J. M. Gorgas operated on Ohio and Mississippi rivers.　　**3** A photographer at Yosemite, the second most popular target (after Niagara Falls).

1 Very early card, labeled on back: "J. C. Dennis, Optician, London."   **2** The Great Eastern. Even card photographs of this ship are rarities.   **3** Typical of colored stereographs mass-produced at the turn of the century.

LITHOPRINT STEREOGRAPHS

Lithoprint stereographs, usually multicolored, were made from plates or mats reproduced from photographs or artist's renderings. The vogue for these items did not start until 1898, with the result that specimens made earlier in the nineteenth century may be considered rare items. High value is frequently attached to all lithoprint card stereographs, but despite their color, this is not warranted. Clean, brightly colored lithoprint cards in first-class condition should be valued more highly than those whose colors have faded or whose image was inferior to begin with. The card stock generally used for lithoprints made after 1898 was thin and of cheap quality, and often became brittle and cracked.[53]

The major publishers of colored lithoprint stereographs were: the American Stereoscopic Company, Griffith and Griffith, H. C. White, Sears Roebuck, Montgomery Ward, World Wide View Company, T. W. Ingersoll, Atlas View Company, W. B. Smith, Barnes and Crosby Company, and the Aste Company (identified frequently only as *A.C.*). The principal publishers of black-and-white lithoprint stereographs were the Continental Art Company and the Cosmopolitan Printing Company.[54]

Firms such as Griffith and Griffith and the H. C. White Company sold cheap lines of lithoprint stereographs along with a finer line of photographic cards which they sold door-to-door. The vast majority of lithoprints were made after 1900, and in many respects their value is close to that of early colored postcards

and apothecary items (cards depicting beauties of the fair sex, cowboys and Indians, baseball heroes, etc.), which made their appearance at about the same time.

A typical line of lithoprint stereographs published by one of the larger establishments, according to the stereograph historian William Culp Darrah, included a complete variety of travel, humorous, and sentimental views. The principal travel views were scenes of America, Europe, Egypt, the Holy Land, and the Orient. The humorous views included boyish pranks, children at play, hunting scenes, inebriated or henpecked husbands, and the stolen kiss.

Darrah lists the following as among the rarest series of lithoprint views because of the small quantity issued, their particular historical value, or their lack of commercial appeal at the time of issue:[55]

San Francisco Earthquake and Fire (1906)
Published by W. B. Smith

The Russo-Japanese War (1904–1905)
Published by Sears Roebuck (boxed set of 100 cards)

The Great White Fleet
Published by several publishers

The Balkan War (1912–1913)
Published by J. Hollinger

Louisiana Purchase Exposition, St. Louis, 1904
Published by Sears Roebuck (boxed set of 100 cards)

The American Indians
Published by Sears Roebuck and Montgomery Ward
(Boxed sets of 25 cards)

1 Circa 1860. Dull gray card mount; square corners; prints on albumen paper.   2 Circa 1870s, by Miller and Best, Boston. Copy print on lemon yellow mount.   3 Circa 1890s. A curved card of style widely adopted after 1880.

DATING CARD STEREOGRAPHS

The earliest card stereographs are often easiest to date. Those made before 1858 are generally extremely thin, and in the case of English and French specimens, they bear no titles or identification of photographers. Cards with images secured on plain paper (calotypes or salt prints) will not exhibit the glossiness that the later albumen prints exhibit. Cards made in the period 1858–65 frequently bear the photographer's or publisher's imprint on the margin of the image side. Cards bearing a revenue stamp on the back can be pinpointed as having been purchased between September 1, 1864, and August 1, 1866, a period when a U.S. federal tax was levied on many small luxuries for purposes of raising additional wartime revenue. After 1868, the policy was adopted by many publishers of affixing to the back of their cards a listing of views in a particular series, each card in that particular series being identified by underlining or otherwise marking the particular card number or title among those listed.[56]

Cards will be found which exhibit a slight difference (sometimes as much as an inch) in the extent of subject matter included in the paired images. The Chicago photographer John Carbutt complained about this in 1870, calling it a "serious error, very detrimental to the interests of the photographic trade."[57] The "Best" series card shown at the left exhibits this difference in subject matter, indicating that Carbutt's complaint evidently went unheeded.

The distribution of card stereographs containing copy photographic prints began in the 1870s. Frequently, these can be identified when it is clear that only a single photographic print (not two) is mounted on a card, the single

	TIME PERIOD
Card Stock	
Very thin	1851–58
Flat with square corners	1851–70
Flat with rounded corners	After 1868
Curved (or "warped") mounts; corners rounded	After 1879
Card Mount Coloring	
White, ivory, cream, and lustrous gray	1851–61
Dull gray (flat cards; square corners)	1860–63
Yellow (lemon or canary yellow in the early 1860s; a deeper chrome yellow after 1870)	1862–72
Purple, pink, violet, red, green, blue	1865–70
Gray (curved cards; rounded corners)	After 1893
Black (curved cards; rounded corners)	After 1902
Card Images	
Original photographic prints pasted on mounts (with or without tinting)	1851 on
Copy photographs (evidencing loss of clarity and detail)	After 1873
Photomechanical prints	After 1874
Lithoprints (hand-colored)	1850s on
Lithoprints (multicolored)	After 1898
Lithoprints (black-and-white)	After 1906

print being in fact a copy photograph made of two similar paired images. By closely examining such copy print images, it will be seen that the line separating the paired images is actually part of the copy print image. This is also true of the "Best" series card, left.

After 1880, curved cards became prevalent. This curving, or "warping," of cards was introduced because it increased the illusion of three dimensions when the cards were viewed in stereoscopes.

Familiarity with the names of nineteenth-century stereo photographers and with their active time periods is particularly helpful in card stereograph dating. So, too, is a knowledge of history and of the changing fashions, architecture, etc., of the period. The table above has been derived principally from data contained in William Culp Darrah's *Stereo Views*, cited earlier, but the reader is cautioned that exceptions will be found in the case of most time periods given.

Card
Photographs

CARTES DE VISITE

The carte de visite (or visiting card) style of photograph was a French invention, hence the continued use of the French nomenclature. It was patented in France in 1854, and an early (but unsuccessful) start was made in making the new style in England in 1857. The style became the fashion when a "Royal Album" was published in August 1860, containing fourteen carte de visite portraits of the royal family.[58]

For more than fifteen years, this style was the principal one used for portraiture in most photographic galleries, although tintypes of similar size were made on a large scale in the United States in special tintype galleries patronized by people of lesser means. The typical carte de visite portrait is a head-and-shoulders or full-length pose 2¼ × 3¾ inches mounted on a card 2½ × 4 inches. This form of photograph was the first used to mass-produce portraits of celebrities, and it matched in popular sales card stereograph views. Multilens cameras were adopted by the larger studios to make four or eight exposures at one time on a single glass negative plate. From this a contact print could be made with four or eight similar photographs on a single sheet of photographic paper. These were then cut apart and mounted separately. Although they are hard to find today, more than 100,000 carte de visite photographs of Abraham Lincoln were produced and distributed in the presidential campaign of 1860. In the mid-1860s, one major New York publisher produced carte de visite portraits of celebrities at the rate of 3,600 a day.[59] In 1864 the London Stereoscopic Company reportedly took four dozen negatives of Prime Minister Palmerston at one sitting in order to get tens of thousands of carte de visite likenesses on the market immediately.[60]

No great value should be placed on the average carte de visite portrait, of which millions are extant. The loss or destruction of many carte de visite negatives made of celebrities (coupled with the loss or destruction of many of the prints made from these negatives) is another matter, however. Any Lincoln carte today, for example, is a highly prized item. A pair of carte portraits of the poet Alfred Tennyson taken in 1861 brought as much as $300 at a New York auction in 1975. Any carte portrait of a celebrity taken by an identified or unidentified photographer in a small city should be given careful attention, since it is likely that the negative has been lost and equally likely that the number of prints originally produced was small. Few photographs were taken of President James Buchanan after he left the White House. A carte de visite portrait of him taken shortly before his death in 1868 brought over $700 at a 1971 auction.

In the pages that follow, examples are given of carte de visite collectors' items, which include outdoor scenes, people in their occupational garb, Indians, a steamboat and horse-drawn fire engine, and portraits of a dog, a black youth, and a finely dressed criminal (after the ambrotype, the carte de visite was adopted for police "rogues' galleries").

A Gallery of Rare Carte de Visite Portraits

1 Julia Ward Howe (1819–1910), first president of the New England Woman Suffrage Association and author of the "Battle Hymn of the Republic."   2 Adolphe Thiers (1797–1877), outstanding figure in French politics, twice premier under Louis Philippe and chief executive of the Third Republic, 1871–1873.   3 Jenny Lind (1820–1887), the Swedish-born coloratura soprano who captivated U.S. audiences in the 1850s.   4 Marie Amélie (1782–1886), queen of the French, 1830–1848, and wife of Louis Philippe. Photo by Antoine Claudet in London, where the queen lived in exile.   5 Christopher "Kit" Carson (1809–1868), the celebrated early western trapper and guide, shown standing with Edwin O. Perrin, seated, who joined Carson in 1861 when the latter was given the rank of colonel to

7   **8**   **9**

10   **11**   **12**

command forces battling Navajo, Apache, Kiowa, and Comanche Indian tribes in the Southwest.[61]   **6** Jean Louis Ernest Meissonier (1815–1891), for many years France's most popular and successful artist, but who has been described by a modern critic as "a rancorous, mean-spirited, smug, and envious little man."[62]   **7** Pauline Cushman (1833–1893), French-born actress who became a Union spy in the Civil War. Captured and condemned to be hanged, she was left behind in a retreat of Confederate forces; after the war she lectured in a Civil War uniform.   **8** The second Mrs. Millard Fillmore, who married America's thirteenth president after he had retired to Buffalo.   **9** Millard Fillmore (1800–1874), thirteenth U.S. president, shown posing for the camera in Paris nearly twenty years after he left the White House.   **10** Thomas Carlyle (1795–1881), the English essayist and historian, shown in a rare montage portrait.   **11** Count Helmuth von Moltke (1800–1891), Germany's greatest nineteenth-century military strategist and tactician.   **12** Samuel L. Clemens, "Mark Twain" (1835–1910), humorist and author.

A Gallery of Carte de Visite Collector's Items

1 A dog   2 Worcester, Mass., police mug-shot of an arrested forger   3 People visiting church ruins
4 A cemetery   5 Machinery   6 Young black boxer   7 Church interior   8 Horticultural image, circa 1860

9 Boy on a toy horse   10 River steamer, circa 1860s   11 Occupational portrait   12 Joining of the Central Pacific and Union Pacific railroads at Promontory, Utah, May 10, 1869   13 A group of Indians   14 A Cincinnati sheriff   15 A street scene with a group of boys, probably Boston, circa 1860s   16 A fire house and engine on Germantown Road, Philadelphia, in September 1865

A City Photographed in Cartes de Visite

Salt Lake City and its Mormon community were photographed in the 1860s by the firm of Savage and Ottinger. The city's population at the time was less than 20,000. The views shown here include:　　1 East Temple Street　2 Southeast view of the city　3 Brigham Young's residence　4 Townsend House　5 A closer view of the Young residence　6 The theater. The carte de visite was little used in recording city views, so this collection is unique. Charles R. Savage and George M. Ottinger worked in partnership from circa 1862 to 1870, after which Savage worked alone. During the partnership, Savage, an Englishman who had emigrated to the United States in 1857, worked as field man, preferring the out-of-doors. Throughout the remainder of the nineteenth century he was the best-known photographer between the Mississippi and Texas. His photograph of the joining of the Central Pacific and Union Pacific railroads at Promontory (previous page) is among the most celebrated documentary photographs of the American West. In 1883, many of Savage's early negatives were destroyed in a fire, but others will be found in the Utah Historical Society. Today a monument to Savage stands on the southeast corner of Temple Square, erected in memory of his concern for the elderly through establishment of Utah's "Old Folks Day."

Entered according to Act of Congress, in the year 1865, by John P. Soule, in the
Clerk's Office of the District Court for the District of Massachusetts.
THE BIRD CATCHERS.
Photo. from the original Drawing and Pub. by J. P. Soule, Boston.

BOTHERIN' A TOURIST.

PIONEER STAGE COMPANY

The Watchful Sentinel.

SEE MY NEW BOOTS.

MY FIRST SERMON.

Genre Cartes de Visite

T. A. Sharpnack, BROWNSVILLE, PA.

Leeper, West Newton, Pa.

H. Sonnenberg PITTSBURGH AND ALLEGHENY CITY, PA.

Leeper, West Newton, Pa.

Black 801 and 803 7th Avenue, Beaver Falls, Pa.

T. A. Sharpnack, BROWNSVILLE, PA.

CABINET CARDS

By 1866 the world was ready for a new style of portrait photograph. This was the cabinet card, first suggested by a British photographer in May of that year and in vogue by the start of 1867. The new prints measured roughly 3¾ × 5½ inches and were mounted on cards 4¼ × 6½ inches.

Like the carte de visite, the cabinet card was produced in the millions, and therefore no particular value should be attached to the average family-style cabinet portrait of identified or unidentified people. The same holds true for cabinet card portraits as for cartes de visite, however, when it comes to likenesses of celebrities of the period 1867 to the turn of the century. Many original photographic negatives, including those by some of the best-known photographic houses of that time, have been lost or destroyed, so surviving prints can be quite valuable. At a 1975 New York photographic auction, for example, a group of twenty cabinet portraits of British and American celebrities brought $225. A single cabinet card portrait of George Sand by the noted French photographer Nadar sold for $200.

The cabinet card brought with it a new appreciation for style in posing, improved lighting, and the use of background objects or scenery to add flair to the photograph. In 1869, the retouching of negatives was begun; they were doctored to improve facial characteristics and to secure a greater variety of intermediate tones that the collodion glass negatives could not by themselves record. A few artists, such as William Kurtz in New York, began applying a "Rembrandt" effect to their photographic portraiture, achieving lighting in cabinet card photographs comparable to that exhibited in oil portraits by the Dutch master two centuries earlier. Another noted New York photographer of the cabinet card era, Napoleon Sarony, broke with convention by seeking special dramatic effects in posing his subjects. The most elaborate backgrounds and accessories were created in the New York studio of J. M. Mora.[63]

The first large-scale production of portraits of celebrities in the performing arts began with the cabinet card era, and those made at the Sarony and Mora galleries are today the most valued of these items. A collection af about one hundred theatrical cabinet card portraits taken by other photographers following the fashion established by Sarony and Mora brought $200 at auction in 1975. The collection was sold in three morocco gilt albums. A group of ten theatrical cabinet portraits brought only $10 at a 1971 New York auction. The largest collection of cabinet card portraits of celebrities was reportedly compiled by the Philadelphia photographer Frederick Gutekunst.[64]

The cabinet card style was utilized after the mid-1870s to make photographic prints by a number of processes other than the traditional (at that time) mode of producing them on albumen paper. Many cabinet cards identified the photographic process used, as for example: Woodburytype; Artotype; Collotype (all photomechanical processes); or as a carbon or platinum print (both examples of the so-called "permanent" photographic print). To some collectors, identification of the photographic process used enhances their value.

1   2

3   4

A Gallery of Cabinet Card Portraits of Celebrities

1 Daniel Webster (1782–1852), copied by James Wallace Black of Boston from a daguerreotype taken circa 1852 by Black or his partner at that time, John A. Whipple.   2 Massachusetts Senator Charles Sumner (1811–1874) and the poet Henry Wadsworth Longfellow (1807–1882).   3 Charles Francis Adams (1807–1886), diplomat and

The Lord Bishop of Massachusetts,
THE RIGHT REV. PHILLIPS BROOKS, D.D.
ELLIOTT & FRY Copyright. 55, BAKER STREET, W.
AND AT 7, GLOUCESTER TERRACE, S.W.

5

PACH,
PHOTO.
N.Y. SENATOR JAMES A. GARFIELD.

6

Wm L Garrison

7

8

statesman who served as Lincoln's minister to England.   4 Julia Marlowe (1866–1950), the celebrated Shakespear-ean actress.   5 Phillips Brooks (1835–1893), renowned Episcopal minister and Bishop of Massachusetts for the last three years of his life.   6 James A. Garfield (1831–1881), twentieth president of the United States.   7 Wil-liam Lloyd Garrison (1805–1879), the abolitionist leader.   8 Otto Eduard Leopold von Bismarck (1815–1898), first chancellor of the German Empire.

Her Majesty The Queen laughing. Copyright.
Photographed in her Carriage
during the Jubilee Celebration at Newport, I.W.
CHARLES KNIGHT, ROYAL STUDIO, NEWPORT, I.W.

1

3

4

2

5

A Gallery of Cabinet Card Collector's Items

1 Queen Victoria laughing (a major photographic coup). 2 The "Siamese Twins," part of the grotesque and gigantic rock formations in the "Garden of the Gods" near Colorado Springs. 3 Tucson, Arizona, jail where Billy the Kid was held briefly before he escaped and was fatally shot seven weeks later on July 15, 1881. The photo was made fourteen years later. 4 Boat docking scene on the Thames River in London. 5 An advertising premium

6

Brady,   New York.

9

7

8

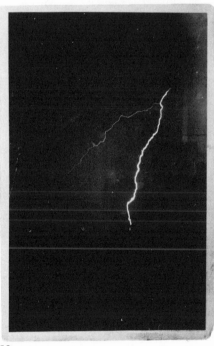

10

from the Carman Manufacturing Co., Madera, Pa.   6 The home of Nathaniel Hawthorne (1804–1864) in Concord, Mass.   7 A street market in Mexico.   8 Crystal Palace, circa 1890s; it had been moved from London in 1854 and reerected on a smaller scale at Sydenham, Kent. It was destroyed by fire in 1936.   9 Brady and other photographers labeled their fashionable cabinet and larger size prints "Imperial" portraits. A New Orleans socialite is pictured in this Brady Imperial.   10 Several daguerreotypes of lightning were reportedly made in the 1840s and 1850s, but any nineteenth-century photograph of lightning—this cabinet card among them—is a rare item.

CARLO NAYA
Fotografo di S.M. · Vittorio Emanuele II
Il solo stabilimento d'Italia premiato con
MEDAGLIA D'ARGENTO
all'Esposizione Universale di Parigi del 1867
MEDAGLIA D'ORO
à quella di Groningen in Olanda nel 1869.
MEDAGLIA DEL PROGRESSO
all'Esposizione Universale di Vienna 1873.
VENEZIA

J. E. McCLEES,
ARTIST,
910 Chestnut Street,
PHILADELPHIA.

THE NEW YORK PHOTOGRAPHIC CO.
No. 639 BROADWAY
NEW YORK.

L. POWERS
FOTOGRAFIA AMERICANA.
VILLINO POWERS
PORTA ROMANA
FIRENZE.

FRITH'S CARTE SERIES

SOMETHING NEW.

At Prof. King's Photograph Gallery, each sitter will be presented with a dozen beautiful Card Photographs of a variety of elegant Engravings.

You are politely requested to place this specimen in your Album for future reference.

Photographs of all sizes made and finished in Crayon, India Ink, Oil or Water Colors, and full satisfaction guaranteed in all cases.

CARTE DE VISITES, plain, per doz. $3 00
    "   vignettes, "   4 00
PHOTO-MINIATURE, on Porcelain, each, 3 50

All other kinds at equally reasonable prices.

Prof. S. A. KING,

No. 30 School Street, corner of Chapman Place,
BOSTON.

Next to the Parker House.

WHIPPLE,
297 Washington Street,
BOSTON.

These Negatives are preserved for years with great care. Photographs can be made from them like this, or enlarged to Cabinet or Life-Size, finished like Oil Paintings or in the style of Crayon Drawings.

F. BEDFORD
PHOTOGRAPHER TO
H.R.H.
THE PRINCE OF WALES

I. ГОФФЕРТЪ
С. ПЕТЕРБУРГЪ
Невскій проспектъ № 26
противъ Гостинаго двора.
НОВАЯ ФОТОГРАФІЯ.

CARTES DE VISITE
D. APPLETON & Co
443 & 445 Broadway N.Y.
A. A. TURNER,
PHOTOGRAPHER.

PHILAD'A PHOTOGRAPHIC CO.
730
PHILADELPHIA
CHESTNUT ST.

DATING CARD PHOTOGRAPHS

People who are most expert in dating card photographs are those who have acquired major collections and are thus able to compare new specimens found with those already in their collections. The more dated specimens there are in a given collection, the easier it becomes to date others, particularly in cases where a photographer's logo is contained on the back side of the card or where the card bears a photographer's imprint on the image side.

Cartes de visite were produced for twenty-five years after 1860. Specimens after 1885 are uncommon. Cabinet cards were produced from circa 1866 to just after the turn of the century. One knowledgeable observer has concluded from examining dated specimens that "extensive production of cabinet-sized photos for the public did not occur until 1880 and lasted no later than 1906."[65] Cartes de visite taken in the 1860s are generally thinner than those produced after 1870 and frequently exhibit two border lines, the outer line being thicker than the inner. Squared corners usually indicate a specimen produced in the 1860s, although cabinet cards with straight, square corners were produced in the 1880s. People steeped in a knowledge of nineteenth-century fashion and of the world's celebrities of the card photograph period can also be helpful in card photograph dating. Other helpful guidelines are the following:

GLOSSINESS OF PRINT   Images that exhibit no gloss were probably secured on plain paper (salt prints) before being mounted on cards. Images secured on albumen paper, widely adopted in Europe in the 1850s and by most U.S. photographers in the 1860s, exhibit a glossier appearance.

TAX STAMPS   Cartes de visite bearing a U.S. postage stamp on the back can be dated as having been produced before or during the period September 1, 1864, to August 1, 1866, when all such photographs transported in the U.S. mail were subject to this form of government tax in order to raise additional wartime revenue.

ACCESSORIES   According to the British photo historian Helmut Gernsheim, "each decade in the carte and later cabinet (photograph) period had its specially characteristic accessories. In the 1860s they were the balustrade, column, and curtain; in the 1870s the rustic bridge and stile; in the 1880s the hammock, swing, and railway-carriage (first-class, of course); in the 1890s palm trees, cockatoos, and bicycles; and in the early twentieth century it was the motorcar, for snobs."[66]

RETOUCHING   Retouching of photographic negatives began in Europe in the late 1860s and was adopted in the United States after 1869. Evidence of this will be found by examining closely the facial characteristics and other elements of a card photograph portrait to determine whether retouching was applied to remove or smooth over any blemishes or imperfections.

PHOTOMECHANICAL PRINTS   Cards bearing imprints beneath the image of such titles as Woodburytype, Artotype, or Collotype are photographs produced in large volume by the photomechanical process of the same name. This was not done prior to the introduction of these processes in the mid-1870s. Cabinet cards were produced with platinum print images in some of the larger and more fashionable galleries, and these date from the 1880s or 1890s.

COLORED MOUNTS   Card photographs on colored mounts usually date from the 1880s, particularly the cabinet variety on maroon or dark green stock.

Photographic
Prints

1

2

3

4

English, Scottish, and French photographers were the principal users of the calotype process in the 1840s and 1850s, some using Talbot's method and others using waxed-paper negatives in the manner of Le Gray. Among the most recent specimens to come to light is a remarkable collection of calotype views acquired from a private owner by the Kodak Museum in Middlesex. They are the works of a wealthy landowner, Samuel Smith (1802–1892), who evidently made it his business to systematically record the changing environs both in and around the eastern English town of Wisbech during the period 1852–1864. Smith dated most of his paper negatives (believed to be waxed-paper negatives) and printed his images on albumen paper (as opposed to the plain paper customarily used in calotype printing). In numerous instances he recorded a scene both before and after an event or change had taken place—ship arrivals, building restoration, and construction work on the canal that runs through Wisbech. The illustrations from Smith's works, above, have the look of brightness and a lack of shadows characteristic of calotype photographs taken in bright sunshine with long camera exposures (fifteen minutes in Smith's case). None of Smith's photographs appears to be known outside of Wisbech, and such a complete photographic record of a provincial town is rare for this early period in photography.   **1** Cornhill, Wisbech, 6 September 1854   **2** Shipping on the River Nene, Wisbech, 1861   **3** The Old Stone Bridge, Wisbech, 1854   **4** Hunstanton Hall, after destruction by fire, 1853 (Smith is the seated figure)

CALOTYPES

Calotypes were the first photographs secured on paper and made with paper negatives. The process was introduced in England by W. H. Fox Talbot concurrently with the daguerreotype process in France. Most calotype prints are hard to distinguish from photographic prints made from glass negatives on plain salted paper (salt prints). Calotypes were produced from the date of Talbot's English patent (1841) until the 1860s, principally by English, Scottish, and French photographers. In 1851, the process was modified by Gustave Le Gray in France, who waxed the calotype paper negatives before use, which prevented some of the graininess in the negatives from being transposed into the paper images and at the same time made the paper negatives more sturdy for in-camera use.[67] Many of the earliest calotypes were subject to fading to a greater extent than paper prints produced by other photographic processes. But prints made from finely prepared waxed-paper negatives are hard to distinguish today from prints made from the more transparent glass negatives.

The largest and most famous collection of calotypes surviving is that produced in the period 1843–47 by the Scottish team of David Octavius Hill and Robert Adamson. A number of books have been published in recent years with reproductions of some of the best of their works. The value of original Hill-Adamson prints, meanwhile, continues to rise. Individual prints sold for between $41 and $255 at a 1972 London auction, and for $300 to $850 at a comparable 1975 auction in New York. An album containing thirty-two original Hill-Adamson prints brought over $11,000 at the 1972 auction. A single print of Edinburgh Castle sold for $1,350 at the 1975 auction.

Frederick and William Langenheim bought the U.S. rights to Talbot's calotype process in 1849, but were unsuccessful in selling licenses to American photographers. Today few American-made calotypes will be found in institutional or private hands. The earliest are a collection at Harvard made by Josiah Cooke in 1841 and later. The Smithsonian Institution possesses a small collection of Langenheim calotypes, and an album of Langenheim calotypes including sixty-seven portraits and views of Philadelphia was found in a Missouri attic in 1939 (the collection is now in the Missouri Historical Society).[68] Other Langenheim calotypes were destroyed in the National Daguerrean Gallery fire in New York City in 1852. Probably the largest U.S. collection is of views of New York City and environs taken in 1851 and 1853–54 by Victor Prevost, who used Le Gray's calotype method, which he learned in France.[69] This collection was retrieved in 1898 from a White Plains, New York, attic, and the surviving negatives and prints (constituting the earliest known photographs of New York extant) are now in the New-York Historical Society.

Many British and French photographers produced calotypes in the 1850s, and as late as 1862 a French journal said the process was the most convenient for traveling, because of the lightness of the paper negatives and the ease with which they could be preserved.[70] Among the foremost British calotypists was Philip H. Delamotte. At a 1972 New York auction, two of his calotype prints, one somewhat faded, brought $150 and $60. Between 1847 and 1851, a photographic club existed in London whose members practiced the calotype and met once or twice a month at each other's homes to exchange prints. A list of the members of this club appears on page 117; collectors should keep a watchful eye out for their works.

1

2

1 The salt print, made by H. H. Snelling in 1857 of the soon-to-be-demolished Columbia College building erected in lower Manhattan in 1790, exhibits a weak, nonlustrous appearance, which contrasts with   2 The stronger, semi-glossy albumen print, made by an unidentified photographer of the dedication of the Thomas Wildey Monument in Baltimore on September 20, 1865.

SALT PRINTS

When photographers began using glass negatives after 1850, they first secured prints on plain paper similar to that used in making calotypes. The paper was treated with ordinary salt before printing from the glass negatives, hence the name "salt prints" for the pictures produced. Salt prints do not exhibit the graniness found in many calotypes (whose images reflect some of the grains in the paper negatives from which they were produced). But they do generally appear nonlustrous, or as having a "dead" surface, as some nineteenth-century experts described their appearance.[71] Because they lacked a glossy surface (the image was more deeply *in* the paper of a salt print, as opposed to being *on* the surface of the paper, as was the case with papers later used), salt prints were ideally suited for hand coloring. Many an "old photograph" of the 1850s that is hand colored can be identified by the coloring as a salt print.

The first glass negatives used in photography were sensitized with albumen (egg white). Different albumen processes were developed independently by Claude Niepce de Saint-Victor in France (1848) and by John A. Whipple in Boston (1850). Both processes are to be distinguished from the principal nineteenth-century glass negative process introduced by Frederick Scott Archer in England (1851), which used wet collodion as the sensitizer (hence the name "wet-plate" photography). Salt prints were produced by either method (albumen or collodion), but are frequently confused with calotypes (produced from paper negatives) because of the similarity of appearance between a fine-quality salt print and a fine-quality calotype. A circa-1852 photograph of Notre Dame Cathedral in Paris by Claude-Marie Ferrier, which was sold at auction in New York in 1971, for example, was described as a calotype print "possibly from an albumen negative." The print sold for $80. Among the most notable salt prints of the 1850s are the wartime views made in the Crimea (1855–56) by the English photographers Roger Fenton and James Robertson. Fenton used the collodion and Robertson the albumen process. Today a collection of Fenton's photographs comprises the largest of salt print collections at the Library of Congress (the collection was purchased during World War II). At a New York auction in 1972, a single Fenton salt print sold for $375. At a 1975 auction, also in New York, a group of Robertson salt prints sold at prices ranging from $200 to $575 each.

Abandoned in the 1860s, the production of salt prints appears to have enjoyed a revival in the 1880s, due to a combination of factors. This resulted from a reaction by many photographers against the glossiness of photographs produced on albumenized paper (which had been adopted in Europe in the 1850s and in the United States in the 1860s). Also, in the 1880s, photographers began producing prints on platinum and mat surface papers, providing an effect not unlike the softness found in the earlier salt prints. In 1888 the *American Journal of Photography* noted the new interest in salt prints, and after pointing out certain drawbacks, concluded: "On the whole we are inclined to favor the revival."[72] Among the revivers was the house of Bachrach in Baltimore.[73] No identified Bachrach photographs from the nineteenth century have appeared to date at major New York or London photographic auctions.

Now faded and discolored at the edges, this albumen print of the Yosemite Falls is typical of the early large photographs made of the world's scenic wonders. In 1871, E. and H. T. Anthony and Company's Christmas selection included views by English and Continental photographers, Yosemite and Niagara views by Anthony photographers, Canadian views by William Notman, Lake George views by S. R. Stoddard, Minnesota views by Upton, and scenes in the Catskills by Beer and Co.

ALBUMEN PRINTS

The vast majority of photographs made from the 1850s to the 1890s were secured on albumen paper. The basic raw paper used was obtained free from all traces of iron (which, if present, would later interfere with sensitizing).[74] The paper was coated with albumen (egg white) and, prior to 1872, was sold to photographers in reams of sheets that were not light-sensitive. After 1872, the paper was sold ready-sensitized, as photographic paper is sold today.[75] The world's largest manufacturer of the paper was the Dresden Albumenizing Company in Germany, which used 60,000 eggs a day in its coating operations. The largest U.S. manufacturer was the J. R. Clemons paper manufactory in Philadelphia.

Albumen prints exhibit a glossy appearance and are sepia toned in color. The albumen coating had the effect of keeping a photographic image more *on* the surface of the paper than *in* the paper, which was the case with the image of a salt print. The Baltimore photographer David Bachrach, Jr., said the distinguishing difference in albumen prints, as compared to salt prints, "is their greater depth, transparency of shadow, brilliance of surface—which latter helps to produce these effects—and the variety of pleasing shades, warm brown, purple, and bluish black, to be obtained in the alkaline toning-baths."[76] The brightness in the appearance of an albumen photograph depended on the quality of the albumen on the paper's surface; that is why surviving prints exhibit different degrees of luster.[77]

Among American-made albumen prints, those made of Niagara Falls and the American West in the 1870s and 1880s are much-sought-after and valued items. Western prints (usually in large folio size) by W. H. Jackson, Timothy O'Sullivan, Carlton E. Watkins, Eadweard Muybridge, Peter Britt, John K. Hillers, and a number of other photographers can be expected to bring a minimum of $100 at any major auction, with collections or albums of prints commanding the highest prices for specimens of this nature. Beginning earlier in the 1850s, large publishing firms were organized in England by Joseph Cundall in London and by Francis Frith in Reigate, and in Scotland by James Valentine in Dundee and by George Washington Wilson in Aberdeen, each of which employed staffs of photographers who made notable albumen photographs of scenery and architecture throughout Great Britain and on the Continent.[78] Among European photographers, Gustave Le Gray in France, Herman Krone in Germany, Charles Clifford in Spain, Samuel Bourne in India, and Robert MacPherson and Carlo Ponti in Italy produced works equally noted today. At a 1975 New York auction, for example, a selection of five albumen photographs of Roman architecture by MacPherson, all taken before 1859, brought $120 to $150 each.

Both albumen prints and salt prints were (and are, in the case of those that have been protected through the years) subject to fading. But albumen prints that become faded also discolor simultaneously.[79] This discoloration exists around the edges of the original photograph of Yosemite Falls reproduced at the left. Albumen prints that appear to have cracks over portions or all of the image were probably given a heavier coating of albumen (with the intention of improving uniformity of coating). As early as 1879, the application of heavier albumen coatings was cited as the principal cause of the cracking and blistering of images.[80]

MELODY   ANNIE W. BRIGMAN

PRINT ON CARBON VELOX

EMULSION-PAPER PRINTS

From 1860 on, numerous technical experts in Britain, France, and Germany endeavored to come up with improved photographic papers that would overcome the principal drawbacks of albumen paper—fading, discoloration, and the slowness with which printing had to be done. The final impetus came with the explosion in amateur photography touched off after 1879 by the perfecting of ready-to-use *dry*, as opposed to individually prepared *wet*, negative plates. Because the first supplied dry-plate glass negatives (followed by celluloid roll-film after 1889) were coated with a gelatin bromide emulsion, the same emulsion (in a weaker state) and other emulsion formulae were coated on photographic papers and supplied ready-to-use. Now the amateur could make a camera exposure ten to twenty times faster, and large printing firms such as Morgan and Kidd in London could make up to a thousand prints in one day from a single negative on bromide paper.[81] This was in 1887. A year earlier, the best another printing firm could do with albumen prints was up to six prints in one day from a single wet-plate negative.[82]

The number of different emulsion papers available was sizeable, including papers of different makes marketed under the same brand name (as, for example, the Aristotype, which was manufactured by one firm with a collodio-chloride emulsion and by another with a gelatin chloride emulsion).[83] A variety of papers were manufactured with a gelatin chloride emulsion, some of which called for exposure and printing without development, others with development. The gelatin chloride papers were sold under such brand names as Omega, Solio, and Velox, one of several papers touted at the time as suitable for printing directly from a negative under gaslight.

Bromide paper was widely adopted almost immediately and was used by many photographers for prints exhibited in 1887 at the first joint exhibit of the New York, Boston, and Philadelphia amateur photographic societies. A critic at the time said he felt that the "delicate grays and pure whites" of the bromides provided "far better exponents of nature than the red tones of the common process" (i.e., prints on albumen paper).[84] Bromide prints were not featured, however, at the major photographic art salons in Europe or America. In 1892 David Bachrach, Jr., said, "I have never made them to any extent—never as a business—and I only consider them suited for commercial work, landscapes, architectural enlargements, etc."[85] Bromide paper allowed fast printing, and this set off a bonanza for enlargement work. Many large "old photographs" of grandparents, which are still to be found in plentiful supply, are bromide prints; but of these Bachrach disparagingly remarked: "It [the bromide print] was used in its earliest days by the 'Cheap Johns' and charlatans of the profession to make 'a life size and a dozen cabinets for $5.00,' and in similar ways to degrade the art."[86]

Fading was common with emulsion-paper prints, and many of those extant will be found to exhibit what can best be described as a "silvering" in the corners or other portions of the image. This is quite noticeable on the original print from which the photograph at left has been reproduced. According to Bachrach, emulsion-paper prints could be successfully made only if the proportions of silver nitrate, chlorides, and organic acids were "maintained in a certain way." He explained: "The fact stares us in the face that less silver is produced in the operation of printing with emulsion papers, and, in consequence, less gold is formed in the final image," and added that this situation could only contribute to print instability.[87]

1

2

3

1 The fashionable New York photographer B. J. Falk produced cabinet card portraits in platinum like this one of R. W. G. Welling, an organizer of a naval battalion in New York in 1891.   **2** A carbon print of Senator Charles Sumner by Allen and Rowell of Boston that served as the frontispiece of a memorial to Sumner published in 1874. **3** The Autotype Company, which acquired the English patent rights to the carbon process in 1868, produced "autotypes" (carbon prints) in sizes up to twelve feet square at the time this "A.B.C." Guide was published.

"PERMANENT" PRINTS

The susceptibility of photographic prints to fading was early recognized, and a committee of experts in London promulgated a series of procedures to insure the proper making of prints as early as 1855. Aside from photomechanical printing methods introduced in the 1870s (described on page 85), the so-called "permanent" photographic printing methods developed in the nineteenth century were those which produced carbon prints and platinum prints.

CARBON PRINTS The black lines of manuscripts and engravings written or printed in carbon in the Middle Ages have not faded or deteriorated, even though the paper or parchment on which they were secured may have faded or yellowed with age. By 1864, an English patent was granted for a workable photographic process by which photographic images could be secured on paper treated with pigments of powdered carbon in gelatin. But it was a process requiring expert hands, since the treated paper (sold as "carbon tissue") could not be worked on, and any desired manipulations or retouching had to be done on the negative before it was exposed in contact with the tissue.[88] The carbon pigment could be tinted by adding coloring matter, but the prints were unsuitable for water coloring or finishing in crayon (which was much in vogue in the 1870s and 1880s). Because they could be produced in varied tints, carbon prints can be difficult to distinguish from other photographic prints, except that they retain their original strength or luster and do not exhibit fading. A *New York World* writer in 1867 thought they resembled "the most delicate drawings in India ink, sepia, Indian red, and other colors never before attained in photography."[89] Carbon prints were produced more extensively in Britain and Europe than in the United States, and many portfolios of foreign-made prints were sold in the United States. Major "art" photographers, such as the British

pictorialist Alexander Keighley, worked principally in carbon. Photographic prints labeled "autotypes" are likely to be carbon prints, since the Autotype Company of London published carbon prints extensively under the autotype name.[90] U.S. rights to the British patent were acquired in 1867, and the first American firm to engage extensively in carbon printing was Allen and Rowell of Boston (see illustration, left). Other major U.S. practitioners were Bradley and Rulofson of San Francisco and the Lilienthal Gallery in New Orleans.

PLATINUM PRINTS Metallic platinum, also black in powdered form, is another substance that remains unaffected by air, moisture, or acids. After 1879, platinotype paper (impregnated with platinum instead of silver salts) was sold as a positive printing paper and was used by many of the principal "art" photographers of the pictorial, Linked Ring, and American Photo-Secession movements. Platinum prints can be fairly readily identified by their soft silver gray or cold black tonal quality (one nineteenth-century photo historian spoke of them as "beautiful black 'engraving-like' pictures").[91] Perhaps the single most celebrated "art" photographer who worked exclusively in this medium was Frederick H. Evans (who gave up photography entirely when he could no longer obtain platinum paper after World War I). Evans's prints were offered at a New York photographic gallery at between $200 and $450 a print in 1971. Similar prints brought between $225 and $650 at a New York photographic auction in 1975. Among the finest, but evidently now rare, platinum photographs are a large number of dramatic portraits of Indians made by F. A. Rinehart of Omaha in the 1890s. Portfolios of these prints were offered, probably for the first time, at the Chicago World's Fair in 1893.

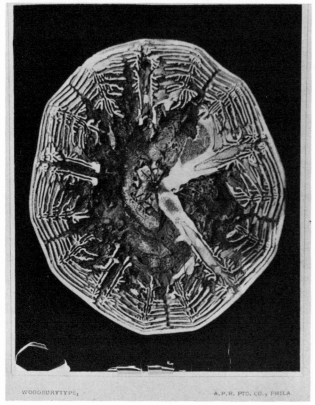

1 When an imported French press fractured in printing, a more powerful R. Hoe and Co. press was developed in the United States in 1871 for Woodburytype and other photomechanical printing. This Woodburytype of a Hong Kong species of sea urchin was made by John Carbutt shortly thereafter.   2 Photography's newest methods were utilized to make this 1883 artotype portrait of the German photographic authority Dr. H. W. Vogel.   3 Brady photograph from which heliotype prints were made to illustrate a report on the Peabody Fund.

PHOTOMECHANICAL PRINTS

By 1870 techniques were perfected which made it possible to secure photographic images on printing plates. Some of the processes were used by larger photographic establishments to make carte de visite and cabinet card portraits; one process (the photogravure) was used extensively for artistic photography renderings; and all were used to prepare illustrations for books and photographic portfolios issued in limited editions.

WOODBURYTYPE The earliest form of photomechanical print, these were made by embossing a photographic image on paper with a metal mold containing the gelatin relief of a photographic negative.[92] The Woodbury Printing Company claimed it could produce a run of as many as 30,000 carte de visite impressions from a single mold, using rotating printing tables; another producer is said to have made 55,000 prints from one mold.[93] No ink was employed in printing; however, the colored gelatin used was referred to as ink. Woodburytypes frequently exhibit a reddish tint and are usually visually quite sharp. The Woodbury Company, Goupil in France, and Adolphe Braun in Switzerland were major producers of Woodburytypes. John Carbutt bought the American rights and established a printing company in Philadelphia in 1870. The Woodburytype illustration at left is an early Carbutt specimen prepared in 1871 for zoologist Alexander Agassiz to illustrate a book on sea urchins.

COLLOTYPES The other principal methods of photomechanical printing were the so-called "photo-gelatin" methods. These were the collotype, Albertype, heliotype, and artotype. Dictionaries today include the collotype, but seldom the other "types." An inked gelatin printing surface was secured on glass in some methods and on metal in others.[94] Colored inks were used, and in all methods the printing surface was both ink-receptive in some parts and ink-repellent in others, producing prints in delicate halftones which are not easily distinguishable from actual photographs. Impressions were limited to about 1,500 to 2,000 before deterioration of the gelatin printing surface.[95] Prints were generally made on plain paper, but were also glazed sometimes (causing them to resemble albumen prints). Among the largest U.S. producers were Edward Bierstadt (brother of the artist) and C. D. Fredericks, both of whom used the nomenclature "artotype" (see illustration, left).

PHOTOGRAVURE The most widely used, expensive, and satisfying of photomechanical printing methods was the photogravure, introduced in Vienna in 1879.[96] Here, the engraver's copper plate is engraved, not by the hand of the engraver, but by photographic sensitizing means. Photogravure plates were shallower and weaker than ordinary engraver's plates, and they rarely allowed more than 1,000 prints off one steel facing.[97] But at the same time it was possible to use transparent inks of soft color (even Vandyke brown), instead of the harsher black or burnt umber inks. This made it possible to produce prints exhibiting a much softer and glowing appearance than was possible from an engraver's plate.[98] Photogravure plates could be altered or doctored by hand (usually the photographer's), and this was frequently done to achieve artistic effects by many European and American "art" photographers (see illustrations on page 86).

HALFTONES The final step in photomechanical printing was to be able to lock up a photographic illustration in typeform for simultaneous inking and printing with textual material (such as has been done in printing this book). This was achieved after 1890 by the halftone method of breaking up the image into fine dots of varying size (by a screening process) and transferring the dot image to a metal plate where it is etched into relief for printing along with type.

WAITING FOR THE BOATS.

1

AN OASIS IN THE BAD LANDS

2

1 Photogravure, 1890, from a photograph by Lyddell Sawyer   2 Photogravure, 1905, from a photograph by Edward S. Curtis

ART PHOTOGRAPHS

As early as 1856, it was suggested that photographs be included in exhibitions of the French Academy of Fine Arts, but the question of whether or not photography could be considered one of the fine arts remained a matter of considerable debate at least until the first major museum exhibition of photographs was held at the Hamburg Kunsthalle in 1893.[99] Earlier in the century, a few names of "artists with the camera" stand out. These include the pioneer calotypists, Hill and Adamson; French masters such as Gustave Le Gray, Maxime Du Camp and Charles Nègre; and the English practitioners, Philip H. Delamotte, Thomas Keith, Francis Frith, and Julia Margaret Cameron. Mrs. Cameron, who took up photography at age 48, was first to apply the use of soft focus, both in her landscape work and in close-up portraiture. The principal "art" photography movements prior to the 1890s were the pictorial and naturalistic schools; the former endeavored in a general way to illustrate the pictorial capabilities of the medium in contradistinction to the mechanical use of cameras, and the latter narrowed its sights on capturing images in photographs the way they are seen in nature.[100] This meant that by differential focusing, chosen portions of the image would be in sharp focus while peripheral areas would be less so.[101] The English photographers Henry P. Robinson and Oscar G. Rejlander, were the guiding lights of the pictorial school; their compatriot Peter H. Emerson was the founder and chief practitioner of the naturalistic school. In 1890 another English photographer, George Davison, hung an "impressionistic" photograph at a Royal Photographic Society exhibition, and this touched off yet another movement (taking its name from the concurrent movement in painting) in which photographers doctored their negatives to secure "controlled" images (or "manipulated" prints) on various pigmented mat-surface papers or canvas.[102]

In 1892 the "artists" of the Royal Photographic Society "began to find they were being tolerated only," according to Robinson. As he expressed it, "some of them left the society; others followed, and a little club was formed to promote the cause of art in photography."[103] This was the British Linked Ring Brotherhood. In America, a counterpart Photo-Secession organization was established in 1902 by Alfred Stieglitz, Edward Steichen, and others. The first publication in England to represent "the artistic position of photography" was *Sun Artists*, a series of large portfolios issued between 1889 and 1891 with collections of artistically rendered photogravures and letterpress material on the photographers represented. The first such publication in the United States was *Camera Notes*, a photographic journal illustrated with original tipped-in art photographs. Alfred Stieglitz edited this journal from 1897 to 1903, when he founded *Camera Work* as the principal medium for Photo-Secession. In 1975, the eight portfolios comprising *Sun Artists* was offered by a U.S. dealer for $1,500. At a New York auction the same year, a complete set of *Camera Work* (1903–17, lacking fifteen photographic plates) sold for $24,000. The price of one particular issue of *Camera Work* (no. 11, 1905, offered separately) brought $425 at the 1975 auction. Another copy of the same issue brought $150 at a 1972 auction.

There were other photographers around the turn of the century who are not now included among the so-called "art" groups, but who, like Emerson, photographed directly from nature, while aiming at the same time for the "painterly" effect. One was James Leon Williams, whose "Home and Haunts of Shakespeare," offered in 1891 (see pages 88–89), provides a charming photographic record of life and landscapes in what is now Warwick County. Another was the American photographer Edward S. Curtis, whose definitive portraits and record of North American Indian life has been much heralded as documentary photography, but is less recognized as an unrivaled achievement in art photography. Neither Williams nor Curtis is known to have been associated in any way with the activities or goals of the Linked Ring or Photo-Secession groups.

1

2

The Home and Haunts of Shakespeare

"The self-same folk meet us here that led their cribb'd and cabin'd life under Shakespeare's eyes so many years ago," said Horace Howard Furnace of the citizenry of Stratford-on-Avon in his introduction to the 1891 portfolio of photographs by James Leon Williams, from which these illustrations have been reproduced. **1** The road to Kenilworth castle "about which [with nearby Warwick castle] the history of England revolved for centuries." **2** The "sylvan solitude" of the forests north of Avon, which prompted Williams in his text to remark: "It is from Athens that Lysander and Hermia [*Midsummer Night's Dream*] steal forth 'when Phoebe doth behold her silver visage on the watery glass,' but it is in English woods that they meet and lie 'upon faint primrose beds,' murmuring words of love." **3** Two villagers remember "when we were boys."

3

1

3

2   4

1 French "instantaneous" card stereograph from a series similar to those first issued in America and England in 1859
2 A London street scene, circa 1876, photographed in Woodburytype by John Thomson   3 A "news" photograph
of the centennial ceremonies at Fort Ticonderoga, N.Y., which was surrendered by the British May 10, 1775, to an
American force of eighty Green Mountain Boys led by Colonels Ethan Allen and Benedict Arnold   4 Group of
workers at an ironworks in Monmouthshire, circa 1860s

SPECIALTY PHOTOGRAPHS

"INSTANTANEOUS" PHOTOGRAPHS Card stereographs of street scenes showing people and carriages in motion were a novelty when they were first published on a wide scale in 1859. By judicious manipulations of the camera and chemicals used in preparing photographic plates, "instantaneous" views (forerunners of today's "candid" photographs) could be secured, but they were the exception to the norm throughout the nineteenth century. In 1875 a photographic magazine raved over prints of snowflakes falling near White Plains, New York.[105] In 1886 the French chemist M. E. Chevreul was photographed while being interviewed, and this was widely heralded as a major new step in photography.[106] Prior to the 1890s, lenses with sufficient aperture to provide the necessary illumination for very short exposures were still not capable of giving anything like accurate definition, except on a small area at the center of the negative plate.[107] Particularly in the 1860s and 1870s, American, British, and European card stereograph manufacturers made a point of identifying various published series as "instantaneous" views (see illustration, left).

NEWS PHOTOGRAPHS Few photographers recorded news events in the nineteenth century, and most of those who did were amateurs who happened to have a camera available at the time of a particular event. This was because photographs had to be converted to engravings for publication in newspapers or popular weeklies such as *Harper's Weekly*, *Leslie's*, or the *Illustrated London News*. There was no such breed as the press photographer. Until the turn of the century, news photographs were published principally in card stereograph form and occasionally as prints. Disasters were the principal subjects of news photographs.

SOCIAL DOCUMENTATION Cameras were little used to record social conditions in the nineteenth century. Carlo Ponti took photographs of Venetian beggars in the 1860s,[108] but such undertakings were rare prior to publication of *Street Life in London* by John Thomson and Adolphe Smith, a photographer-journalist team, which was issued in 1877–78 with thirty-six Woodburytype photographs (see left). This is now among the rarest of nineteenth-century photographically illustrated books. Individual prints extracted from a copy of the book sold for between $175 and $450 at a 1975 New York auction.

KODAK CIRCULAR PRINTS By 1889 there were an estimated 13,000 owners of the Kodak I camera with roll film, and the Eastman Kodak Company was by that time processing some 7,500 prints a day sent in by the growing cadre of amateur photographers.[109] Until 1896 the images secured by Kodak I and Kodak II cameras were round, because of the shape of the image frame. Because of the scarcity of these round-image prints, rather than their subject matter, they are major collector's items.

BLUE PRINTS Blue paper photographs (also called cyanotypes) made their appearance briefly in the early days of photography, principally in the form of images of plant leaves. Their reappearance occurred in the mid-1880s with the explosion in amateur photography. They could be made in three easy steps: (1) a chemical solution (potassium ferricyanide and ferric ammonium citrate) was brushed on sized paper and allowed to dry; (2) the sensitized paper was exposed under a negative to sunlight or intense artificial light; (3) the paper was then washed in ordinary water (no hypo was required), at which time an intense blue image was formed on the paper's surface.[110] Blue prints will be found today in many turn-of-the-century photograph albums and scrapbooks.

Bishop Wilberforce.. Died July 19.. 1873..
Oxford and Winchester..

Rev: J. M. Neale.. D.D... Died Aug: 6.. 1866..
East Grinstead..

An English album of carte de visite photographs, mostly of clergymen, cathedrals, and churches (interior as well as exterior views), but also of other views and family-style portraits, circa 1870s and 1880s. Bishop Samuel Wilberforce (1805–1873), whose portrait begins the album, was a noted conservative Anglican leader and critic of the Darwinian theory of evolution.

PHOTOGRAPH ALBUMS

PERSONAL ALBUMS Many of the earliest photograph albums extant today were prepared by wealthy English or European amateurs with the leisure time to obtain and mount photographs (calotypes, salt prints, or albumen prints) in albums of their own making. A number of specific albums of this kind, together with dealer values or their sale prices at public auctions, are described in the pages that follow. Special albums with recessed pockets to hold carte de visite, tintype, and cabinet card portraits made their appearance in 1860. These were the first "family" albums and were filled by their owners with portraits not only of family members, in-laws, and friends, but also celebrities of the day. By 1870, E. and H. T. Anthony and Company's list of family albums comprised upwards of 500 styles suited for cards, cabinets, or larger pictures and holding from 12 to 500 portraits.[111] The explosion in amateur photography in the 1880s sparked new styles, and in 1883 Anthony was offering morocco-bound albums 7½ x 10½ inches in size for prints 5 x 8 inches in size, and larger morocco-bound albums (11 x 14) for photographs obtained and exhibited by members of the newly proliferating amateur photography clubs.[112] In 1876 Harroun and Bierstadt placed a patented album on the market which was designed to hold card stereographs and contained a fold-out pair of lenses for viewing the cards stereoscopically.

Greater attention should be paid to some of the better albums prepared by amateurs around the turn of the century. Items of this nature may still be in the hands of their original owners or may have been passed on to first- or second-generation offspring. In many cases the negatives for photographs in such albums have been lost or destroyed, so even greater importance can be attached to those albums possessing unusual or historically significant images.

SPECIALTY ALBUMS These were prepared for special events or occasions. In 1867, for example, a full green morocco album containing 130 carte de visite portraits of prominent U.S. statesmen and literary figures was presented by a group of American friends to Mrs. Peter Alfred Taylor in London in recognition for her "services in the cause of justice to the Negro during the American struggle." When the album was auctioned in New York in 1975, it brought $2,200. Another example, reported in an 1876 photographic journal, was an album inlaid with Tiffany silver containing photographs by J. M. Mora of many of the "most prominent belles of New York Society," each costumed to represent a different nationality. The cost of the album, labeled "Mora's Centennial Album," was stated to be $3,000. It was prepared for, and later auctioned at, a benefit for the Ladies Centennial Union.[113]

OFFICIAL ALBUMS During the 1850s the French government sponsored the taking of photographs (mostly calotypes) of architecture and monuments throughout France. In the 1860s when wars and other economic factors put an end to this practice, many albums were commissioned privately. In 1860, for example, the Bisson brothers of Paris were commissioned to portray Mont Blanc and its surrounding glaciers as a souvenir of the royal family's excursion into the area. The same year, Charles Nègre documented the Imperial Asylum at Vincennes for the emperor. Probably at the same time, Edouard Baldus was commissioned by Baron James de Rothschild to photograph views, now famous, of the architecture along several railroad lines outside Paris.[114] Private albums, distributed in some instances in limited copies, were prepared by many royal heads of state, depicting their palatial residences and estates, and in some instances portraying the members of the royal family, their pastimes, etc.

Determining the Value of Nineteenth-Century Photograph Albums

Vintage photograph albums are not easy to value; much depends on the subject matter of the photographs, the taste with which the album was prepared, its date, condition, etc. A good way to determine value is to study specific specimens handled by dealers or auctioneers. These are examples:

	PRICE	SOURCE	DATE
Album of English albumen prints (circa 1850–70), some of prominent personages, others of an English family, together with views of Somerset, the Lake District, and Shropshire. Full morocco with brass clasp; condition fair.	$ 500	Auction	1975
Album labeled *America* on half-morocco cover, containing 28 circa-1880 photographs, most by identified U.S. photographers. Album prepared by a British author and fellow traveler on trip to major U.S. cities and scenic localities. Condition fair.	75	Auction	1975
Harvard University album containing 125 oval albumen prints of faculty and members of the class of 1858, plus 12 college views. Pages separated from half-morocco binding.	300	Auction	1975
Gilt-stamped leather album (14 × 10½ inches), typical of specimens prepared by the English aristocracy in the 1850s, containing 268 photographs of the family and friends of Lord Uxbridge, and views of estates. Album contained 253 albumen prints (175 in carte de visite size), 13 salt prints, and 2 calotypes of Vice Consul F. H. Vyse in his residence in Japan. Condition good.	4,500	Dealer	1975
Portfolio of ten 4 × 5 albumen prints of Heidelberg in the early 1860s (tourist souvenir). Spine damaged; contents good.	25	Dealer	1973
Album of 55 photographs (early 1880s), *Views-Manila*, providing a complete portrait of life in Manila at the time. Views include destruction in 1882 hurricane. Photography unusually well executed.	450	Dealer	1973
Album of 46 mounted albumen prints (mostly 7 × 9) of Irish castles and estates, some of hunting hounds, horses, and interiors (circa 1880s). Cover missing.	65	Dealer	1972
Personal album of 250 photographs of varying nature and size taken in early 1860s. Includes small oval photographs of U.S. presidents (Lincoln and earlier), and salt prints of other prominent U.S. statesmen and literary and military personages. Condition good.	125	Dealer	1972
Personal album containing 97 albumen prints of English scenes and colonial life in India (1868). Full black leather with a watercolor and pencil sketch included.	65	Dealer	1972
English album with 59 photographs (mostly 1860s) of scenes and leisure activities on a country estate. Condition excellent.	125	Dealer	1972
Small carte de visite album with 46 portraits of theatrical personages of the 1860s.	150	Dealer	1972
Album with 58 pages of mounted photographs (mid-1860s) of Gibraltar, Africa, India, Spain, Malta, etc. Includes scenes of British military life, natives of Kaffraria, etc.	150	Auction	1972
Album of 32 mounted photographs (size 7½ × 11) of Nepal, including villages, temples, carvings, occupations, etc. (circa 1870). Half morocco; condition worn, some plates detached.	35	Auction	1972
Leather album containing 110 identified French literary and theatrical personages in Woodburytype prints (circa 1880s).	110	Auction	1972

	PRICE	SOURCE	DATE
Album of 136 albumen prints and 9 calotypes depicting the life of Sir William Muir and family in India (1845–75). Sir William later served as head of Edinburgh University.	500	Dealer	1972
Personal red leather album of 81 mounted albumen prints (mostly 2½ × 4) of European cities and landmarks in 1877. Some wear.	65	Dealer	1971
Album of 47 photographs (size 7 × 9) of Italian architecture, some with firm name imprints on borders (Pozzi; Brogi; etc.), circa 1880. Condition fair.	45	Dealer	1971
Brown University class of 1863 album containing 43 salt prints (one scene, one group portrait, and 41 portraits, many signed, of students and faculty). Condition excellent.	95	Dealer	1971
Album of 83 photographs (mostly 4 × 6½) of Colorado and California scenes in the 1870s. Photographers include W. H. Jackson, I. W. Taber, and C. R. Savage. Cover loose.	125	Dealer	1971
Small album of carte de visite portraits of unidentified people (family-style album). Embossed brown leather; pages dampstained.	20	Auction	1971

Photographic
Literature

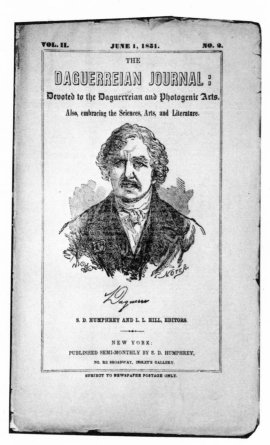

VOL. II.   JUNE 1, 1851.   NO. 2.

THE
DAGUERREIAN JOURNAL:
Devoted to the Daguerreian and Photogenic Arts.

Also, embracing the Sciences, Arts, and Literature.

S. D. HUMPHREY AND L. L. HILL, EDITORS.

NEW YORK:
PUBLISHED SEMI-MONTHLY BY S. D. HUMPHREY,
NO. 311 BROADWAY, INSLEY'S GALLERY.

SUBJECT TO NEWSPAPER POSTAGE ONLY.

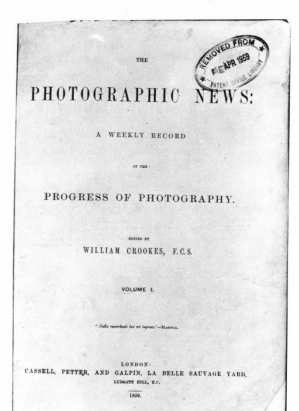

THE
PHOTOGRAPHIC NEWS:
A WEEKLY RECORD
OF THE
PROGRESS OF PHOTOGRAPHY.

EDITED BY
WILLIAM CROOKES, F.C.S.

VOLUME I.

"Nulla recordanti lux est ingrata."—MARTIAL.

LONDON:
CASSELL, PETTER, AND GALPIN, LA BELLE SAUVAGE YARD,
LUDGATE HILL, E.C.

1859.

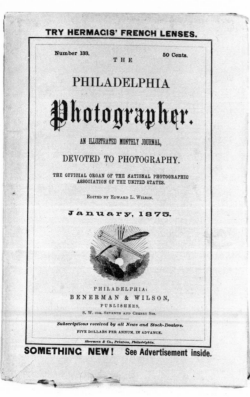

TRY HERMAGIS' FRENCH LENSES.

Number 133.   50 Cents.

THE
PHILADELPHIA
Photographer.
AN ILLUSTRATED MONTHLY JOURNAL,
DEVOTED TO PHOTOGRAPHY.

THE OFFICIAL ORGAN OF THE NATIONAL PHOTOGRAPHIC
ASSOCIATION OF THE UNITED STATES.

EDITED BY EDWARD L. WILSON.

January, 1875.

PHILADELPHIA:
BENERMAN & WILSON,
PUBLISHERS,
S. W. COR. SEVENTH AND CHERRY STS.

Subscriptions received by all News and Stock-Dealers.
FIVE DOLLARS PER ANNUM, IN ADVANCE.

Sherman & Co., Printers, Philadelphia.

SOMETHING NEW!   See Advertisement inside.

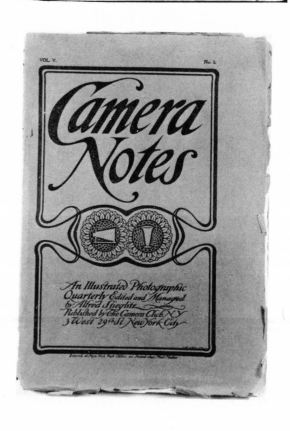

VOL. V.   No. 1.

Camera Notes

An Illustrated Photographic
Quarterly Edited and Managed
by Alfred Stieglitz
Published by The Camera Club, N.Y.
3 West 29th St. New York City

Entered at New York Post-Office as Second-class Mail Matter

Although no photographic journals are known to have been published during photography's first decade, there were reportedly some sixty periodicals circulating in the world by the medium's fiftieth anniversary in 1889.[115] The first journal was an American publication, *The Daguerreian Journal*, which was begun in New York on November 1, 1850. This was followed by *The Photographic and Fine Arts Journal*, begun in New York in January 1851, and by the French journal *La Lumière*, begun in Paris a month later. The first British journal appeared on March 3, 1853, the *Journal of the Photographic Society of London*. The name was changed to *The Photographic Journal* in 1859, and it has been published under this title ever since.

Britain's earliest journals, *The Photographic Journal* and *The British Journal of Photography* (begun in 1854 in Liverpool under a different title) have both survived to the present day, as has France's monthly *Bulletin de la Société Française de Photographie*, begun in Paris in 1855. No American photographic journal of the 1850s, however, survived beyond 1900, and the two earliest were gone by the time American photographers attended the first annual convention of the National Photographic Association in 1868. The regional U.S. journal that lasted the longest was *The St. Louis and Canadian Practical Photographer*, begun in 1878 and published (except for the three-year period 1883–85) until 1905. Other regional journals were attempted in Chicago, Baltimore, and Brooklyn, New York, but were short-lived.

No library or institution houses complete sets of America's three earliest photographic journals. The *National Union Catalog*, which will be found in major U.S. libraries, includes photographic journals among its alphabetical listing of all known periodicals, together with their dates of publication, and provides the names of U.S. libraries (in coded form) where copies of yearly bound volumes of each periodical can be found. Most libraries contain only a few such yearly bound volumes of nineteenth-century photographic journals, and those they do possess have been consigned in many cases to rare book rooms.

The first U.S. journals were not widely circulated, and they contain little information as to who was doing what in photography at the time. The editor of one of these journals complained in later years that his own publication and others as well "were largely made up from French and English publications, and that for the simple reason that for years after the establishment of our first journals there was not half a dozen men in the United States capable, or willing, to write upon the subject of photography, while such as were capable of authorship preferred communicating their information to the philosophical and photographic press of England as the best means of being appreciated."[116]

American journals were illustrated with original, separately-bound-in photographs printed by various new photographic processes up until the 1890s, when the invention of the halftone process allowed reproduction of photographs from the same plates used to print the text. Most of the publications were monthly, and none was issued more frequently than biweekly. Only England maintained a weekly photographic press. Yearly bound issues of photographic journals from the nineteenth century rarely appear at photographic auctions today.

Principal Nineteenth-Century American Photographic Journals

HUMPHREY'S JOURNAL

Began as *The Daguerreian Journal*—New York, Nov. 1, 1850–Dec. 15, 1851.

Humphrey's Journal—New York, April 1852–April 1862; June 15, 1862–April 15, 1863; May 1, 1863–April 15, 1868.

Supplement: *The American Photographic Almanac*—New York, 1865–1868.

PHOTOGRAPHIC AND FINE ARTS JOURNAL

Began as *The Photographic Art Journal*—New York, Jan. 1851–Dec. 1853.

The Photographic and Fine Arts Journal—New York, 1854–1860.

AMERICAN JOURNAL OF PHOTOGRAPHY
Began as *American Journal of Photography and Allied Arts*—New York, 1855–1858 (vols. 1-6); 1858–1867 (n.s. vols. 1-9).
American Journal of Photography—Philadelphia, 1879–1900 (n.s. vols. 1-20).

PHOTOGRAPHIC JOURNAL OF AMERICA
Began as *The Philadelphia Photographer*—Philadelphia, 1864–1888.
Wilson's Photographic Magazine—New York, 1889–1914.
Photographic Journal of America—New York, 1915–1923.
Supplement: *The Photographic Mosaics*—Philadelphia, 1867–1887; New York, 1887–1901 (annual publication).

ANTHONY'S PHOTOGRAPHIC BULLETIN
New York, Feb. 1870–1902.
Supplement: *International Annual of Anthony's Photographic Bulletin*—New York, 1888–1902.

PHOTOGRAPHIC TIMES
New York, 1871–1915.

ST. LOUIS AND CANADIAN PRACTICAL PHOTOGRAPHER
Began as *The St. Louis Practical Photographer*—St. Louis, 1878–1882.
St. Louis Photographer—St. Louis, 1886–1887.
St. Louis and Canadian Practical Photographer—St. Louis, 1888–1905.

PHOTOGRAPHIC WORLD
Philadelphia, 1871–1872.

PHOTOGRAPHERS FRIEND
Baltimore, 1871–1874.

WESTERN PHOTOGRAPHIC NEWS
Chicago, July–December, 1874.

PHOTOGRAPHIC RAYS OF LIGHT
Baltimore, 1878–1907.

AMERICAN ANNUAL OF PHOTOGRAPHY
New York, 1887–1953.

SUN AND SHADE
New York, Photo-Gravure Co., July 1888–March 1896.

PHOTO BEACON
Chicago, 1889–1907.

PHOTO-AMERICAN
Stamford, Conn., 1889–1907.

AMERICAN AMATEUR PHOTOGRAPHER
New York, 1889–1907.

CAMERA NOTES
New York, 1897–1903.

PHOTO ERA
Boston, May 1898–March 1932.

CAMERA AND DARK ROOM
Brooklyn, N.Y., 1899–1906.

PHOTO MINIATURE
New York, 1899–1932.

CAMERA WORK
New York, 1903–1917.

Principal Nineteenth-Century British Photographic Journals

THE PHOTOGRAPHIC JOURNAL
Began as *The Journal of the Photographic Society of London*—London, March 3, 1853–Dec. 1858.
Photographic Journal—London, Jan. 1859–present.

BRITISH JOURNAL OF PHOTOGRAPHY
Began as *The Liverpool Photographic Journal*—Liverpool, Jan. 14, 1854–Dec. 1856.
Liverpool and Manchester Photographic Journal—Liverpool, Jan. 1857–Dec. 1858.
The Photographic Journal—Liverpool, Jan. 1859–Dec. 1859.
British Journal of Photography—Liverpool, Jan. 1860–1863; London, 1864–present.

PHOTOGRAPHIC NOTES

Jersey and London, Jan. 1, 1856–Aug. 1856 (monthly); Sept. 1856–Dec. 1867 (fortnightly).

PHOTOGRAPHIC NEWS

London, Sept. 10, 1858–May 12, 1908 (weekly). Incorporated (1908) with *The Amateur Photographer*.

PHOTOGRAPHIC ART JOURNAL

London, Feb. 1858–Dec. 1858 (monthly). Republished as one volume with original illustrated photograph in 1859.

THE PHOTOGRAPHIC TIMES

London, Nov. 1, 1861–Jan. 15, 1865 (title adopted thereafter by the American publication of the same name).

Principal Nineteenth-Century French Photographic Journals

LA LUMIÈRE

Paris, Feb. 9, 1851–Dec. 30, 1860 (12 vols.).

BULLETIN DE LA SOCIÉTÉ FRANÇAISE DE PHOTOGRAPHIE

Paris, Jan. 1, 1855–present (monthly).

REVUE PHOTOGRAPHIQUE

Paris, Nov. 5, 1855–Dec. 1865 (monthly).

LE MONITEUR DE LA PHOTOGRAPHIE

Paris, 1861–1914 (fortnightly).

Principal Nineteenth-Century German Photographic Journals

PHOTOGRAPHISCHES JOURNAL

Leipzig, Jan. 1, 1854–1865.

PHOTOGRAPHISCHES ARCHIV

Elberfeld, Jan. 1860–1897 (monthly).

PHOTOGRAPHISCHE MITTHEILUNGEN

Berlin, 1864–1911 (monthly; semi-monthly).

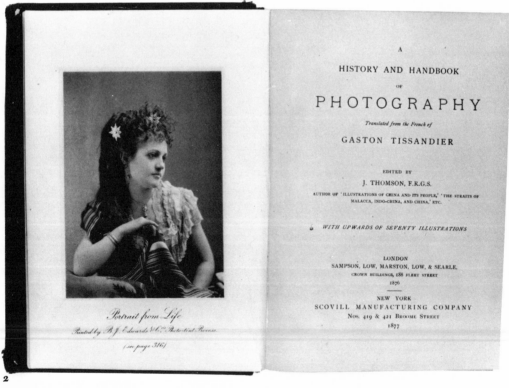

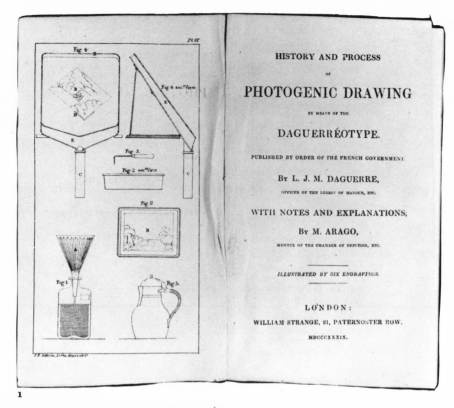

1 World's first photographic manual (English edition) 2 An 1877 manual published in three languages

PHOTOGRAPHY BOOKS, MANUALS, AND CATALOGS

BOOKS AND MANUALS   The vast majority of books published in the nineteenth century that dealt with the history of photography or the development and practice of particular photographic processes were published in England and France. Up until 1872, only one U.S. firm (Beneman and Wilson in Philadelphia) devoted itself principally to photographic publishing.[117] The volume of publishing became quite sizeable; forty-four new books were produced in the year 1888 alone, according to one historian.[118] The American photographic journal editors Henry Hunt Snelling and Edward L. Wilson were perhaps the foremost early U.S. publishers of photography books and manuals, but also prominent among the authors of such books published in America was Dr. Herman W. Vogel (1834–99), editor of a German photographic journal and director of the Royal Photochemical Laboratory in Berlin (see page 84). Dr. Vogel was a guest of honor at the 1871 and 1883 annual conventions of the National Photographic Association and served as the German government's imperial commissioner at international photographic exhibitions held in Philadelphia during the U.S. Centennial and in Chicago in 1893.[119]

It is sometimes difficult to determine what constitutes a book, a manual, or a handbook on a photography subject. For example, a New York dealer listed a Vogel work as a book in 1973, whereas another Vogel work had been listed among an offering of handbooks at a New York auction the previous year. Rare books, manuals, handbooks, and even catalogs will frequently be found included in groups of publications offered as a single lot at photographic auctions. Even the choicest nineteenth-century items will occasionally turn up in such lots. Within the past decade several U.S. publishers have begun issuing reprints of selected nineteenth-century photography books and manuals; these publishers include the Arno Press and Dover Publications in New York; Morgan and Morgan in Dobbs Ferry, New York; and the Helios Press, Pawlet, Vermont.

CATALOGS   The significance and importance of manufacturers' catalogs covering the availability of equipment, supplies, photographic literature, or actual photographs can be appreciated only when such items are studied. Frequently, a particular catalog will provide information not recorded elsewhere or will shed new light or a different perspective on the state of the photographic art of the period. Catalogs produced in the 1840s or 1850s are extremely rare. Catalogs issued in the 1860s by the publishers of card stereographs, carte de visite portraits, etc., provide the only complete record of the subject matter, places, and people photographed in this period. In 1851 the California photographer Robert Vance provided a catalog of more than one hundred of the daguerreotype views he had taken the previous two years during the gold rush. Since this provides the only record of the subject matter of these photographs, which are now lost (or destroyed), the list is reproduced in the Appendix as a point of reference in the event any of the daguerreotypes turn up in future. One publisher of catalogs of available photographs, the Soule Company of Boston, evidently operated as a pioneer in the field of supplying photographs for book illustration as well as for private sale.[120] Illustrations were not used to a large degree in catalogs published before 1870. By the latter part of the nineteenth century and during the early decades of the twentieth, catalogs began to be lavishly illustrated with art nouveau motifs, then in vogue.

SKETCHES

OF A

SUMMER TOUR.

The Brig o' Doon.

Magyar Nobleman.

Norwegian Peasants.

The Grand Canal (Venice).

NEW YORK:
PRINTED BY WILLIAM J. READ,
(AT BROWNSON'S STEAM JOB PRINTING ESTABLISHMENT,)
No. 45 Fulton Street.
1866

The Mode of Traveling in Norway.

Throughout publishing history, individuals have privately printed books in limited editions for distribution to family, friends, libraries, etc. This is among the earliest of such items produced in the United States to contain original photographs bound in with the text. The book consists of a series of letters addressed to a friend in America describing a voyage to the British Isles and Europe, and includes eleven albumen prints made in Ireland, Scotland, Norway, Austria, and Italy.

BOOKS ILLUSTRATED WITH
ORIGINAL PHOTOGRAPHS

Beginning in 1844, publishers began issuing limited editions of books containing original photographs, printed separately but bound with the text. This process was carried on until the turn of the century, when the halftone process for reproducing photographs was perfected, allowing the printing of text and photographic illustrations simultaneously on the same press.

W. H. Fox Talbot was first to prepare a photographically illustrated book, *The Pencil of Nature*, which was published in six parts (London, 1844–46). The first installment was limited to approximately two hundred copies, but the number of subscribers dwindled in the course of the later installments, owing to the high price, delay in delivery, and deterioration of the images.[121] The entire work consists of twenty-four calotype photographs, each accompanied by a commentary. Only a dozen complete sets are known to be extant. In 1971 one sold at auction in England for $6,500. In 1845 Talbot issued a second publication, *Sun Pictures in Scotland*, illustrated with twenty-three calotypes.

Books illustrated with original photographs made their appearance in France in 1850 and in America in 1854. The earliest American book, *Homes of American Statesmen* (New York, 1854), contains a mounted photograph of the John Hancock house in Boston as a frontispiece. American photographically illustrated books published in the 1850s are extremely rare. No copy is known to exist, for example, of *The Crystallotype* (New York, 1855), an illustrated record of the New York Crystal Palace Fair of 1853 (the New York Crystal Palace was built for the 1853 fair and was destroyed by fire in 1858). In 1866 the editor of an American photographic journal lamented: "In England, books illustrated by photographs are quite common and obtainable at a reasonable price. A few faint attempts at it have been made in this country, but we hope before another holiday season we shall have something really fine."[122] Beginning in 1868, books were prepared in the United States with biographies and original photographic illustrations of noteworthy citizens of a number of cities. The first, *Biographical Sketches of the Leading Men of Chicago*, was published in a limited edition of five hundred by John Carbutt. Many copies were subsequently destroyed in the 1871 Chicago fire, however, so copies of this book are rare. Similar books published in the 1870s provided biographies and photographs of leading citizens of Baltimore, Cincinnati, Syracuse, and the state of Nebraska.

Probably the most expensive book illustrated with original photographs and published in the nineteenth century was *The Queen's Bible*, which was prepared for Queen Victoria and issued in a limited edition of 170 copies in 1862.[123] From the 1860s to the 1890s, English and European publishers adopted the practice of illustrating new and limited editions of literary and poetical works by noted authors and poets with photographs specially taken for the publications.

The distinction was sometimes blurred between what one publisher might offer as a photographically illustrated book and another as an album of photographic views. Thus *San Francisco Album* by George F. Fardon, a book of photographs issued by Herre and Bauer circa 1856, was described by the publishers as "the earliest collection of views of an American city." Many "portrait gallery" style books published in England and Europe with photographs of prominent people were also classed, or referred to in subtitles, as albums.

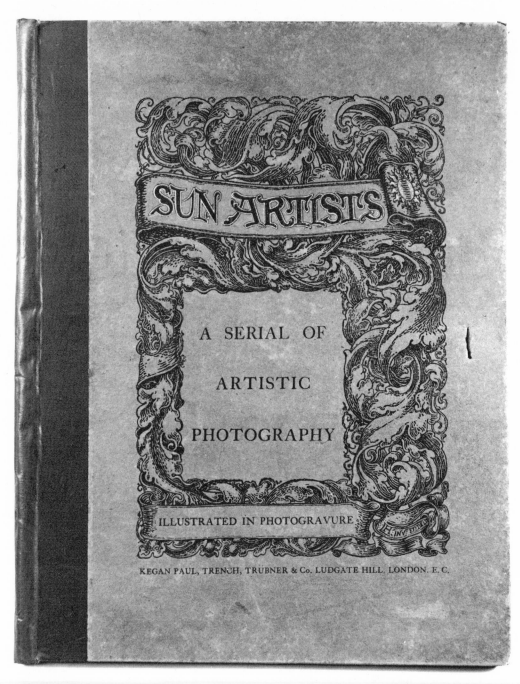

Portfolio jacket of *Sun Artists,* which contains eight monographic booklets issued between October 1889 and July 1891. Edited by W. Arthur Boord, the series includes text by various authors and 32 photogravures size 11½ × 15 inches by Joseph Gale, H. P. Robinson, J. B. Wellington, Lyddell Sawyer, Julia Margaret Cameron, B. G. Wilkinson, Mrs. F. W. H. Myers, and F. M. Sutcliffe. This publication was said to be the first to represent the "artistic" position of photography.

PHOTOGRAPHIC PORTFOLIOS

Today most major photographic galleries offer portfolios of photographs prepared by various contemporary photographers. Some museums and institutions do likewise, as for example the International Museum at Rochester, which has offered portfolios of prints made from the museum's collection of negatives by Lewis Hine (whose early twentieth-century photographs of child labor conditions led to the passage of a child labor law in 1916). The modern photographic portfolio was defined by Jacob Deschin in 1973 in these words: "A portfolio is a sampling of photographs by one or more photographers, either in reproduction or originals, and varying in price from a few dollars to a thousand or more, in editions of a few copies to several thousands."[124]

Nineteenth-century photographic portfolios, with a few exceptions (see below), generally consisted of the works of only one photographer. Prior to the invention of the halftone process for reproducing photographs in the 1890s, portfolios were issued with original photographs or with prints made by a photomechanical process; editions were seldom larger than a thousand. The publication in England of a series of photographic portfolios under the title *Sun Artists* during the period 1889–91 (see illustration, left) might be cited as an example of a portfolio containing photographs of more than one photographer; however, the edition consisted of five separate portfolios of works by different photographers, which were prepared consecutively during the three-year period, and it might have continued with additional portfolios prepared separately by others, had sales warranted.

The vast majority of nineteenth-century portfolios were issued in England and on the Continent (see Appendix). Many such publications were issued simultaneously by (or distributed through) American publishers. James Leon Williams's five-portfolio edition of *The Home and Haunts of Shakespeare* (see pages 88–89),

for example, was published simultaneously in London and in New York (by Charles Scribner's Sons) in 1891. An 1867 portfolio of early carbon prints made by Adolphe Braun (of landscape views in Dornbach, France) was offered through Wilson and Hood of Philadelphia.[125] An 1873 portfolio entitled *Twenty-five English Photographs*, by R. M. Gordon, was issued simultaneously by W. J. Stillman in London and by C. F. McKim in New York.[126]

One of the most prolific publishers of portfolios and books illustrated with photographs was the naturalistic photographer Peter H. Emerson, who photographed life and landscapes in rural England. In 1974, at what was billed as Emerson's first one-man exhibition (posthumously at a New York gallery), copies of two of Emerson's portfolios, *The Compleat Angler* (1888) and *Wild Life on a Tidal Water* (1890), were offered at $1,500 and $5,000 respectively. The most noted American portfolio editions are probably those made in the 1870s and 1880s of scenic wonders in the Rocky Mountains and the Far West. At a 1971 New York auction, a portfolio of forty-one photographs by W. H. Jackson of Yellowstone National Park and other western views brought $5,750. At the same auction, a portfolio of sixty photographs by Timothy O'Sullivan and William Bell, taken on the Wheeler surveys (1871–74) of territory west of the hundredth meridian, brought $6,000.

Perhaps the most noteworthy nineteenth-century work published in the United States was Eadweard Muybridge's summarized report on his photographic studies of human and animal locomotion at Stanford University. This was *Animal Locomotion* (Philadelphia, 1887), which consisted of eleven volumes and a series of portfolios containing 781 large photographs. One portfolio from this work, containing ninety-nine collotypes of nude or partially nude persons and of horses, birds, and other animals in motion, sold for $1,000 at a 1972 New York auction.

Photographic
Miscellany

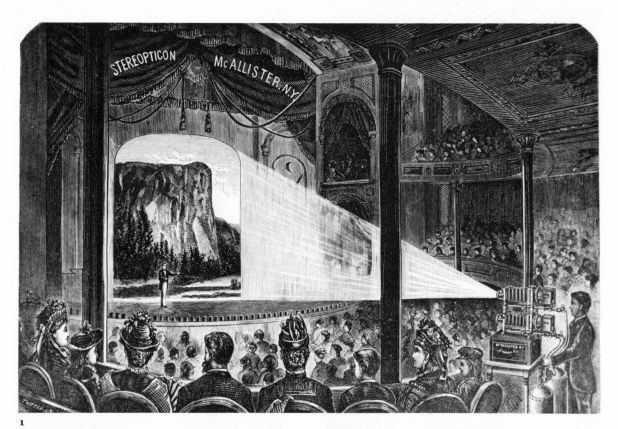

1 Artist's rendering of a stereopticon slide lecture, as depicted in an 1893 catalog of T. H. McAllister Manufacturing Optician, New York City   2 Lantern slide view of a monument in Munich, one of thousands of American and European slide views advertised by McAllister at fifty cents each   3 Slide of a New York City fire, circa 1890, made by George Rockwood from a Kodak Model I or II camera with a rounded image frame

PHOTOGRAPHIC SLIDES

The projection of hand-drawn and hand-painted glass slides for audience viewing began as early as the seventeenth century. Photographic slides were introduced in 1850 in America and were exhibited at the Crystal Palace exhibition in London the following year. The term *magic lantern* was applied to the projection equipment used; hence the nomenclature *lantern slides* usually applied to photographic slides manufactured in the nineteenth century.

American and European slides customarily measure 3½ x 4 inches, while those manufactured in England were normally 3½ inches square. Slides can also be found that are circular, egg-shaped, rectangular, and crown-shaped. Novelty slides were also produced which were capable of giving the effect of motion. These included, for example, slip glass slides where human or animated movement could be effected by moving one slide of a particular image in front of another slide having a slightly different version of the same image. Slides were painted with watercolors or transparent oils or were dyed.

The term *stereopticon* applied to a combination of two projectors which made it possible to dissolve views while showing them in sequence. This type of projector utilized limelight as opposed to oil for illumination and was the principal type used after 1870. Another version of the basic instrument was the *artopticon*, which was designed to use oil but could be adapted for the gases. In the stereopticon, oxygen and hydrogen gases were burned against a pellet of lime. By using large parabolic reflectors with a stereopticon, it was possible to spotlight the stage, which gave rise to the expression that a speaker or performing artist so spotlighted was "in the limelight."[127]

Frederick and William Langenheim of Philadelphia are credited with introducing the first photographic slides, and they served as the principal suppliers until 1874, when their business was sold to a Massachusetts competitor, Casper W. Briggs, who dominated the market thereafter until World War I. Casper Briggs has been described as something of a forerunner of Hollywood, since his firm produced a wide variety of religious, literary, historical, humorous, and scientific sets of slides which were quite popular on the lecture circuit.[128] The principal U.S. manufacturer of projection equipment was C. T. Milligen, also of Philadelphia.

Good photographic slides were made by any of the various photographic processes practiced in the nineteenth century, but a process that might yield excellent results in some hands failed altogether in others. The English photographer Frederick Evans, who worked principally in platinum printing, produced exceptionally fine slides, for example. T. C. Roche, who photographed for Mathew Brady during the Civil War, and for E. and H. T. Anthony for several decades after the war, maintained as late as 1891 that the collodion glass negative process yielded "the best results in the matter of detail in the pictures, and cleanness in the highlights."[129]

Photographic slides from the nineteenth century remain quite plentiful, perhaps because their owners viewed them as being more worthy of preservation than ordinary photographic prints. Value varies according to the rarity, date, and subject matter of particular specimens. In 1971 a large group of slide views taken in New York City in the 1880s and 1890s brought approximately $4 to $10 apiece, depending upon image subject matter. An early slide (circa 1860) by C. E. Watkins of the mammoth trees in California was offered for $17.50 by a New York dealer in 1973.

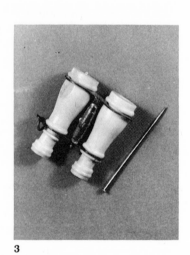

1

2

3

4

1 Ivorytype portrait on glass   **2** Same portrait, back-lighted; coloring (not visible in this reproduction) makes it appear like a lighted oil painting.   **3** Miniature pair of opera glasses (shown here in actual size) containing two microphotographs visible to the naked eye when the "glasses" are aimed at a light source   **4** Photographic portrait secured on porcelain

PHOTOGRAPHIC VARIANTS

IVORYTYPES   By a process patented in England in 1855, photographic images were secured on the surface of artificial ivory sensitized with a coating of either albumen or collodion. When colored, these photographs resembled an ivory miniature portrait, but were produced at a fraction of the normal cost of such miniatures. Ivorytypes made of prominent statesmen, such as Prime Minister Gladstone, were quite popular. An ivorytype portrait 8 x 10 inches of the Civil War general P. G. T. Beauregard made at a New Orleans gallery sold for $100 at a New York auction in 1970.

An American ivorytype process was introduced and exhibited for the first time by F. A. Wenderoth at the 1859 fair of the Franklin Institute in Philadelphia. By this and other competitive processes, a photograph could be colored and sealed on plate glass so as to exhibit the effect of an oil portrait when lighted from behind (see illustration, left).[130]

PHOTOGRAPHS ON LEATHER   Photographs secured on leather resemble tintypes, except that the overall appearance is more brown than black. Although such specimens are now rare, it was easier to impregnate leather with photographic chemicals than it was many other substances. At a 1975 New York auction, an image of two seated men on a piece of leather 3¼ x 2½ inches (taken circa 1855) brought $120.

CERAMIC PHOTOGRAPHS   The first successful method of securing colored photographic images on enamel, porcelain, china, etc., was introduced and patented in England in 1854. After an image was secured by conventional photographic sensitizing techniques, it was colored, baked in an oven, and coated with a varnish.[131] A different method, by which a positive image on glass was transferred from the glass to enamel or porcelain and then baked in an oven, was developed in France in 1867.[132] Ceramic photographs remained popular throughout the nineteenth century and like miniature portraits were fitted into lockets, brooches, leather cases, etc. *American Artisan*, in referring to a method of producing porcelain photographs introduced by Black and Case in Boston, noted that the pictures were "especially beautiful when suspended where the light can pass through the porcelain, which renders the shading soft and delicate and brings out many effects which cannot be produced in an ordinary picture."[133]

MICROPHOTOGRAPHS   In the 1850s, methods were perfected of securing photographic images $\frac{1}{16}$ inch in size on microscope slides for viewing through a microscope. The novelty became a fad after a pinhead-size photograph of the Ten Commandments was produced, and in 1867 a microphotographic portrait mosaic of all 450 members of the French Chamber of Deputies was exhibited at the International Exhibition held that year in Paris. Microphotographic images were secured by copying other small images through a microscope objective and printing them on slides with specially prepared collodion, which would allow the copied image to remain grain-free when magnified for viewing.[134] Microphotographs were set in jewelry, buttons, and numerous other objects, and well into the twentieth century were sold as souvenirs at tourist sites, particularly in the form of tiny opera glasses incorporating a small magnifying lens over the picture (see illustration, left).

OTHER VARIANTS   By 1856 photographs had been secured on wood, stained glass, silk, and canvas. A silk photograph secured in the 1850s by A. S. Southworth of Boston was a featured item at the third national convention of the National Photographic Association held in June 1871.[135]

Photographer
Listings

ENGLISH AND SCOTTISH PHOTOGRAPHERS OF THE DAGUERREAN ERA

London Daguerreotypists

Beard, Richard, Establishment
    Cooper, J. T.
    Goddard, John F.
Claudet, Antoine
Cocke, Archibald Lewis
Kilburn, William E.
Mayall, John J. E.
Telfer, William
Williams, T. R.

Daguerreotypists Outside London

Booth, H. C. *Low Harrowgate*
Dancer, J. B. *Liverpool and Manchester*
Davidson, Thomas *Edinburgh*
Hughes, C. Jabez *Glasgow*
Lowe, R. *Cheltenham*
Pumphrey, William *York*
Ross and Thompson *Edinburgh*
Sharp, Thomas *Somerset County*
Shaw, George *Birmingham*
Sims, Thomas *Weston-Super-Mare*
Werge, John *Glasgow*
Whitlock, H. J. *Warwickshire*

Principal Calotype Practitioners

Buckle, Samuel *Peterborough*
Collen, Henry *London*
Cundall, Joseph

Delamotte, Philip H. *London*
Fenton, Roger
Heath, Vernon
Henneman, Nikolaas
Hill, D. O. and Adamson, Robert *Edinburgh*
Jones, Rev. Calvert
Keith, Dr. Thomas *Edinburgh*
Owen, Hugh
Pumphrey, William *York*
Sedgfield, Russell
Smith, John Shaw
Smith, Samuel *Wisbech*
Talbot, W. H. Fox
Turner, Benjamin Bracknell

London Members of the Calotype Club*

Fry, Peter Wickens (founder)
Ansdell, Richard
Archer, F. S.
Berger, Frederick W.
Cundall, Joseph
Diamond, Dr. Hugh
Fenton, Roger
Foster, Peter Le Neve
Herbert, John Rogers
Hunt, Robert, F.R.S.
Kater, Edward, F.R.S.
Knight, John Prescott
Newton, Sir William
Owen, Hugh
Vignoles, Charles, F.R.S.
Wilson, Sir Thomas M.

SOURCES *The History of Photography*, Helmut and Alison Gernsheim, Thames and Hudson, London, 1969.
Evolution of Photography, John Werge, London, 1890. Kodak Museum, Kodak, Ltd.

*Operated 1847–1851

REGIONAL LISTING OF AMERICAN PHOTOGRAPHERS OPERATING IN THE 1840s AND 1850s

Boston

Bemis, Samuel
Black, J. W.
Bond, William C.
Bradlee, J. E.
Campbell, B. F.
Channing, W. F.
Charter, Miss S. R.
Chase, L. G.
Cooke, Josiah
Cutting, James
Davis Brothers
Davis, J. J. P.
Drew, Clement
Fessenden, Benjamin
French, Benjamin
Fuller, George
Hale, L. H.
Hawes, Josiah
Hayward, G. W.
Ives, L. M.
Jones, J. Wesley
Masury, Samuel
Moore, J. B.
Nicols, John P.
Ormsbee, Marcus
Ormsbee and Silsbee
Pennell, Joseph
Plumbe, John
Plumbe, Richard
Rice, J. L.
Sawyer, John
Sharp, Philip T.
Shew, William
Silsbee, George M.
Southworth and Pennell
Southworth and Hawes
Wetherby, Isaac A.
Whipple, John Adams
White, Asa
Winslow, Abraham
Woodward, William

New England

Adams, George *Worcester, Mass.*
Baker, E. H. *Providence, R. I.*
Bartlett, H. H. *Hartford, Conn.*
Bowen, N. O. *Norwich, Conn.*
Brown, F. A. *Manchester, N.H.*
Cathan, Lucius H. *Townshend, Vt.; Boston*
Champney, L. C. *Itinerant (Mass.; Vermont)*
Chapin, Moses *Worcester, Mass.*
Clark, Anson *West Stockbridge, Mass.*
Cone, D. D. *Fisherville, N.H.*
Cooley, O. H. *Springfield, Mass.*
Ellis and Burnham *Bangor, Me.*
Foster, B. *Portland, Me.*
Gage, Franklin P. *St. Johnsbury, Vt.*
Gay, C. H. *New London, Conn.*
Gilchrest and Currier *Lowell, Mass.*
Goddard, Emerson *New Woonsocket, R.I.*
Hartshorn, W. S. *Providence, R.I.*
Hartshorn and Masury *Providence, R.I.*
Hawes (Howes), Samuel P. *Lowell, Mass.*
Hayden, Hiram W. *Waterbury, Conn.*
Holcomb, J. G. *Augusta, Me.*
Holcomb, Sarah *Itinerant (Mass.; N.H.)*
Howe, Elias *Cambridgeport, Mass.*
Kimball, W. H. *Concord, N.H.*
Litch and Graniss *Waterbury, Conn.*
McKeney, E. H. *Biddeford, Me.*
McIntosh, H. P. *Newburyport, Mass.*
Manchester Brothers (Henry and Edwin)
  Providence, R.I.
Masury, Samuel *Providence, R.I.*
Moore, Henry *Lowell, Mass.*
Moulthroup, M. *New Haven, Conn.*
Pardee, Phineas *New Haven, Conn.*
Peck, Samuel *New Haven, Conn.*
Ritten, E. D. *Danbury, Conn.*
Stancliff, J. W. *Hartford, Conn.*
Van Alsten, A. *Worcester, Mass.*
Warren, Gardner *Woonsocket, R.I.*
Warren, George K. *Lowell, Mass.*
Weller, F. G. *Littleton, N.H.*

Wells, J. D.   *Northampton, Mass.*
White, Franklin   *Lancaster, N.H.*
White, L.   *Springfield, Mass.*

New York State

Armstrong, Mrs. Agnes   *Peekskill*
Appleby, R. B.   *Rochester*
Barnard, George N.   *Oswego*
Barnes, Marcelia   *Salem Cross Roads*
Beech, W. P.   *Homer*
Benedict, P. H.   *Syracuse*
Churchill, R. E.   *Albany*
Clark Brothers   *Utica; Syracuse; Boston*
Clark, F. J.   *Utica*
Davie, D. D. T.   *Utica; Syracuse*
Davis, W. P.   *Union Springs*
Denney, C. B.   *Rochester*
DeReimer, C. B.   *Auburn*
Dodge, Edward S.   *Poughkeepsie*
Dunning, U.   *Utica*
Evans, G.   *Utica*
Evans, O. B.   *Buffalo*
Everett, R., Jr.   *Utica*
Fairchild, A.   *Deriter (De Ruyter?)*
Finley, M.   *Canandaigua*
Geer and Benedict   *Syracuse*
Goddard, M. J.   *Lyons*
Graves, E. R.   *Lockport*
Gray, L.   *Oswego*
Hall, W. H.   *Rouse's Point*
Hartman, Henry G.   *Rochester*
Higgins, B. L.   *Syracuse*
Hill, Levi   *Westkill; Saugerties*
Hill, R. H.   *Kingston*
Hovey, Daniel   *Rochester*
Hoyt, Mary S.   *Syracuse*
Hudson, E. A.   *Syracuse*
Huntley, P. C.   *Paris*
Johnson, C. N.   *Batavia*
Johnston, D. B.   *Utica*
Kelsey, John   *Rochester*
McDonald, A.   *Buffalo*
McDonald, D.   *Buffalo*
McDonald, R.   *Buffalo*
Marcus, J. B.   *Chenango*
Myers, J. S.   *Poughkeepsie*
Nicols, A. C.   *Fulton*
Parsons, L. V.   *Auburn*
Pruden, Henry   *Lockport*
Ragg, G. S.   *Denmark*

Sissons, N. E.   *Albany*
Thompson, S. J.   *Albany*
Tomlinson, W. A.   *Poughkeepsie; Troy; N.Y.C.*
Walker, S. L.   *Albany; Poughkeepsie*
Wentworth, Henry   *Fort Plain*
Westcott, C. P.   *Watertown*
Whitney, C. B.   *Rochester*
Whitney, Edward T.   *Rochester; Norwalk, Ct.*

New York City

Anson, Charles
Anson, Rufus
Anthony, Edward
Atkins, J.
Beals, A. T.
Beckers, Alexander
Beckmann, Madam
Beekman & Brothers
Bogardus, Abraham
Brady, Mathew
Brinckerhoff, J. DeWitt
Brown, Eliphalet M.
Brown, James A.
Burgess, Nathan G.
Butler, William H.
Cady, James
Carden and Co.
Carvalho, S. N.
Chilton, James R.
Cook, Jane
Dobyns, T. C.
Duchochois, P. C.
Durang, W. H.
Edwards, J. M.
Field, Erastus S.
Fredericks, C. D.
Gavit, Daniel E.
Gurney, Jeremiah and Son
Haas, Philip
Hanson, Peter
Harrison, Charles C.
Harrison, Gabriel
Holmes, Silas A.
Holt, G. M. A.
Howell, E. M.
Insley, Henry
Jacquith, N. C.
Johnson, John
Landy, James
Lawrence, M. M.

[119]

Lewis, W. and W. H.
Mayr, Christian
Meade, Charles R.
Metcalf, W.
Morand, Augustus
Morse, S. F. B.
Muller, C. J.
Pearsall, Alva
Perry, Edward
Piard, Victor
Plumbe, John
Prevost, Victor
Prud'homme, J. F. E.
Reese and Co.
Rice, S. N.
Robinson, Joseph C.
Rockwood, George
Root, Marcus
Root, Samuel
Seager, D. W.
Seely, Charles
Selleck, S.
Snelling, Henry Hunt
Stansbury, B.
Tomlinson, W. A.
Turner, A. A.
Turner, G. R.
Venino, Francis
Weston, R.
Whipple, A. W.
White, Edward
Whitehurst, Jesse
Whittemore, H.
Wolcott, Alexander S.
Wood, John
Woodridge, John T.

Philadelphia

Broadbent, Samuel
Canfield, Dr.
Collins, David
Cornelius, Robert
Cresson, Charles
Currie, William
Ehrmann, Charles
Ennis, T. L.
Frazer, John
Germon, Washington L.
Goddard, Dr. Paul B.
Housekeeper, Cheney H.

Johnson, Walter R.
Kern, Edward M.
Langenheim, Frederick and William
McClees, James E.
Mason, William G.
Mayall, J. J. E.
Rhenn, Isaac
Richards, Frederick De B.
Shew, Myron
Shew, Trueman
Spieler, William F.
Swift, H. B.
Thompson, Warren
Van Loan, Samuel
Williams, J. B.

New Jersey and Pennsylvania

Campbell, John   *Jersey City, N.J.*
Clark, David   *New Brunswick, N.J.*
Frost, D. V.   *Augusta, Pa.*
Haskell, M.   *Jersey City, N.J.*
Hough and Anthony   *Pittsburgh, Pa.*
Martin, Jane P.   *Paterson, N.J.*
Moses, Morris   *Trenton, N.J.*
Prosch, George W.   *Newark, N.J.*
Stauffer, Jacob   *Mt. Joy, Pa.*
Vail, J. H.   *New Brunswick, N.J.*
Ward, Charles V.   *Bloomfield, N.J.*
Ward, Jacob   *Bloomfield, N.J.*

Maryland and District of Columbia

Baker, F. S.   *Baltimore, Md.*
Bennett, N. S.   *Washington, D.C.*
Byerly, Jacob   *Frederick, Md.*
Coale, George B.   *Baltimore, Md.*
Fitz, Henry   *Baltimore, Md.; Washington, D.C.*
Gardner, Alexander   *Washington, D.C.*
Marks, H. R.   *Baltimore, Md.*
Page, Charles G.   *Washington, D.C.*
Paige, Blanchard P.   *Washington, D.C.*
Shew, Jacob   *Baltimore, Md.; Philadelphia, Pa.*
Stanley, J. M.   *Washington, D.C.*
Walker, L. E.   *Washington, D.C.*
Walzl, Richard   *Baltimore, Md.*
Warner, L. T.   *Washington, D.C.*
West, George R.   *Washington, D.C.*
Whitehurst, J. H.   *Baltimore, Md.; Washington, D.C.*

The South

Adams, Dan *Nashville, Tenn.*
Anderson, D. H. *Richmond, Va.*
Anthony, J. B. *Poplar Grove, S.C.*
Bailey, Thomas *Columbia, Tenn.*
Barnard, F. A. *Alabama*
Barnes, C. *Mobile, Ala.*
Bennett, John A. *Mobile, Ala.*
Bolles, Jesse H. *Charleston, S.C.*
Bryant, Henry *Virginia*
Cary, P. M. *Savannah, Ga.*
Cook, George S. *New Orleans, La; N.Y.C.; Charleston, S.C.*
Cridland, T. W. *Lexington, Ky.*
Dobyns, T. J. *New Orleans, La.; Louisville, Ky.; Nashville, Tenn.; Memphis, Tenn.; St. Louis, Mo.; N.Y.C.*
Elliott, E. *Chester, S.C.*
Fahrenberg, Albert *Louisville, Ky.*
Hewitt, John M. *Louisville, Ky.*
Hough, Eugenio *Petersburg, Va.*
Jacobs, Emil *New Orleans, La.*
Leinback, T. *Salem, N.C.*
L'Homdieu, Charles *Charleston, S.C.*
Lilienthal, Theodore *New Orleans, La.*
Lion, Jules *New Orleans, La.*
Lloyd, John R. *Tallahassee, Fla.*
Maguire, James *New Orleans, La.*
Moissenet, F. *New Orleans, La.*
Partridge, A. C. *Wheeling, W. Va.*
Shorb, J. R. *Winnsboro, S.C.*
Simons, M. P. *Richmond, Va.*
Troendle, Joseph *Louisville, Ky.*
Webster, I. B. *Louisville, Ky.*
Wenderoth, F. A. *Charleston, S.C.*
Whitehurst, J. H. *Richmond, Va.; Norfolk, Va.; Petersburg, Va.; Lynchburg, Va.*
Wood, R. L. *Macon, Ga.*

Midwest

Alschuler, S. D. *Chicago, Ill.*
Balch, H. A. *Joliet, Ill.*
Bardwell, Jex *Detroit, Mich.*
Battersby, Joseph *Chicago, Ill.*
Benson, W. *Boonville, Mo.*
Bisbee, A. *Dayton, Ohio*
Boisseau, Alfred *Cleveland, Ohio*
Brand, Edwin L. *Chicago, Ill.*
Brown, H. S. *Milwaukee, Wis.*
Canfield, H. D. *St. Louis, Mo.*
Clifford, R. A. *Milwaukee, Wis.*

Combs, Fred *St. Louis, Mo.*
Easterly, Thomas *St. Louis, Mo.*
Farris, Thomas *Cincinnati, Ohio*
Fassett, Samuel M. *Chicago, Ill.*
Finley, A. C. *Jerseyville, Ill.*
Fitzgibbons, J. H. *St. Louis, Mo.*
Fontayne, Charles *Cincinnati, Ohio*
Fuller, John S. *Madison, Wis.*
Garlick, Theodatus *Cleveland, Ohio*
Gatewood, E. H. *Boonville, Mo.*
Gorgas, John M. *Floating gallery on Ohio and Mississippi Rivers*
Griswold, Victor M. *Tiffin, Ohio; Lancaster, Pa.*
Hawkins, Ezekiel *Cincinnati, Ohio*
Hesler, Alexander *Galena, Ill.; Chicago, Ill.*
Hopes, Caroline *St. Louis, Mo.*
Howell, W. B. *Lexington, Mo.*
Hunter, John *Chicago, Ill.*
Johnson, Charles E. *Cleveland, Ohio*
Kelsey, Calvin C. *Chicago, Ill.*
Knight, W. M. *Racine, Wis.*
Long, H. H. and Enoch *St. Louis, Mo.*
Martin, J. E. *Detroit, Mich.*
Merrick, Dr. G. W. *Adrian, Mich.*
Miles, Charles T. *Fayette, Mo.*
Moore and Ward *St. Louis, Mo.*
Nicholson, John *Columbus, Ind.*
Porter, William *Cincinnati, Ohio*
Ryder, James *Cleveland, Ohio*
Smith, Hamilton *Cleveland, Ohio; Gambier, Ohio*
Stamm and Upman *Milwaukee, Wis.*
Sutton and Brothers *Chicago, Ill.*
Von Schneidau, Polycarpus *Chicago, Ill.*
Whitney, Joel E. *St. Paul, Minn.*
Whitney, T. R. *St. Louis, Mo.*

West

Bradley, Henry *San Francisco, Calif.*
Britt, Peter *Highland, Ill.; Jacksonville, Ore.*
Chamberlain, W. G. *Denver, Colo.*
Coombs, F. *San Francisco, Calif.*
Edouart, Alexander *San Francisco, Calif.*
Ford, J. M. *San Francisco, Calif.; Sacramento, Calif.*
McIntyre, S. S. *San Francisco, Calif.*
Nahl, Hugo, W. A. *San Francisco, Calif.*
Rulofson, W. H. *San Francisco, Calif.*
Selkirk, J. H. *Matagorda, Tex.*
Shew, William *San Francisco, Calif.*
Vance, Robert H. *San Francisco, Calif.*

STEREOPHOTOGRAPHERS OF THE
1850s AND 1860s

The United States

Adams, S. F.   *New Bedford, Mass.*
Adams, S. F.   *Oak Bluffs, Mass.*
Allen, E. L.   *Boston, Mass.*
Alley, E. H.   *Toledo, Ohio*
American Stereoscopic Co.   *Philadelphia, Pa.*
Anthony, E. and H. T. and Co.   *New York City*
Babbitt   *Niagara Falls, N.Y.*
Barker, George   *Niagara Falls, N.Y.*
Barnes, O. C.   *Stowe, Vt.*
Barnum, DeLoss   *Boston, Mass., and Roxbury, Mass.*
Bartlett and French   *Philadelphia, Pa.*
Battelle, W.   *Taunton, Mass.*
Beal's Art Gallery   *Minneapolis, Minn.*
Beckel Brothers   *Lockport, N.Y.*
Beers Brothers   *New York City*
Bell, William   *Washington, D.C.*
Benecke, R.   *St. Louis, Mo.*
Bierstadt, Charles   *Niagara Falls, N.Y.*
Bierstadt Brothers   *New Bedford, Mass.*
Boehl and Koenig   *St. Louis, Mo.*
Bowie's Stereoscopic Views   *Corry, Pa.*
Bowman, W. E.   *Ottawa, Ill.*
Brown, Josiah   *Mauch Chunk, Pa.*
Browne, J. C.   *Philadelphia, Pa.*
Bundy   *Middletown, Conn.*
Bundy and Williams   *New Haven, Conn.*
Carbutt, John   *Chicago, Ill.*
Chase, William M.   *Baltimore, Md.*
Cooley, Sam A.   *Hilton Head, S.C.*
Cooley, Sam A.   *Jacksonville, Fla.*
Coonley and Wolfersberger   *Philadelphia, Pa.*
Cremer, George   *Philadelphia, Pa.*
Davis, S.   *Niagara Falls, N.Y.*
Doerr and Jacobson   *San Antonio, Tex.*
Duchochois, P. C.   *New York City*
Fifield, H. S.   *Lincoln, N.H.*
Gage, F. B.   *St. Johnsbury, Vt.*

SOURCE   *Stereo Views, A History of Stereographs in America and Their Collection,* William Culp Darrah, Times & News Publishing Co., Gettysburg, Pa., 1964.

Gardner, Alexander   *Washington, D.C.*
Gates, G. F.   *Watkins, N.Y.*
Gill, William L.   *Lancaster, Pa.*
Gurney, Jeremiah and Son   *New York City*
Hart, Alfred A.   *Sacramento, Calif.*
Heywood, J. B.   *Boston, Mass.*
Holmes, William B.   *New York City*
Holt and Gray   *New York City*
Houseworth, Thomas   *San Francisco, Calif.*
Ingersoll, W. B.   *New York City*
Kilburn Brothers   *Littleton, N.H.*
Lakin   *Montgomery, Ala.*
Leland, E. J.   *Worcester, Mass.*
Macurdy, J. C.   *Oil City, Pa.*
Mason, S. J.   *Niagara Falls, N.Y.*
Mather, John A.   *Titusville, Pa.*
Meinerth, Carl   *Newburyport, Mass.*
Moran, John   *Philadelphia, Pa.*
Muybridge, E. J.   *San Francisco, Calif.*
N.Y. Stereoscopic Co.
O'Sullivan, T. H.   *Washington, D.C.*
Paradise   *New York City*
Pike and Sons   *New York City*
Purviance, W. T.   *Pittsburgh, Pa.*
Quinby and Co.   *Charleston, S.C.*
Reilly, J. J.   *Niagara Falls, N.Y.*
Roche, T. C.   *New York City*
Rogers, John   *New York City*
Rood and Emerson   *New York City*
Rope's, H. and Co.   *New York City*
Savage, C. R.   *Salt Lake City, Utah*
Sellers, Coleman   *Philadelphia, Pa.*
Smillie, T. W.   *Washington, D.C.*
Soule, John P.   *Boston, Mass.*
Stacey, George   *New York City*
Surdam and White   *New York City*
Taylor, A. S., Jr.   *New York City*
Taylor and Lamson   *New York City*
Thompson, F. F.   *Canandaigua, N.Y.*
Thorne, G. W.   *New York City*
Towler, John   *Geneva, N.Y.*
Tubbs, G. L.   *Geneva, N.Y.*
Tyson, C. J.   *Gettysburg, Pa.*
Waldack, Charles   *Cincinnati, Ohio*
Watkins, C. E.   *San Francisco, Calif.*

Watson, A.   *Philadelphia, Pa.*
Weaver, Peter S.   *Hanover, Pa.*
Wheeler and Barton   *Boston, Mass.*
White, Franklin   *Lancaster, N.H.*
Whitney   *St. Paul, Minn.*
Whitney and Paradise   *New York City*
Williams, J. A.   *Newport, R.I.*
Wood, H., Jr.   *New York City*
Wood and Murray   *Chicago, Ill.*

Canada

Armstrong, Beere and Hime   *Toronto, Ont.*
Ellison, William   *Quebec, Que.*
Ewing, R. D.   *Peterborough, Ont.*
Henderson, Alexander   *Montreal, Que.*
Notman, William   *Montreal, Que.*
Parks, J. G.   *Montreal, Que.*

Great Britain

Bedford, Francis   *London*
Buckman, C. H.   *Dover*
Burns, Archibald   *Edinburgh*
Campbell, G.   *Edinburgh*
Child, W.   *Leeds*
Crowe, A.   *Stirling*
Duthis, Andrew   *Glasgow*
Dutton, J. and J.   *Bath*
England, William   *London*
Good, Frank M.   *London*
Hills and Saunders   *Oxford*
Latham, John   *London*
Petschler, H. and Co.   *Manchester*
Reed, S.   *Whitby*
Stuart, J.   *Inverness*
Taylor, W. F.   *London*
Valentine and Sons   *Dundee*
Wilson, George W.   *Aberdeen*
York, F.   *London*

Germany

Bottger, G.   *Munich*
Christman, S. P.   *Berlin*
Die Creifelds   *Cologne*
Herzog, L.   *Hanover*
Konig, Christian   *Nuremberg*
Kruss, A.   *Hamburg*
Linde, E.   *Berlin*
May und Widmater   *Munich*
Moser   *Berlin*
Richard, Franz   *Heidelberg*
Schmidt, C.   *Nuremberg*

France

Disderi   *Paris and London*
Ferrier   *Paris*
Fietta, Édouard   *Strasbourg*
Hautecoeur, A.   *Paris*
Ledot   *Paris*
Leon, M. et J. Levy   *Paris*
Martinet   *Paris*
Muzet et Joquet   *Lyon*

Switzerland

Braun, Adolphe
Charnaux, F.   *Geneva*

Italy

Bernoud, Alphonse   *Naples and Florence*
Degoix, C.   *Genoa*
Duroni, A.   *Milan*
Emilia   *Bologna*
Godard, Adolphe   *Genoa*
Luswergh   *Rome*
Mang, M.   *Rome*
Naya, Carlo   *Venice*
Ponti, Carlo   *Venice*
Rive, R.   *Naples*
Sommer and Behles   *Rome and Naples*
Sorgato   *Bologna*
Spithover   *Rome*
Van Lint   *Pisa*

TURN-OF-THE-CENTURY "ART" PHOTOGRAPHERS

(From the Linked Ring Brotherhood, founded in London in 1892, through the American Photo-Secession movement, which ended with the outbreak of World War I)

JAMES CRAIG ANNAN [1864–1946] Member of the Linked Ring and first president of the International Society of Pictorial Photographers. He was the son of the noted Glasgow photographer Thomas Annan (1829–87), and with his father led the movement at the turn of the century to "rediscover" the calotype works of Hill and Adamson taken in the period 1843–47. Annan introduced the photogravure process in Great Britain in 1883.

JEAN EUGENE AUGUSTE ATGET [1856–1927] At first a sailor, then an actor, Atget took up photography at age 42, and from 1898 made an extensive documentary record of Paris and Parisian life. The Museum of Modern Art in New York possesses roughly 3,500 Atget prints and 1,200 plates, and has yet to determine whether Atget's principal purpose in photography was documentary or simply an attempt to present a visual understanding and artistic rendering of the subject matter he chose to photograph. Atget's works are now widely celebrated, but of the photographer's life most of what is known, according to officials at the Museum of Modern Art, is "rumor or myth."

ALICE BOUGHTON [1865/6–1943] Miss Boughton first studied painting, then took up photography and became associated for a time with Gertrude Käsebier. She opened her own studio in New York in 1890 and remained active, principally as a portraitist, for over 40 years. Her works were included in *Camera Work*.

ELIZABETH BUEHRMANN [1866/7–after 1962] Miss Buehrmann became associated with Eva Watson Schütze in Chicago at the age of sixteen. She worked primarily in portraiture, but may also have worked in advertising and illustration. She visited Paris in 1906, where she met Robert Demachy.

ALVIN LANGDON COBURN [1882–1966] Founder-member of the Photo-Secession movement in 1902, the year he opened his first studio in New York City. He established his reputation with one-man shows in London in 1906 and 1913. He illustrated novels and books on New York and London and published *Men of Mark* (1913) and *More Men of Mark* (1922), illustrated with hand-photogravure portraits of English and French celebrities. He resided in England and Wales after 1912.

GEORGE DAVISON [1856–1930] Founder (in 1890) of the impressionistic school of photography and founder-member (in 1892) of the Linked Ring Brotherhood. He served as managing director of Kodak, Ltd., from 1898 to 1912, when he was asked to resign because of his anarchistic views and activities.

F. HOLLAND DAY [1864–1933] Day was a distant cousin of Alvin Langdon Coburn. Both were native Bostonians and traveled together to England in the summer of 1899. Day was a very private photographer. In 1896 he accepted membership in the Linked Ring, but later declined membership in Photo-Secession. He is most noted for his renderings of the head of Christ and the dead Christ.

ROBERT DEMACHY [1859–1938] A banker residing in Paris, Demachy popularized the gum-bichromate print style in 1896 and was a frequent exhibitor of impressionistic works. According to experts at the Metropolitan Museum of Art, Demachy's writings "constitute the most comprehensive statement that exists on manipulated photographic imagery." His works were repeatedly reproduced in *Camera Work*.

PETER HENRY EMERSON [1856–1936] Emerson, in the 1880s, maintained that the aim of art was imitation of the effect of nature on the eye, and advocated use of images that were slightly out of focus as most like those seen by the human eye. This "soft focus" approach to photography, together with the merits of retouching, were among the most disputed matters of photographic practice during this decade.

In 1891 Emerson reversed himself, claiming that photography "is not an art but solely a means of knowing reality." Today he is best known for the series of seven photographically illustrated books on the life and landscapes of East Anglia that he published between 1886 and 1895.

HUGO ERFURTH [1874–1948] Erfurth became a portrait photographer in Dresden and a supporter of the aesthetic movement in Germany after 1896. His specialty was gum prints and later oil pigment prints. In the 1920s, he was recognized as one of the foremost portrait photographers on the Continent.

FRANK EUGENE [1865–1936] Eugene was a City College of New York graduate who studied at the Royal Academy of Fine Arts in Bavaria. He was a founder-member of Photo-Secession in 1902. He settled in Germany in 1906, dropping his family name, Smith. A skilled etcher, he marked, scratched, or otherwise manipulated his photographic negatives so that they would conform to his own artistic perception of subject matter. His works were repeatedly reproduced in *Camera Work.*

FREDERICK H. EVANS [1853–1943] Until he was forty-five, Evans was a London bookseller. Abut 1895, he began taking photographic portraits of his many artistic friends, including G. B. Shaw and Aubrey Beardsley. Today, he is best known for his images of English and French cathedrals, done in a style that later had great influence on Alfred Stieglitz. He was a member of the Linked Ring, and gave up photography after World War I, when platinum paper could no longer be obtained.

JOSEPH GALE [?–1906] Little is known about Gale, other than that he was an English army colonel whose photographs were the first to be included in *Sun Artists* (his was the first of eight monographic booklets comprising *Sun Artists*, published from 1889 to 1891).

HUGO HENNEBERG [1863–1918] Henneberg, Heinrich Kühn, and Hans Watzek comprised what was known in Austria as the "Viennese Triforium," working principally with the gum-bichromate process. Henneberg is today most noted for his landscape gum prints, which were appreciated for their close resemblance to paintings. Some of his works were included in *Camera Work.*

A. HORSLEY HINTON [1863–1908] Editor of the British journal *The Amateur Photographer* and principal spokesman for the Linked Ring. He is described as having a "strong, yet tolerant personality" and as being "admirably suited to unite men of widely different interests and divergent views," which contributed to the alliance of other pictorial movements with Linked Ring. Hinton is also noted for his landscape photographs.

THEODOR HOFMEISTER [1865–?] and OSKAR HOFMEISTER [1869–?] Active in Hamburg, these brothers first exhibited landscape photographs in 1896. In 1897 they took up the gumbichromate process, about which Theodor published two literary works in 1898. Today they are most noted for their photographs of landscapes and of the life of fishermen in the Hamburg area.

FREDERICK HOLLYER [1837–1933] Hollyer became a professional portrait photographer in 1870, but worked only one day a week. Mainly his time was spent as Britain's leading specialist in the photographic reproduction of paintings. He is also noted for his photographs of artists in their own surroundings, achieved in platinotype.

ERNEST W. JUHL [1850–1915] Founder of the Society for the Advancement of Amateur Photography in Hamburg and organizer of international photographic exhibitions held at the Hamburg Kunsthalle from 1893 to 1903. Juhl was also an influential writer.

GERTRUDE KÄSEBIER [1852–1934] Gertrude Käsebier studied painting from 1888 to 1893 at the Pratt Institute in Brooklyn, New York, and in Paris. Then she took up photography and opened her own studio in New York in 1897. She was a founder-member of Photo-Secession and became one of New York's most fashionable portrait photographers. Her commitment to the pictorial style of photography caused her to break with Alfred Stieglitz and his following after 1914.

ALEXANDER KEIGHLEY [1861–1947] Regarded as Britain's foremost pictorialist photographer after the death (in 1908) of A. Horsley Hinton, Keighley worked in his family's woolen business before taking up photography in the early 1880s. He joined the Linked Ring in 1892 and became noted for printing large, idealized landscape photographs, using the carbon process.

JOSEPH T. KEILEY [1869–1914] An active organizer of Photo-Secession and an associate editor of *Camera Work*, Keiley was a Wall Street lawyer in New York. Along with Alfred Stieglitz, he helped refine the glycerine process, which allowed brush development of a platinum print, giving the photograph a painterly effect. Keiley was the third American elected (in 1900) to membership in the Linked Ring.

HEINRICH KÜHN [1868–1944] Kühn took up photography in 1879 in his native Dresden, then moved to Innsbruck in 1888. He became one of the three celebrated members of the "Viennese Triforium" (the others were Hugo Henneberg and Hans Watzek) and organizer of the first international exhibition of the Vienna Camera Club in 1891. In 1897 he introduced a gum-bichromate process of multiple pigments, which enabled production of color gum prints. He was a member of the Linked Ring, and in 1937 was named an honorary doctor of Innsbruck University.

RENÉ LE BÈGUE [dates unknown] Although he attempted to conceal the fact that real persons were portrayed in his imitation crayon and charcoal photographic renderings, Le Bègue was ranked high among French pictorialists. His gum-bichromate work was reproduced in *Camera Work* and in 1973 was included in an exhibition of painterly photographic works at the New York Metropolitan Museum of Art.

ALFRED LICHTWARK [1852–1914] Director of the Hamburg Kunsthalle, he was one of the first art historians to recognize the importance of photography as a means of artistic expression (although his motive for doing so was reportedly to revitalize painting, particularly portrait painting).

CHARLES PUYO [1857–1933] A French army artillery officer, Puyo took up photography about 1885, and after 1900 concentrated on technical refinements of the gum-bichromate and oil transfer photographic processes. His works were reproduced in *Camera Work*, but his subject matter was considered inferior to his mastery of technical aspects of photographic printing.

HENRY P. ROBINSON [1830–1901] Recognized as the most influential pictorial photographer in the world during the latter half of the nineteenth century, Robinson began as an amateur painter. After one of his paintings was hung at the Royal Academy, he took up photography and opened a portrait gallery in Leamington in 1857. He made composition photographs for the annual exhibitions of the Photographic Society of London and wrote several works on the pictorial medium available today in reprint. He was a founder-member of the Linked Ring.

LYDDELL SAWYER [1856–?] Founder-member of the Linked Ring, Sawyer worked at first with his father, a portrait painter and photographer at Newcastle, then established his own photographic studio in 1885. In 1893 he opened a second studio in Sunderland, and in 1895 left the management of his Newcastle and Sunderland establishments to brothers and set up a third studio on London's Regent Street. In addition to his portraiture, he is noted for landscape photographs taken in the naturalistic style.

EVA WATSON SCHÜTZE [dates unknown] A founder-member of Photo-Secession, Miss Schütze took up photography in the late 1890s and enjoyed a wide reputation for her gum-bichromate and other prints exhibited at Philadelphia salons. She was a close friend of Alfred Stieglitz, and her works were reproduced in *Camera Work*.

GEORGE H. SEELEY [1880–1955] Seeley attended art school in Boston and probably studied photography at the same time. By 1902 he had established a reputation for landscapes and figure studies taken around his native Stockbridge, Massachusetts, and exhibited at photographic salons. His works were reproduced in *Camera Work*.

EDWARD STEICHEN [1879–1973] Steichen came from his native Luxembourg to America with his parents in 1881, settling in Wisconsin. He took his first photographs in 1894, and his works drew considerable notice at the second Philadelphia Salon in 1899. He met Alfred Stieglitz in 1900 on his way to Paris, where he exhibited paintings and photographs in 1901 and 1902. A founder, with Stieglitz, of the Photo-Secession gallery at 291 Fifth Avenue, New York, in 1905, Steichen produced many works in gum print (which he later burned, along with many of his paintings, after World War I). In 1906 he settled in Voulangis, near Paris, where he chose and sent to Stieglitz in New York the avant-garde paintings and sculpture that made the Photo-Secession gallery famous. Steichen was chief of aerial photography for U.S. expeditionary forces in World War I and chief of U.S. Navy combat photography in World War II. From 1923 to 1937, he was chief photographer for *Vanity Fair* and *Vogue*, and in 1947 was appointed director of the photographic department at the New York Museum of Modern Art.

ALFRED STIEGLITZ [1865–1946] A native of Hoboken, New Jersey, Stieglitz was educated in New York and studied mechanical engineering and photography at the Berlin Polytechnic from 1882 to 1890. Returning to New York, he began taking street-life photographs in New York with a hand camera, and became editor of *Camera Notes*, organ of the New York Camera Club. After organizing the now-famous Photo-Secession exhibition at the National Arts Club in 1902, he founded *Camera Work*, which he edited from 1903 to 1917, and established the Photo-Secession gallery at 291 Fifth Avenue, which he operated during those years with the help of Edward Steichen in Paris (who sent works of avant-garde artists to match the works of numerous modern photographers). Stieglitz compiled the single most important collection of photographic works of the painterly school, which is now housed at the Metropolitan Museum of Art.

FRANK M. SUTCLIFFE [1859–1940] Sutcliffe was the son of an English watercolor artist. He opened a photographic portrait studio in Whitby in 1875. Today he is most noted for his landscape works and genre subjects executed in the manner of the naturalistic school. He was a founder-member of the Linked Ring.

HANS WATZEK [1848–1903] Professor Watzek was the third member, with Hugo Henneberg and Heinrich Kühn, of the "Viennese Triforium," and considered the leading artistic photographer of Austria at the turn of the century. Long a prominent exhibitor at European international salons, he favored the gumbichromate process and introduced a "monocle" lens to maximize diffusion in his impressionistic-style portraits, landscape views, and still lifes.

J. B. WELLINGTON [dates unknown] Member of the Linked Ring, he was a self-taught carpenter and made all of his own cameras, small and large. He worked principally in platinotype and frequently used hand cameras. He is noted for his figure studies and landscapes, and endeavored to pose the figures in his photographs rather than capture them in a candid fashion.

CLARENCE H. WHITE [1871–1925] White began taking photographs during off-duty hours as head bookkeeper in a wholesale grocery business in Newark, Ohio. He exhibited works at the first Philadelphia Salon in 1898, and a few years later was proposed for honorary membership in the New York Camera Club by Alfred Stieglitz. White moved to New York and was a lecturer on photography at the Teachers College of Columbia University from 1906 to his death. He also founded the Clarence H. White School of Photography, first during summers in Maine, then permanently in New York after 1914. His photographs were in the style of American impressionism.

BENJAMIN G. WILKINSON [1857–1927] During all of his life, photography remained a holiday pursuit for Wilkinson. Yet he was a prominent practitioner of the naturalistic landscape photography pioneered by Peter H. Emerson and in 1892 became a founder-member of the Linked Ring.

Photographic
Archives

MAJOR REPOSITORIES

The vast majority of significant collections of nineteenth-century photographs and photographic literature will be found in national libraries, in other libraries in large cities and universities, and at a small number of major museums and institutions. The latter include the International Museum of Photography, Rochester, New York; the Victoria and Albert Museum in London; the Smithsonian Institution, Washington, D.C.; the Metropolitan Museum of Art, New York; the Museum of Modern Art, New York; the Folkwang Museum, Essen; and the American Antiquarian Society, Worcester, Massachusetts. Important collections will also be found in certain American state and city historical societies and at various commercial establishments that make a business of collecting and selling the rights to reproduce and use vintage and contemporary photographs.

In 1971 Britain's National Portrait Gallery in London established a department of film and photography, which has begun the task of building a national collection of photographs. In the United States, the National Portrait Gallery in Washington, D.C., has been prevented from taking similar steps. The problem was described by Robert Ketchum in 1962 in these words:

The acquisition problem, difficult under any circumstances, is made more so by restrictions placed by Congress upon the Gallery's permanent collection. The enabling legislation stipulated that the term "portraiture" meant "painted or sculptured likenesses." Which rules out, among other likenesses, those taken with a camera, or a substantial percentage of all likenesses made during the past century and a quarter, when the dominant form of portraiture was photography, not painting. Congress, being part of a bureaucracy, behaves in a manner common to officialdom: it is the nature of things that each branch of government has its special fields of interest which must be protected at all costs, and in the case of photography, the Library of Congress was adjudged to have prior claim.[138]

An exhaustive study, or compilation, of information covering photographic archives is hard to come by. The record set down in these pages is by no means complete, but it does identify and provide brief data on some of the principal archives holding nineteenth-century material.

UNIVERSITY OF TEXAS AT AUSTIN Although such men of stature as Sir Julian Huxley and J. B. Priestly urged the establishment of a national photographic archives in Great Britain at the time the Gernsheim collection was offered for sale in the 1950s, the suggestion was not followed, and the collection was acquired by the University of Texas in 1964. The collection was described at that time as the largest set of photographic antiquities in private hands. It includes photographs by noted practitioners of the art and a significant library of books and journals extending from the sixteenth-century prehistories of photography to the present. It also contains outstanding examples of the earliest experiments in photography and much of the finest European photography of the Victorian era.[139]

INTERNATIONAL MUSEUM OF PHOTOGRAPHY After its opening in 1949, the museum (at George Eastman House, Rochester, New York) acquired a number of significant private collections of nineteenth-century material. These included the Philip Jay Medicus collection of Civil War photographs, the Gordon Lightfoot collection of over 5,000 stereographs, and the Gabriel Cromer collection rich in nineteenth-century French photographs. In 1951 the museum was given the Alden Scott Boyer collection of over 3,000 books, albums, and periodicals, including long runs of the *Daguerreian Journal* (*Humphrey's Journal* after April 1852) and *Philadelphia Photographer* (*Wilson's Photographic Magazine* after 1888). In 1968 the museum acquired the Zelda Mackay collection of rare daguerreotype, ambrotype, and tintype portraits and views. The museum has also acquired major collections and works of twentieth-century photographers and photographic literature.[140]

SMITHSONIAN INSTITUTION The institution maintains a History of Photography Collection, begun in 1888, and a Hall of Photography, opened in 1913 and substantially enlarged and given new quarters in 1973. The collection was launched principally as a result of the selfless dedication of the collection's first curator, Thomas W. Smillie (who reportedly paid for Samuel F. B. Morse's daguerreotype equipment out of his own pocket). The collection was not designated a curatorial unit until 1896, and official policy prohibited use of federal funds for acquisitions until 1913. During this period there were no individuals possessing major private collections which could be donated to the institution, and as a result the Smithsonian's holdings in photography principally comprise small, specialized collections of particular significance. Among these are countless items of photographic equipment transferred from the U.S. Patent Office (including, for example, the first patented U.S. camera, introduced by Alexander S. Wolcott in America and England in 1840; the first japanned iron plates used in making tintypes; two carbon photographs supplied at the time the American rights were secured for the British carbon process (in 1867); and two broken glass plate negatives of Lincoln by Alexander Hesler, which were broken in the mails, retained by the U.S. Post Office after the insurance claim was settled, and transferred thereafter. A large proportion of photographs in the collection remains uncatalogued to the present day; the total number is estimated to be several hundred thousand. The new Hall of Photography provides exhibition space rivaling that of the International Museum of Photography in Rochester. Included are a print gallery with shows that change about three times a year and a number of "period" rooms containing examples of original photographic apparatus and paraphernalia.[141]

3M COMPANY, ST. PAUL, MINNESOTA Once there was an American Museum of Photography. Its doors were opened in Philadelphia in 1940, but after about two decades the museum was closed and its contents were acquired by the 3M Company. At the time of the sale, the collection included the assets of the principal American manufacturer of lantern slides in the nineteenth century; early photographs and negatives from the estates of Frederick and William Langenheim; one of the largest private collections of nineteenth-century American photographic journals; and a unique assortment of graphic arts items which had belonged to the principal American and German pioneers of photomechanical, halftone, and three-color photographic printing. The nucleus of the museum's collection at the time of its opening was the assets of the Casper W. Briggs Company. Briggs had been a competitor and then (after 1874) the successor to the Langenheims' lantern slide business. For a few years prior to his death, he served on the museum's advisory board. To Briggs's extensive inventory and memorabilia were added a complete assortment of lantern projectors and other devices associated with their use. These were acquired from the Charles T. Milligan firm, which in 1876 succeeded to the W. Y. McAllister Company, previously the largest of the nineteenth-century equipment manufacturers. The museum's collection of Langenheim photographs and negatives included the earliest glass negatives and glass stereographs produced in the United States; contact prints made from the Langenheims' early lantern slides; Langenheim catalogs issued in the 1860s and 1870s; and some of the earliest calotype photographs made after the Langenheims acquired the U.S. rights to the British process in 1847. Among the extensive assortment of graphic arts items were early examples of photoengraving works by such masters as Frederic E. Ives, Louis Levy, and John C. Moss. Included, too, were early photomechanical specimens by Stephen H. Horgan, pioneer developer of the halftone process for photo reproduction, and specimens from the three-color photographic printing method developed in Germany by Dr. Herman Vogel, director of the Royal Photo-Chemical Laboratory in Berlin.[142]

COLUMBIA UNIVERSITY One of the most important private collections of photographic literature covering the history, art, science, and technical aspects of the medium was that compiled by Edward Epstean, a photoengraver. This collection is rich in French and German literature, much of it translated into English. The collection was donated to Columbia in 1934.

MUSEUM OF THE CITY OF NEW YORK

Founded in 1923, the museum houses one of the largest collections of photographs of New York City and environs, taken in the nineteenth and twentieth centuries. Included among nineteenth-century items is the Jacob Riis collection of approximately four hundred photographs depicting immigrant life on New York's Lower East Side, which Riis took while preparing his noted work, *How the Other Half Lives* (New York, Charles Scribner's Sons, 1890). Although Riis's photographs were reproduced as artist's renderings in the 1890 edition (the halftone process for reproducing photographs for book illustration was not then perfected), a 1971 Dover Publications reprint edition of the 1890 work has replaced the artist's renderings in most cases with the corresponding actual photographs. A second major acquisition is the Byron collection of 10,000 prints and photographs of scenes in New York taken principally during the period 1890–1910. Among the museum's notable collections of architectural photographs is a group of 1,046 glass negatives of buildings designed by the New York architectural firm of McKim, Mead and White during the period 1880–1915.[143]

HISTORICAL SOCIETIES

According to Walter Muir Whitehill, director of the Boston Athenaeum, the three principal motivating forces in nineteenth-century movements to establish state and city historical societies were Jeremy Belknap, a Boston clergyman and founder of the Massachusetts Historical Society (in 1791); John Pintard, a New York merchant and founder of the New York Historical Society (in 1804); and Isaiah Thomas, a scholar-printer and founder of the American Antiquarian Society in Worcester, Massachusetts (in 1812). Until the founding of the American Historical Association in 1884, universities and colleges concerned themselves relatively little with American history. But by 1860, according to Whitehill, every state east of Texas, with the exception of Delaware, had established a state society, many emulating the patterns set by the three earliest.[144]

Today these state and city historical societies concentrate for the most part on acquiring material relating to their particular areas, and this applies as much to photographic collections as to other historical material. Thus the Kansas State Historical Society houses approximately 70,000 photographs (with as many as 40 per cent taken in the nineteenth century) dealing primarily with people, places, and events in Kansas and the West; the Society of California Pioneers in San Francisco houses a major collection of glass and card stereographs taken from the 1860s on by the noted photographer Carlton E. Watkins; the Virginia Historical Society houses a large collection of glass negatives on the Reconstruction years in the South; and the Oregon Historical Society houses early photographs documenting the advent of steamboats, railroads, mining, and agriculture in the Far West. Few societies have organized their collections in such a fashion that they know exactly how many different styles of photographs they have. One exception, the State Historical Society of Colorado, estimates that it possesses 50 daguerreotypes, 75 ambrotypes (five of them ambrotype views), 200 tintypes (50 of them views), and 5,000 lantern slides. The Ohio Historical Society estimates that its photographic

collection houses 250 daguerreotypes, 50 ambrotypes, 100 tintypes, 400 stereographs, 500 cartes de visite, 1,000 cabinet cards, 15,000 lantern slides, 250,000 emulsion-paper prints, and negligible holdings of calotypes, salt prints, albumen prints, carbon prints, platinum prints, and photomechanical prints.

The collections of three major societies are summarized below.

NEW-YORK HISTORICAL SOCIETY   The photographic archives of this society were launched after the turn of the century (in 1906) with a donation (by the president of the society) of forty-two wax-paper negatives made by Victor Prevost in New York City and its environs in 1851 and in 1853–54. This is the collection retrieved in 1898 from a White Plains, New York, attic (see page 75) that contains the finest photographs made in the United States by the Le Gray calotype method and also the earliest known surviving photographs of New York. Today the society's collection numbers over 100,000 photographic items, including 1,300 portraits made by the Pach Brothers studio in New York; 1,200 Civil War views; 900 photographs of East Coast steamboats; 1,200 views of New York lighthouses; 2,000 lantern slides of archeological excavations in New York and elsewhere; 4,000 photographs by Arnold Genthe (who photographed in San Francisco until his gallery was destroyed in the 1906 earthquake and fire, and then established himself in New York); 2,000 records of buildings by the architectural firms of R. M. Hood and McKim, Mead and White; and 750 social documentary photographs by Jacob Riis and Robert Bracklow. The society also possesses glass negatives which have not yet been counted or catalogued.[145]

CHICAGO HISTORICAL SOCIETY   This society is rich in photographs made before and during the American Civil War and has one of the foremost collections of daguerreotype portraits made of American celebrities in that period. This includes one of the finest assortments of daguerreotypes of American presidents made prior to the war. The society also possesses daguerreotype views of landmark buildings in Chicago and Galena; ambrotype views of steamboats, Chicago street scenes, grain elevators, and private residences; and several panoramic views (paper photographs) of Chicago taken in 1858 by Alexander Hesler. The society also houses major photographic works by Alexander Gardner and George N. Barnard.[146]

MISSOURI HISTORICAL SOCIETY As early as 1866, this society purchased twelve daguerreotypes from an early St. Louis photographer, Thomas Easterly, who had established his gallery there in 1847. The society's collection of daguerreotypes now numbers in excess of 100 views (including the ruins of an 1849 St. Louis fire) and several hundred portraits by Easterly and the more renowned St. Louis photographer, John Fitzgibbons. Among thousands of other nineteenth-century photographs, the society owns the Gen. William S. Harney collection of Indian photographs (75 in number) taken in the period 1862–68 by Alexander Gardner and other photographers; 115 views by Gardner of the Kansas-Pacific railroad construction (1867–68); a large collection of card stereographs taken from the 1860s to the turn of the century; and 101 calotype views of Philadelphia, Washington, D.C., and Niagara Falls made in 1850 by Frederick and William Langenheim (following their purchase of the U.S. rights to the British calotype process the previous year). This collection, among the largest Langenheim calotype collections extant, was recovered from a Missouri farmhouse attic in 1939.[147]

Comprehensive summaries or catalogs of photographic collections in libraries also remain elusive. In 1973 the number of surveys being made prompted the editors of *Picturescope* to comment: "To some of them [librarians and curators in charge of picture collections], it must seem that a new questionnaire arrives in the mail every week." In any event, there are many libraries as well as historical societies and other institutions that will freely admit to ignorance as to the full significance or even total count of photographs in their collections. In 1974 a retired Montclair, New Jersey, banker, for example, "found" a small collection of copies of the earliest card stereographs of the American West (taken in 1859 by Albert Bierstadt) in the photographic archives of both the New York Public Library and the New-York Historical Society. Taken on a U.S. Army survey of a wagon route to the Pacific, these views were long thought to have been lost. In all probability, the New York Public Library views were among the 40,000 stereographs that the library acquired in 1938 (and later) from Robert Dennis of Williamsburg, Virginia.

In a number of libraries, a particular collection of photographs donated by a local citizen constitutes the nucleus of, or a celebrated portion of, that library's holdings. The personal collection of 8,000 photographs, prints, and clippings compiled in forty-six scrapbooks by a Philadelphian, Samuel Castner, is a major adjunct of the archives of the Free Library of Philadelphia; after eluding the library at a 1943 auction, it was acquired at another auction in 1947. This collection comprises prints and photogravures covering the history of Philadelphia, the Schuylkill River, old houses, streets, churches, theaters, prisons, and areas of the Delaware River. Similarly, the Birmingham, Alabama, public library boasts a collection of over 1,000 photographs taken between 1878 and 1943, which were assembled and donated by a streetcar conductor.[148]

Library of Congress
Major Special Collections of Photographs in the Prints and Photographs Division

SUBJECT	DESCRIPTION OF COLLECTION	PHOTOGRAPHER
	Nineteenth-Century Photographic Prints	
Brady items	Over 3,000 glass negs.; 24 daguerreotypes	M. B. Brady
Brady items	7,500 negs.; 2,500 copy negs. and films	M. B. Brady
Brady items	4,500 Civil War prints and duplicates	M. B. Brady
Colorado, 1867	38 mounted prints	W. G. Chamberlain
Colorado, 1864	25 mounted prints	G. D. Wakely
B & O Railroad, 1871	Album of 125 photographs	Unidentified
Mississippi steamboats	Approx. 400 prints, mainly 1870–90	Unidentified
Hayden Survey, 1870–79	27 albumen prints; 31 card stereographs; 15 other mounted prints	W. H. Jackson
Walt Whitman	800 items; photographs, paintings, prints, drawings, sculpture, caricatures, etc.	Not specified
Mexico, 1883–84	800 original photographs, together with other prints made elsewhere, 1900–05	W. H. Jackson

SUBJECT	DESCRIPTION OF COLLECTION	PHOTOGRAPHER
Pennsylvania Oil Fields, 1861–70	12 photographs (from 3,274 negs. at Drake Museum, Titusville, Pa.)	J. A. Mather
Powell Survey, 1871–72	20 large photographs	J. K. Hillers
Yale, 1868	2 albums containing approx. 200 photographs of class members, faculty, and buildings	Warren (probably G. K. Warren)
Tennessee, 1867	25 photographs; Chattanooga and Tennessee River valley towns	Unidentified
Western, 1890s	3 albums with approx. 400 photographs of ranches, cattle, scenes on Indian reservations, etc.	C. E. Watkins
Crimean War	265 unmounted salt prints, 1855	Roger Fenton
Egypt and Near East, 1852	33 salt prints taken by an American student of archaeological monuments	Leavitt Hunt
New York and New England, 1858–61	7 scrapbooks containing 176 half-stereographs and duplicates, 30 stereo pairs (duplicates of above) and 24 proofs from enlarged negs. of the same views, mostly salt prints	Franklin and Luther White
Turkey, 1893	2,250 albumen prints of military and facilities	Abdullah Frères
Alaska, 1890s	Album of approx. 125 photographs	Unidentified
Woodrow Wilson	250 photographs, including family, buildings, residences, etc.	Not specified
U.S. Navy	Approx. 30 photographs received in 1888 from George Barrie	Not specified
Clara Barton	Approx. 150 photographs, about 100 in Cuba in 1899 of yellow fever camp and other views	Not specified
Catskill Mts., circa 1871	10 photographs; scenery, waterfalls, etc.	Adolphus Beer
Yachting, 1890s	Approx. 1,500 photographs of racing yachts in action, schooners, steam yachts, and other craft	C. E. Bolles
Paris Exposition, 1889	215 photographs of U.S. exhibits	Not specified
West Point, 1882	Album of approx. 75 photographs of class, instructors, and views; includes photos of Presidents Garfield and Hayes	G. W. Pach and Brothers
Nebraska, 1880s	13 photographs of settler families	S. D. Butcher
East Africa, 1891	Album of 47 photographs of railroad activity and facilities	Unidentified
Ft. Scott, Kan., 1840–69	24 photographs copied from daguerreotypes and other earlier photographs of town, street scenes, woolen mill, etc.	Unidentified
French and English cathedrals	28 turn-of-the-century platinum prints	F. H. Evans
Western views, 1888–91	Approx. 100 photographs of towns, scenery, and daily life in South Dakota, Wyoming, Colorado	J. C. H. Gabrill
Benjamin Harrison	Approx. 200 items, including photographs pertaining to life and career of 23rd president	Not specified
U.S. Navy, 1890s	Approx. 2,500 photographs of vessels, yards, portraits, shipboard life, etc.	E. H. Hart
South America, 1868	2 albums of approx. 100 photographs, mostly of Lima; also earthquake in Arequipa	Courret Hermanos

SUBJECT	DESCRIPTION OF COLLECTION	PHOTOGRAPHER
Latin-American Conference, 1889–90	Album of 40 photographs of delegates to first International American Conference, held in Washington, D.C.	M. B. Brady studio
Hague Conference, 1899	Album of approx. 60 photographs of delegates and other views	Not specified
Kiel Canal construction	10 photographs of construction in 1889–92	Constabel and Knackstedt
Chicago "street types"	Approx. 40 posed photographs of organ grinders, icemen, beggars, bill posters, etc.	Sigmund Krausz
Krupp Works, 1890s	23 photographs of guns and artillery manufactured at Krupp works in Essen, 1890–93	Unidentified
Turkestan Survey, 1871–72	Approx. 750 photographs in 4 albums of Russian sector of Turkestan	N. V. Bogaevskii
Kurile Islands, 1891–92	100 photographs of villages, terrain, harbors, and people of the islands north of Japan	Not specified
Klondike gold rush, 1897	Approx. 40 photographs	Frank LaRoche
Hudson River and New York scenes, 1890s	Approx. 225 photographs of naval vessels, yachts, excursion steamers, ocean liners, and views in New York City	A. Loeffler
Astronomy	Approx. 100 photographs of Simon Newcomb and other astronomers and scientists; also of telescopes; all in period 1862–1900	Not specified
Nautical and Western, 1886–1902	Approx. 475 photographs; some in 4 albums of yachts, river steamers, sloops, and schooners; series of naval vessels; canyon and western storm views	H. G. Peabody
Italy and France, 1870–85	23 photographs of cities, monuments, buildings, and landscapes	Carlo Ponti
Russian Railroad construction, 1890–94	Portfolio of 30 photographs of construction, route, stations, and equipment along southwest railroad on Dniester River and in the Ukraine	Not specified
Yachting, 1890s	Approx. 125 photographs of yachts, races, and naval vessels; a few oceangoing steamships	N. L. Stebbins
Stieglitz items, 1894–1910	40 photographs on chloride paper; 2 platinum prints; Europe, New York, upstate New York	Alfred Stieglitz
Upstate New York, 1880–1900	Approx. 200 photographs of scenery, resorts, West Point, and Adirondack Mountains	S. R. Stoddard
India, 1870s	141 photographs of scenery, architecture, and native activities; Edward VII as Prince of Wales	Samuel Bourne
Civil War	Album of 61 photographs of Sherman's campaign	George N. Barnard
Civil War	5 photographs of Chattanooga River and railroad bridge and tracks in city's vicinity	R. M. Cressey
Civil War	500 items, including photographs of Gettysburg and other battlefields; a personal collection	W. H. Tipton and P. S. Weaver
Civil War	41 photographs of fortifications and batteries at Fort Sumter and Fort Wagner, 1863	Haas and Peale
Civil War	72 photographs of Washington, D.C., and Alexandria, made for U.S. Military Railroad Construction Corp.	A. J. Russell
Lincoln	6 photographs of president's funeral	S. M. Fassett

SUBJECT	DESCRIPTION OF COLLECTION	PHOTOGRAPHER
Lincoln	Estimated 750 photographs and other portraits from Meserve, Rabinowitz, Stern, and other collections	M. B. Brady and others
Indians	22 photographs of Comanche, Kiowa, and Apache warriors and camps	John P. Soule
Indians	Approx. 400 photographs of Sioux and other Indians, singly and in groups	Heyn and Heyn, and Matzen
Indians	Album of 23 photographs and photocopies of portraits of Cherokee chiefs, 1828–1911	Not specified
Indians	Approx. 100 photographs (some salt paper proofs) of Indians at Isleta, N.M. (received 1888–94)	C. F. Lummis
U.S. presidents	Album of 150 oval portraits from Lincoln to Benjamin Harrison; includes other statesmen	Not specified
Spanish-American War	Approx. 125 photographs in album of Havana, U.S. Marines, wrecked Spanish vessels, U.S. troops at Manila, etc.	Files of Detroit Publishing Co.
Spanish-American War	Approx. 60 photographs of views in Puerto Rico, British tramp steamers, wharf at Charleston, S.C., newspaper correspondents, etc.; presented by Gen. Sherman Miles	Not specified
Aviation (Chanute items)	Album of 102 photographs of experimental gliders demonstrated by Octave Chanute; sea gulls in flight, etc.	Not specified
Adm. D. D. Porter	Scrapbook of 12 portraits of Porter and 8 cartes de visite of naval vessels	Not specified

Cartes de Visite

SUBJECT	DESCRIPTION OF COLLECTION	PHOTOGRAPHER
Paris Commune, 1871	2 albums with portraits of officials, anarchists, journalists, arsonists, etc.	Not specified
European notables	Album with approx. 200 portraits of royalty, statesmen, literary figures, etc.	Not specified
U.S. notables	Portraits in larger collection; includes Carl Schurz, Lee, Joseph E. Johnston, and others	Various photogs.
U.S. and European notables	5 albums with 540 portraits assembled by the actress Charlotte Cushman	Not specified
Mexican notables	Album with 184 portraits of statesmen and military and operatic notables	Various photogs.
China, 1860s	46 carte de visite and 4 cabinet portraits of missionaries, waterfront views, etc.	Various photogs.
European musicians	45 portraits and other portraits cut to same size of musicians in 1860s and 1870s	Not specified
Goldmark items, 1848–70	20 portraits of Joseph Goldmark and associates, some possibly connected with 1848 revolutions	Not specified
Portland, Ore., residents	Album with 55 portraits (and 2 tintypes) of Portland residents in 1860s and 1870s	Not specified
Pennsylvania Convention, 1872	90 portraits (autographed) of members of the Pennsylvania Constitutional Convention	Not specified
Confederate items	37 portraits of Conferate leaders, U.S. Army officers, etc.	Not specified
Confederate items	50 photographs, principally carte de visite portraits of men prominent in the Confederacy; battle scenes; blockade runners; other items relating to Confederacy	Not specified

SUBJECT	DESCRIPTION OF COLLECTION	PHOTOGRAPHER
Civil War nurses	Album of approx. 100 portraits; includes Union officers	Not specified
U.S. statesmen, 1864	Album with 194 portraits of Lincoln, Johnson, cabinet members, 34 senators, 151 representatives, and others	Brady studio
U.S. notables	Album with approx. 50 portraits of prominent figures in the period 1860–70	Not specified
U.S. notables	487 carte de visite and other photographs of the 1860s and 1870s	Not specified
McClellan items	Personal album of Gen. George McClellan with 13 mounted and other loose portraits	Not specified
Civil War	Approx. 45 portraits of Union officers and other Americans of Civil War period	Not specified

Cabinet Cards

SUBJECT	DESCRIPTION OF COLLECTION	PHOTOGRAPHER
U.S. statesmen	Two bound volumes, *Senate of the United States, 41st Congress*, with 60 portraits of senators, President Grant, cabinet members, etc.	M. B. Brady
Gen. Logan items	Approx. 360 cabinet and carte de visite photographs relating to the life, career, residences, etc., of the Civil War general, senator, and vice-presidential candidate	Not specified
U.S. senators, 41st Congress	Album with 50 cabinet and 1 carte de visite portraits taken 1871–73	Brady studio

Card Stereographs

SUBJECT	DESCRIPTION OF COLLECTION	PHOTOGRAPHER
Eastern U.S. scenery, 1882–95	Approx. 100 stereoviews and 200 additional photographs of scenes, buildings, daily life in Niagara Falls, Virginia, Georgia, and Florida	George Barker
Humorous items	Approx. 300 stereoviews (2 collections) taken in period 1876–1910	Not specified
California and Nevada, 1866	860 half-stereoviews of mining towns, missions, landscapes, Indians, etc.	George S. Lawrence and Thomas Houseworth
New York Fair, 1864	15 stereoviews of building and exhibits	Not specified
Little Big Horn Battleground	5 stereoviews of activities not long after the battle in 1876	S. J. Morrow
Powell Survey, 1871–72	32 stereoviews	J. K. Hillers, E. O. Beaman, and James Fennemore
Geyser Springs Calif., c.1870	13 stereoviews of hotels and tourists	Not specified
Yosemite, 1870	Approx. 125 stereoviews of Yosemite and other California scenery	John P. Soule
Union Pacific Railroad, 1866	9 stereoviews of construction	John Carbutt
Union Pacific Railroad, 1868–69	71 stereoviews of scenes in Kansas, including cities, towns, buildings, depots, army forts, farm homes, cattle, etc.	Alexander Gardner
Mammoth Cave, 1866	10 stereoviews of interior of the Kentucky tourist attraction, made with magnesium light	Charles Waldack

SOURCE: *Guide To Special Collections of Prints and Photographs in the Library of Congress*, U.S. Government Printing Office, Washington, D.C., 1955.

Photographic
Societies

LATE NINETEENTH-CENTURY
PHOTOGRAPHIC SOCIETIES

The list of American societies was published in 1889, photography's fiftieth anniversary. The list of those outside the United States was published in 1892. For collectors who reside in the modern-day locales where these organizations functioned, the various names and addresses given may provide leads to the retrieval of lost records or photographic items that may yet survive in the hands of succeeding generations.

American Societies (1889)

AGASSIZ ASSOCIATION, MANHATTAN CHAPTER, N. Y. (Photographic Section) *President*, W. T. Demarest; *Treasurer*, W. S. Miller; *Corresponding Secretary*, Edward B. Miller. Meeting, 103 Lexington Avenue, New York City. Date of meetings, third Friday of each month at 8 P.M.

ALBANY CAMERA CLUB Albany, N. Y. Organized January, 1888. *President*, Dr. Samuel B. Ward; *Treasurer and Secretary*, M. H. Rochester. Place of meeting, 20 North Pearl Street. Meetings, first Friday in month.

AMERICAN INSTITUTE, N. Y. (Photographical Section) New York City. Organized March 26, 1859. *President*, Henry J. Newton; *Vice-President*, John B. Gardner; *Treasurer*, Edward Schell; *Secretary*, Oscar G. Mason, Photographic Department, Bellevue Hospital, New York City. Place of meeting, Institute Hall, Clinton Buildings. Ordinary meetings at 8 P.M. on the first Tuesday of each month, except July and August.

AMERICA, PHOTOGRAPHERS' ASSOCIATION OF Organized, 1879. *President*, H. McMichael, Buffalo; *First Vice-President*, G. H. Hastings, Boston; *Second Vice-President*, J. M. Appleton, Dayton, Ohio; *Treasurer*, G. M. Carlisle, Providence, R. I.; *Secretary*, O. P. Scott, Chicago. Tenth Annual Convention will meet at Boston, August 6th to 9th inclusive, 1889.

AMERICAN LANTERN SLIDE INTERCHANGE *Manager*, George Bullock; *Assistant-Managers*, William H. Rau, Philadelphia; Frederick C. Beach, New York. The members of the Interchange are the Society of Amateur Photographers of New York, represented by F. C. Beach; The Philadelphia Photographic Society, by W. H. Rau; Pittsburg Amateur Photographer's Society, by W. S. Bell; Cincinnati Camera Club, by George Bullock; Louisville Camera Club, by W. A. Peaslee; Chicago Lantern Slide Club, by W. A. Morse; St. Louis Camera Club, by H. B. Alexander; New Orleans Camera Club, by H. T. Howard; The New Brunswick (N. J.) Camerads, by Prof. Peter T. Austen. From December 1st to June 20th, of each year, exchanges of lantern slides are made monthly between each association, and annually with the Camera Club of England.

ATLANTA (GA.) CAMERA CLUB *President*, Prof. Sumner Salter; *Treasurer*, Dr. Frank O. Stockton; *Secretary*, F. J. Paxton, 66½ Whitehall Street; *Corresponding Secretary*, Miss E. Marguerite Lindley, 124 Peachtree Street. Place of meeting, 66½ Whitehall Street. Meetings, second Monday of each month.

BALTIMORE (MD.) AMATEUR PHOTOGRAPHIC ASSOCIATION *President*, Isaac T. Norris; *Treasurer*, John H. Kimble; *Secretary*, Harry D. Williar. Place of meeting, 106 N. Charles Street. Meeting, third Friday of each month.

BOSTON (MASS.) CAMERA CLUB (Formerly Boston Society of Amateur Photographers) *President*, Geo. E. Cabot; *Treasurer*, Wm. Garrison Reed; *Secretary*, Edw. F. Wilder, 47 Tremont Street, Boston. Place of meeting, Club Rooms, 50 Bromfield Street; meetings, first Monday of month, excepting June, July and August; entertainment meetings, third Mondays, except as above, and often when occasion requires.

BROOKLYN (N. Y.) ACADEMY OF PHOTOGRAPHY Incorporated April, 1887. *President*,

Wallace Gould Levison; *Treasurer*, Edward H. Quantin; *Recording Secretary*, Geo. S. Wheeler; *Corresponding Secretary*, Willis Dodge, 346 Schermerhorn Street, Brooklyn. Place of meeting, Hoagland Laboratory, cor. Henry and Pacific Streets. Meetings, second Tuesday of each month.

BROOKLYN (N. Y.) SOCIETY OF AMATEUR PHOTOGRAPHERS *President*, Allan Ormsbee; *Vice-President*, Homer Ladd; *Treasurer*, Charles Blake; *Secretary*, George R. Sheldon, Jr., 57 Clark Street.

BROOKLYN (N. Y.) PHOTOGRAPHIC ASSOCIATION *President*, E. Wagner; *Treasurer*, A. Roussel; *Secretary*, Chas. M. Heid, 412 Wyckoff Street. Place of meeting, Arion Hall, Wall Street. Meetings, first and third Wednesday of each month, 8:30 P.M.

BROOKLYN ACADEMY OF SCIENCE (Photographic Section) Organized March 26, 1888. *Secretary*, J. W. Holbrook, Jr., 462 Hart Street, Brooklyn, N.Y.

BROOKLYN INSTITUTE (Photographic Department) Brooklyn Institute, Washington Street, Brooklyn. *President*, Alexander Black, Brooklyn *Times* office; *Secretary*, Anna L. Meeker.

BROOKLYN CAMERA CLUB Organized January 3, 1888. *President*, Wm. F. Miller; *Vice-President*, M. E. Baker; *Treasurer*, M. L. Allen; *Secretary*, H. C. Mettler, 442 Fulton Street. Brooklyn. Place of meeting, 442 Fulton Street. Ordinary meetings, first Thursday of each month, 8 P.M.

BUFFALO (N. Y.) CAMERA CLUB *President*, George F. H. Bartlett, M.D.; *Treasurer*, Charles E. Hayes; *Recording Secretary*, Edwin L. Burdick; *Corresponding Secretary*, Thomas Carey Welch, 33 Law Exchange Building. Place of meeting, Buffalo Library Building. Meetings, twice a month. Regular meeting, first week; lantern slide, third week.

COLUMBIA COLLEGE (N. Y.) Amateur Photographic Society, New York Organized 1886. *President*, C. E. Gudewill; *Treasurer*, J. T. Davies, Jr.; *Secretary*, H. R. Taylor, School of Arts, Columbia College. Place of meeting, Columbia College. Meetings, twice a month during college term.

COLUMBIAN COLLEGE (WASHINGTON, D. C.) CAMERA CLUB Organized 1888. *President*, Allan J. Houghton; *Vice-President*, Edwin W. Ashford; *Treasurer*, A. J. Houghton; *Librarian*, W. B. Asmussen; *Secretary*, Chas. P. Spooner. Place of meeting, Columbian College, Washington, D.C. Ordinary meetings, every Wednesday afternoon.

CASE SCHOOL CAMERA CLUB (CLEVELAND, OHIO) Organized February, 1889. *Hon. President*, Prof. C. F. Mabery, S. D.; *Hon. Vice-President*, Albert W. Smith, Ph. C.; *President*, Frank E. Hall; *Vice-President*, Lafayette D. Vorce; *Secretary* and *Treasurer*, J. Frank Moore; *Corresponding Secretary*, Milton B. Punnett. Meetings, Case School of Applied Science.

COLUMBUS (OHIO) CAMERA CLUB *President*, Rev. Geo. W. Lincoln; *Treasurer*, Jos. N. Bradford; *Secretary*, Frank H. Howe, King Building. Place of meeting, room 40, Pioneer Block. Date of meeting, third Thursday of each month.

CHICAGO (ILL.), PHOTOGRAPHIC SOCIETY OF *President*, Judge J. B. Bradwell; *Executive Committee*, F. A. Place, M. J. Steffins, H. D. Garrison, M.D.; *Treasurer*, G. A. Douglas; *Secretary*, C. Gentile, 134 Van Buren Street. Place of meeting, Art Institute. Meeting, first Tuesday of each month.

CHICAGO (ILL.) LANTERN SLIDE CLUB *President*, Col. A. F. Stevenson; *Secretary*, W. A. Morse, 185 Wabash Avenue. Place of meeting, Art Institute. Meetings, third Tuesday in month.

CAMBRIDGE CAMERA CLUB (CAMBRIDGEPORT, MASS.) *President*, J. A. Darling; *Treasurer*, C. W. Wilson; *Secretary*, H. Sumner Yates. Place of meeting, 23 William Street. Meetings, first Tuesday in month.

CINCINNATI (OHIO) CAMERA CLUB (Photographic Section of Society of Natural History) *President*, Geo. Bullock; *Treasurer*, T. H. Kelly; *Secretary*, Emery H. Barton, 171 Race Street. Place of Meeting, Natural History Society Rooms, 108 Broadway. Meetings, first and third Mondays of each month.

CORNELL CAMERA CLUB (ITHACA, N. Y.) *President*, W. E. Reed; *Treasurer*, Geo. A. Bliss; *Secretary*, A. Vickers, Ithaca, N.Y. Place of meetings, Physical Lecture Room, Campus. Meetings, every two weeks; every other meeting a lantern slide exhibit.

CLEVELAND (OHIO) CAMERA CLUB *President*, Rev. Charles Pomeroy; *Treasurer*, D. Cole; *Secretary*, Charles Potter; *Corresponding Secretary*, Robert Dayton, M.D. Place of meeting, 5 Euclid Avenue, Cleveland, Ohio. Meetings, first and third Tuesdays.

CRANFORD (N. J.) CAMERA CLUB *President*, R. M. Fuller; *Treasurer*, J. C. Wagstaff; *Secretary*, Wm. Chamberlain, Cranford, N.J. Place of meeting, Club Rooms, Meetings, every other Monday.

GERMAN PHOTOGRAPHIC SOCIETY OF NEW YORK Organized 1868. *President*, A. Mildenberger; *Vice-President*, H. Fruwirth; *Treasurer*, G. E. Pellnitz; *Financial Secretary*, L. Schill; *Corresponding Secretary*, H. G. Borgfeldt, 192 Washington Street, Hoboken, N.J. Place of meeting, 62 East Fourth Street, New York City. Ordinary meetings, second and fourth Wednesday of every month at 8:15 P.M.

GRAND RAPIDS (MICH.) PHOTOGRAPHIC CLUB *President*, Dr. J. C. Parker; *Treasurer*, N. Fred. Avery; *Secretary*, J. B. Barlow. Place of meeting, 15 Fountain Street. Meetings, first and third Monday evenings each month.

HARTFORD (CONN.) CAMERA CLUB *President*, James B. Cone; *Secretary*, Edw. H. Crowell; *Treasurer* and *Corresponding Secretary*, Elmer M. White, P. O. Box 708. Place of meeting, Club Room, Room 61, Ætna Life Insurance Co. Building. Meetings, second Monday in each month, except July and August.

HAWAIIAN CAMERA CLUB (HONOLULU, SANDWICH ISLANDS) *President*, C. Hedemann; *Secretary*, A. W. Richardson. Meeting night, first Friday after first Monday in each month. Club Rooms, Campbell's Block, corner Fort and Merchant Streets, Honolulu, H.I.

HOBOKEN (N. J.) CAMERA CLUB Organized at the residence of Mr. William Sachs, 432 Garden Street. W. Allen, *President;* C. Beckers, *Custodian*, and F. A. Huench, *Secretary*, 76 Bloomfield Street, Hoboken, N.J.

INDIANAPOLIS (IND.) CAMERA CLUB Organized November 25, 1887. *President*, Charles McBride; *Vice-President*, H. C. Chandler; *Treasurer* and *Secretary*, Carl H. Lieber; *Executive Committee*, J. T. Harris, Remo Steele, Henry Kothe. Place of meeting, 33 South Meridian Street. Meetings, first Tuesday every month.

LOWELL (MASS.) CAMERA CLUB (Formerly Lowell Association Amateur Photographers) *President*, W. P. Atwood; *Treasurer*, H. W. Barnes; *Secretary*, G. A. Nelson, 81 Appleton Street. Meetings, every third Tuesday. November to March inclusive with special meetings, subject to call of president.

LYNN (MASS.) CAMERA CLUB *President*, W. H. Drew; *Treasurer*, E. F. Bacheller; *Secretary*, J. W. Gibboney. Place of meeting, 347 Union Street, Lynn, Mass. Meetings, first Tuesday of each month. Club nights, Tuesdays and Thursdays of each week.

LOUISVILLE (KY.) CAMERA CLUB *President*, C. R. Peaslee; *Vice-President*, Alex. Griswold; *Treasurer*, R. L. Stevens. Place of meeting, Polytechnic Building, Louisville, Ky. Date of meeting, second and fourth Tuesdays of each month.

MINNEAPOLIS (MINN.), CAMERA CLUB OF *President*, R. D. Cleveland; *Treasurer*, F. Read; *Secretary*, C. A. Hoffman, 22 Fourth Street, South. Place of meeting, 20 Fourth Street, South. Meetings, two Tuesdays each month.

MILBURY (MASS.) CAMERA CLUB *President*, T. D. Bristol, M. D.; *Treasurer* and *Secretary*, Miss E. R. Benson. Place of meeting, rooms of the Millbury National History Society. Meetings, third Monday of each month.

NEW BRUNSWICK (N. J.) CAMERADS Organized February, 1889. *President*, Prof. P. T. Austen; *Secretary*, Dr. Harry Tredwell. Meetings, Rutgers College. No regular. On call.

NEWARK (N. J.) CAMERA CLUB *President*, Wm. A. Halsey; *Treasurer*, J. M. Foote; *Secretary*, C. G. Hine. Place of meeting, 833 Broad Street, Newark, N.J. Meeting, second Monday of each month.

NEW YORK (N. Y.), SOCIETY OF AMATEUR PHOTOGRAPHERS OF *President*, C. W. Canfield; *Vice-President*, David Williams; *Treasurer*, J. E. Plimpton; *Secretary*, Harry T. Duffield. Place of meeting, 122 West Thirty-sixth Street. Meetings, second Tuesday in each month, except June, July and August.

NEW YORK CITY CAMERA CLUB *President*, Wm. T. Colbron. *Treasurer* and *Secretary*, J. H. Wainwright. Place of meeting, 314 Fifth Avenue. Meetings, second Wednesday in January, April, July and October.

NEW ORLEANS (LA.) CAMERA CLUB *President*, H. T. Howard; *Vice-President*, J. A. Hincks; *Treasurer*, P. E. Carriere; *Secretary*, Chas. H. Fenner. Meetings at Tulane University, the third Wednesday of each month.

OREGON CAMERA CLUB (PORTLAND, OREGON) *President*, W. W. Bretherton; *Vice-President*, M. Goldsmith; *Secretary* and *Treasurer*, Edward Norton. Meetings at Club Rooms, Third and Morrison Streets, third Friday of each month.

OLD COLONY CAMERA CLUB (ROCKLAND, MASS.) *President*, W. G. E. Freeman; *Treasurer*, David Smith; *Secretary*, Burton O. Estes. Meetings at Club Rooms, Liberty Street, Wednesdays.

PROVIDENCE (R. I.) CAMERA CLUB Organized as Providence Amateur Photographic Association, 1884. Incorporated February, 1889. *President*, R. C. Fuller; *Treasurer*, J. E. Dansin; *Secretary*, J. E. Dansin; *Librarian*, A. B. Ladd. Place of meeting, Swarts' Block, 81 Weybosset Street. Meetings, first Saturday and Tuesday after third Saturday. Annual meeting, first Saturday in March.

PHILADELPHIA (PA.), PHOTOGRAPHIC SOCIETY OF *President*, Frederic Graff; *Treasurer*, Samuel Fox; *Secretary*, Robert S. Redfield, 1601 Callowhill Street. Place of meeting, 1305 Arch Street. Meetings, stated, first Wednesday evening of each month. Conversational, third Monday.

PHILADELPHIA AMATEUR PHOTOGRAPHIC CLUB Organized December 21, 1883. Incorporated February 12, 1887. *President*, Francis A. Cunningham; *Vice-President*, P. S. Chase; *Treasurer*, W. S. Buchanan; *Secretary*, Alfred Thompson, 1311 Butler Street. Place of meeting, 907 Filbert Street. Ordinary meetings, third Monday, 8 P.M. Annual meeting, third Monday in December.

PACIFIC COAST AMATEUR PHOTOGRAPHIC ASSOCIATION *President*, A. J. Treat; *Treasurer* and *Secretary*, J. H. Johnson, 414 Buchanan Street, San Francisco, Cal. Place of meeting, 605 Mercantile Street. Meetings, first Thursday after first Monday in each month.

PITTSBURGH (PA.) AMATEUR PHOTOGRAPHERS' SOCIETY *President*, W. S. Bell; *Treasurer*, G. A. Hays; *Secretary*, F. R. C. Perrin, Crafton, Allegheny Co., Pa. Place of meeting, 59 Fourth Street. Meetings, second Monday of each month, 7:30 P.M.

PLAINFIELD (N. J.) CAMERA CLUB *President*, Oscar S. Teale; *Treasurer*, W. H. Lyon, Jr.; *Secretary*, G. Harry Squires, 108 Broadway. Place of meeting, Club Rooms, 12 Park Avenue. Meetings, first Monday in each month.

POSTAL PHOTOGRAPHIC CLUB *President*, Randall Spaulding; *Treasurer* and *Secretary*, Dr. J. Max Mueller. Secretary's address, West Chester, Pa.

ROCHESTER (N. Y.), CAMERA CLUB OF *President*, George Hanmer Croughton; *Treasurer*, James Streeter; *Secretary*, Peter Maudsley, 42 Smith Avenue. Place of meeting, Kirley Block, East Main Street. Meetings, every alternate Thursday. Intervening Thursday evenings devoted to informal gatherings.

SELMA (ALA.) Y. M. C. A. CAMERA CLUB *President*, Chas. E. Bailey; *Treasurer* and *Secretary*, S. Orlando Trippe. Place of meeting, Y. M. C. A. Building, Broad Street. Meetings, first Thursday of each month.

SYRACUSE (N. Y.) CAMERA CLUB *President*, Arthur P. Yates; *Vice-President*, Amos Padgham; *Treasurer*, Charles R. Jones; *Secretary*, Wallace Dickson, P. O. Box 129. Place of meeting, Club Rooms, 72 South Salina Street. Meetings, every Friday evening.

SPRINGFIELD (MASS.) CAMERA CLUB *President*, W. P. Draper; *Treasurer*, N. P. Amos Carter; *Secretary*, John Leshun. Place of meeting, Cor. Main and Sanford Streets. Meetings, third Wednesday of each month.

STEVENS PHOTOGRAPHIC SOCIETY (HOBOKEN, N. J.) *President*, A. R. Whitney, Jr.; *Treasurer*, C. E. Pearce; *Secretary*, E. W. Franzar. Place of meeting, Stevens Institute, Prof. De Volson Wood's Lecture Room. Meetings, first Wednesday in month.

SOUTHERN TIER PHOTOGRAPHIC ASSOCIATION *President*, W. L. Sutton; *Treasurer*, J. S. Ryder; *Secretary*, A. B. Stebbins, Canisteo, N. Y. Place of meeting, decided from time to time. Meetings, third Thursday of each month.

SAINT LOUIS (MO.) CAMERA CLUB *President*, Robert E. M. Bain; *Vice-President*, Rev. C. M. Charroppin, S. J.; *Secretary* and *Trea-*

surer, W. M. Butler, 2636 Osage Street, St. Louis, Mo. Place of meeting, St. Louis University, Cor. Grand Avenue and Pine Street. Meetings, first and third Tuesdays of month.

TEXAS STATE (TEX.) PHOTOGRAPHERS' ASSOCIATION *President*, J. S. Webster and six *Vice-Presidents; Treasurer*, S. T. Blessing; *Secretary*, C. F. Cooke. Place of meeting, at different places in the State. Meetings, conventions twice a year.

WATERTOWN (N. Y.) CAMERA CLUB *President*, H. M. Hill, A. M.; *Treasurer*, L. C. Child; *Secretary*, George I. Woolley. Watertown, N. Y. Place of meeting, Watertown High School. Meetings, first Monday of month.

WASHINGTON (D. C.) CAMERA CLUB Organized November, 1883, as the Argents; re-organized March, 1887; incorporated May, 1888, as the Washington Camera Club. *President*, R. J. Fisher, Jr.; *Vice-President*, B. Perry Pierce; *Secretary* and *Treasurer*, S. H. Griffiths, M. D., M. S. N.; *Corresponding Secretary*, J. Albert Cole, office of Supervising Architect, United States Treasury Department, Washington, D. C.

WATERBURY (CONN.), PHOTOGRAPHERS' SOCIETY OF *President*, Chas. R. Pancoast; *Treasurer*, E. W. Mooney, Jr.; *Secretary*, Wm. L. White, 100 Cooke Street. Place of meeting, room 18, Baldwin's Block, 63 Bank Street. Meetings, Friday evenings.

WORCESTER (MASS.) LANTERN SLIDE CLUB *President* and *Corresponding Secretary*, Dr. Geo. E. Francis. Meetings, every second Tuesday, 4 Elm Street. Exchanges slides with other similar organizations.

WORCESTER (MASS.) CAMERA CLUB *President*, Dr. E. V. Scribner; *Treasurer*, Geo. H. Corbett; *Secretary*, Paul B. Morgan. Place of meetings, Natural History Society Rooms, Foster Street. Second Tuesdays in month. Annual meetings in January.

YONKERS (N. Y.) AMATEUR PHOTOGRAPHERS' CLUB Organized February 15, 1889. *President*, G. Livingston Morse; *Treasurer* and *Secretary*, Robert M. Reevs, Box 720, Yonkers, N. Y. Place of meeting, Dey's Building, Cor. Warburton and Well's Avenues. Meetings, first Friday in month. Annual, first Friday in April. (Informal every Friday.)

Canadian Societies (1889)

CANADA, PHOTOGRAPHIC ASSOCIATION OF *President*, A. T. Barraud; *Secretary*, E. Poole, St. Catherines, Ontario. Place of meetings, Toronto. Meetings, August 20, 21, 22.

MONTREAL (CAN.) AMATEUR PHOTOGRAPHIC CLUB *President*, Captain James G. Shaw; *Hon. Treasurer*, W. E. Bradshaw; *Hon. Secretary*, J. W. Davis, Alois Dept., G. T. Ry. Place of meeting, 2204 St. Catherine Street. Meetings, first Monday each month. Annual meeting, 1889, December 2. Use of rooms at disposal of visiting photographers.

QUEBEC (CANADA) CAMERA CLUB *President*, Captain Jas. Peters; *Treasurer*, Jas. Brodie; *Secretary*, Ernest F. Würtele, 93 St. Peter Street, Quebec. Place of meeting, Captain Imlah's Quarters, Citadel. Annual meetings, second Monday of December.

TORONTO (CAN.) AMATEUR PHOTOGRAPHERS' ASSOCIATION *President*, G. O. E. Bethune; *Vice-President*, W. B. McMurrick; *Treasurer* and *Secretary*, F. D. Manchee. Place of meeting, College of Physicians and Surgeons, Bay Street, Toronto. Meetings, first Monday of month. Weekly club night, Monday evening.

Societies in the British Isles (1892)

ABERDARE AMATEUR PHOTOGRAPHIC AND SCIENTIFIC SOCIETY Established 1891. Annual Meeting in January. *President*, H. C. Lewis; *Vice-Presidents*, D. P. Davies, J. P. and E. Arnoll; *Committee*, G. Davies, J. Finnucane, G. George, A. E. Dewsbury, D. M. Richards, S. Williams, D. Tudor Williams, Iago Lloyd; *Treasurer*, Leonard Acomb, Lloyd's Bank; *Secretary*, D. P. Davies, 17 Commercial Street, Aberdare.

ABERDEENSHIRE AMATEUR PHOTOGRAPHIC SOCIETY Established 1891. Headquarters 35A Union Street. Meetings held on the last Tuesday of each month. *Hon. President*, Dr. J. Mackenzie Davidson; *Hon. Vice-President*, Thomas Ferguson; *President*, W. Todd Moffatt; *Vice-Presidents*, J. Clark and W. G. Lindsay; *Committee*, James Main and Alexander Mackilligan;

Hon. Secretary and *Treasurer*, G. Brodie, 35A Union Street, Aberdeen.

ABNEY CAMERA CLUB   Established 1889. Meetings held on Friday evenings at 8 P. M. during the winter months at the houses of members. *Secretary*, F. H. Leeds, F.I.C., F.C.S., 26 East Bank, Stamford Hill, N.

ALBANY INSTITUTE AMATEUR PHOTOGRAPHIC SOCIETY   Established 1888. Meetings are held on alternate Thursday evenings at 8:30 P.M., at the Albany Institute, 345 Albany Road, Camberwell, S. E., starting from the second Thursday in January. *President*, Berkeley Chappell; *Council*, Messrs. Bucknole, Harvey and Rhodes; *Hon. Treasurer*, A. B. Smith; *Hon. Secretary*, Alfred B. Gee, 3 Welby Street, Camberwell, S. E.

ALTRINCHAM AMATEUR PHOTOGRAPHIC SOCIETY   *Secretary*, James Davenport, Albert Road, Altrincham.

AMATEUR PHOTOGRAPHIC ASSOCIATION   Established 1861. No stated times for meetings. *President*, His Royal Highness the Prince of Wales; *Vice-Presidents*, H. R. H. the Duke of Cambridge, H. H. the Duke of Teck, G. C. B., etc., The Most Noble the Marquis of Drogheda, General the Right Hon. the Lord of Ros, The Right Hon. the Earl of Rosse, F.R.S., James Glaisler, Esq., F.R.S., F.R.A.S., etc.; *Council*, Sir J. Whittaker Ellis, Bart., Sir Spencer Maryon Wilson, Bart., Charles Stephens, M.A. (Oxon), W. D. Howard, F.I.C., Walter Wood, F.R.G.S., W. S. Hobson, John Aird, M.P., R. O. Milne; *Hon. Secretary*, Arthur James Melhuish, 58 Pall Mall, London, S.W.

AMATEUR PHOTOGRAPHIC FIELD CLUB   Established 1852. Monthly outings during the summer. Indoor meetings monthly during the winter. Annual meeting in March. *President*, C. Burton Barber; *Treasurer* and *Secretary*, B. G. Wilkinson, Jr., 151 Bermondsey Street, London, S.E.

ARBROATH AMATEUR PHOTOGRAPHIC ASSOCIATION   Established 1890. Headquarters, Brothock Bridge. Meetings last Tuesday of each month. *President*, Robert Moodie; *Vice-President*, George R. Reid; *Council*, W. Webster, D. Kyd, A. Malcolm, Robert McLush; *Hon. Secretary* and *Treasurer*, E. J. Ritchie, Clifburn, Arbroath.

ASHTON UNDER LYNE PHOTOGRAPHIC SOCIETY   Established 1891. Headquarters, Henry Square, open from 9 A. M. to 10 P. M. *President*, Dr. A. Hamilton; *Vice-Presidents*, J. W. Kenworthy, C. E. Redfern, Rev. H. J. Palmer, Major Bradley; *Council*, W. Chadwick, T. Glazebrook, W. Greenwood, W. Leigh, R. Matthews, J. H. Storey, Geo. Weild and I. Hutchinson; *Hon. Treasurer*, R. T. Marsland; *Hon. Secretary*, Geo. H. Dean, 8 Egmont Terrace, Stalybridge; *Librarian*, L. Tornbull.

AYLESBURY AMATEUR PHOTOGRAPHIC SOCIETY   *Secretary*, J. F. Roche, 2 St. Mary's Square, Aylesbury.

BARNSTAPLE AND NORTH DEVON PHOTOGRAPHIC SOCIETY   Established 1890. Ordinary meetings held at 7:30 P. M. on the first Wednesday in each month, at the Society's Room, North Devon Althenaeum, Barnstaple. Annual meeting first Wednesday in October. *President*, Rev. Thos. Newton, LL.D.; *Vice-President*, W. Ridd; *Council*, W. Britton, W. M. Jones, J. J. H. Sanders, L.D.S., and Officers; *Secretary* and *Treasurer*, Arthur C. King, Hills View, Barnstaple, North Devon.

BARROW-IN-FURNESS NATURALIST FIELD CLUB (Photographic Section)   Meetings every fourth Tuesday. *President*, A. Blechynden; *Vice-Presidents*, W. Dunlop and R. Westos; *Treasurer*, J. P. Smith; *Secretary*, J. Redhead, 9 Spring Street, Barrow-in-Furness.

BATH PHOTOGRAPHIC SOCIETY   Established 1888. Ordinary meetings last Thursday in each month. Annual meeting last Thursday in February, at 8 o'clock, at the Royal Literary and Scientific Institution, Terrace Walks. *President*, Austin J. King; *Vice-President*, Philip Braham; *Committee*, E. J. Appleby, A. F. Perren, G. F. Powell, Rev. E. A. Purvis, Canon Williams, D. Williams, W. Pumphrey (permanent member of Committee); *Hon. Secretary* and *Treasurer*, W. Middleton Ashman, 12A Old Bond Street, Bath.

BATLEY AND DISTRICT PHOTOGRAPHIC SOCIETY   *President*, Percy Sheard; *Secretary*, Charles Naylor, Clark Green Street, Batley.

BEDFORD AND DISTRICT CAMERA CLUB   *President*, Rev. H. Victor Macdona, M. A.; *Hon. Secretary* and *Treasurer*, W. E. Ison; *Committee*, Rev. H. Victor Macdona, M. A., Deputy

Surgeon-General A. H. Beaman, Mr. H. W. Stewardson, Mr. Alex Kirby, Mr. P. Hill, Mr. Montague Troup, Mr. W. E. Ison.

BIRKENHEAD PHOTOGRAPHIC ASSOCIATION Established 1881. Meetings held every second Thursday in the month, commencing at 7:30 P.M. Annual meeting, November. *President*, G. E. Thompson; *Vice-President*, G. A. Carruthers; *Council*, F. S. Eaton, F. H. Jones, Paul Lange, J. L. Mackrell, T. S. Mayne, A. F. Stanistreet, E. M. Tunstall; *Auditors*, A. Bradbury and H. Wilkinson; *Librarian*, J. A. Forrest; *Treasurer*, H. R. Millar, 72 Merton Road, Bootle; *Secretary*, C. B. Reader, Mouniside, Rowson Street, New Brighton, Birkenhead.

BIRKENHEAD YOUNG MEN'S CHRISTIAN ASSOCIATION CAMERA CLUB *President*, Edward Whalley; *Secretary*, J. C. Walker, 42 Conway Street, Birkenhead.

BIRMINGHAM PHOTOGRAPHIC SOCIETY Established 1884. Lantern evenings on Wednesdays, Demonstrations on Thursdays and Elementary Papers for Beginners one Tuesday a month, time given in published programmes. These are held respectively at the Y. M. C. A. Lecture Hall, the Midland Institute, and the Club room, Colonnade Hotel, Birmingham. *President*, J. E. Stone, J.P., F.L.S., F.R.G.S.; *Vice-Presidents*, W. Jerome Harrison, F.G.S., E. H. Jaques, B. Karleese; *Council*, A. A. Bonehill, A. R. Longmore, E. C. Middleton, William Rooke, J. Simkin, G. A. Thomason, George Wilkes; *Treasurer*, Thomas Taylor; *Secretaries*, Arthur J. Leeson, 20 Cannon Street, Birmingham, and J. T. Mousley, Portland Road, Edgbaston.

BLACKBURN AND DISTRICT PHOTOGRAPHIC SOCIETY Established 1890. Meetings are held on Thursday evenings at 8 P.M. Annual meeting the last Thursday in October at 8 P.M. *President*, Major Baron, of Darwen; *Vice-Presidents*, R. C. Pilling and Peter Jackson; *Council*, W. Y. Gowans, R. P. Gregson, Dr. Hasler, Sagar J. Mitchell; *Treasurer*, A. P. Garland; *Secretary*, W. B. Burrows, 20 Richmond Terrace, Blackburn.

BLACKBURN LITERARY CLUB (Photographic Section) Established 1884. Each Section of the Club is managed by its own Secretary. Meetings and excursions at intervals during the season. *President*, T. J. Syckelmoore, B.A.; *Vice-President*, Charles Smithies; *Hon. Secretary*, E. S. Johnson, Literary Club, Blackburn.

BLACKHEATH CAMERA CLUB Established 1891. Headquarters, Art Club, Bennett Park. Meetings Tuesdays and Wednesdays, fortnightly. *President*, W. H. M. Christie, M.A.; F.R.S.; *Vice-Presidents*, Ernest Clarke, M.D., and J. T. Field; *Hon. Treasurer*, A. W. Young; *Hon. Secretary*, Thos. B. Earle, The Cottage, Handen Road, Lee, Kent.

BOLTON CAMERA CLUB Established 1889. Meetings held at 21 Bury New Road, Bolton, on the second and fourth Wednesdays during the summer, at 8 P.M. *President*, J. Johnson, M.D.; *Vice-President*, C. A. Mackechnie, M.B.; *Council*, J. Turner, J. Berry, J. Royle, A. Harper, T. Parkinson, Jr., W. Russell; *Treasurer*, W. Bromley, 155 Blackburn Road, Bolton; *Secretary*, T. Parkinson, 331 St. Helen's Road, Daubhill, Bolton.

BOLTON PHOTOGRAPHIC CLUB Established 1883. Meetings are held every Tuesday evening, at the Studio of the Club, Chancery Lane, Bolton, at 8 o'clock P.M. *President*, Jabez Boothroyd; *Vice-President*, Thomas Jukes; *Committee*, Messrs. Hawksworth, Banks, Bradshaw, Ashworth, Sewell; *Treasurer*, John Bradshaw; *Secretary*, James Slater, Town Hall Square, Bolton.

BOLTON PHOTOGRAPHIC SOCIETY Established 1879. Meetings held at 10 Rushton Street, on the first Thursday in each month from September to May, at 8 P.M. Annual meeting, first Thursday in October. *President*, J. R. Bridson; *Vice-Presidents*, E. N. Ashworth, R. Harwood, William Banks, W. Knowles, B. H. Abbott, J. Boothroyd, John Taylor; *Council*, C. J. P. Fuller, J. Johnston, M.D., J. E. Austwick, James Leach, Thomas Davis, R. Flintoff, A. Harper, W. Green, J. S. Roscow; *Treasurer*, C. K. Dalton; *Secretary*, Charles Mackechnie, M.D., 355 Blackburn Road, Bolton.

BOURNEMOUTH SOCIETY OF NATURAL SCIENCE (Photographic Section) Founded October, 1890. Headquarters, Fine Art Gallery, 76 Old Christchurch Road. Meets alternate Wednesdays. *President*, Rev. J. R. Husband, M.D.; *Vice-Presidents*, Dr. Hyla Greves, Dr. NanKevit; *Hon. Secretary*, Wm. Jones, on Old

Christchurch Road, Bournemouth; *Ass't Secretary*, Mr. Greenleave, Priory Mansion, Bournemouth.

'BOYS' OWN' POSTAL PHOTOGRAPHIC CLUB Established 1868. At present there are twelve members; open to any number under twenty. *President* and *Secretary*, J. E. Hardwich, 4 Gloucester Terrace, Weymouth.

BRADFORD PHOTOGRAPHIC CLUB *President*, Charles Holmes. *Hon. Secretary*, Frederick North, 27 Kirkgate, Bradford.

BRADFORD PHOTOGRAPHIC SOCIETY Established 1882. Meetings, second Thursday in the month. *President*, Isidor Sonnenthal; *Vice-Presidents*, W. H. Scott and Walter Leach, F.C.S.; *Committee*, W. Halstead, W. S. Smith, W. Judson, F. J. R. Sutcliffe, George Firth, Rev. T. Mellodey, M.A., J. P. Burgess; *Secretary* and *Treasurer*, F. B. Pickles, 15 Beech Grove, Pollard Lane, Bradford.

BRECHIN PHOTOGRAPHIC ASSOCIATION Established 1888. Meetings in Rooms, 14 St. Mary Street, on the third Wednesday of each month, at 15 minutes past 8, from September to May. Annual meeting, September. Dark room open to vistors, being members of other societies, at a nominal charge of 1*s*. per month. *President*, William Shaw Adamson, Jr., of Careston. *Vice-Presidents*, W. Lawrence and Henry Braid; *Committee*, G. F. Robertson, B.Sc., A. Brown, J. Buchanan; *Curator*, J. C. Middleton; *Treasurer*, Alexander Innes; *Secretary*, James D. Ross, 6 High Street, Brechin, N.B.

BRIGHTON AND SUSSEX NATURAL HISTORY AND PHILOSOPHICAL SOCIETY (Photographic Section) Founded March, 1892. Headquarters, Free Library and Museum, Brighton. Meeting on the first Friday in the month. *Chairman*, J. P. Slingsby Roberts, Esq.; *Hon. Secretary*, Dr. W. Harrison, 98 Western Road, Brighton.

BRISTOL AND WEST OF ENGLAND AMATEUR PHOTOGRAPHIC ASSOCIATION Established about 1866. Meetings, first Friday in the month; Annual meeting, January, at the Association's Rooms, Literary and Philosophic Club, 28 Berkeley Square, Bristol. *President*, H. A. Hood Daniel, F.S.I.; *Vice-President*, Colonel F. L. Playfair and Edward Brightman; *Secretary* and *Treasurer*, Frederick Bligh Bond, 36 Corn Street, Bristol.

BRISTOL CAMERA SOCIETY Established 1887. Meetings at University College, Tyndall's Park, Bristol, on the second and fourth Thursdays in each month at 7:30 P.M. *President*, Harvey Barton; *Hon. Secretary*, T. T. Genge, 68 Berkeley Road, Bishopston, Bristol.

BRITISH ASSOCIATION FOR THE ADVANCEMENT OF SCIENCE Established 1831. The next meeting will be held at Nottingham, September 13–20, 1893. *President*, Sir Archibald Geikie, F.R.S.; *President-Elect*, Prof. J. S. Burdon Sanderson, F.R.S.; *Treasurer*, Prof. A. W. Rücker, F.R.S.; *General Secretaries*, Sir Douglas Galton, K.C.B., and A. Vernon Harcourt, F.A.S.; *Assistant General Secretary*, G. Griffith, M.A. Office, Burlington House, London, W.

BRIXTON AND CLAPHAM CAMERA CLUB Established 1889. The ordinary meetings of the Club are held on the first and third Tuesdays each month at 8 P.M., at The Clarence Rooms, 376 Coldharbour Lane, Brixton. *President*, John Reynolds, M. D. F.R.G.S.; *Vice-Presidents*, J. W. Coade and W. H Harrison; *Committee*, Messrs. Bartrop, Bevins, Butler, Edwards, Howard and Kent; *Assistant-Secretary*, Mr. R. G. F. Kidson; *Secretary* and *Treasurer*, Fred W. Levett, 376 Coldharbour Lane, Brixton, S.W.

BROCKLEY AND ST. JOHN'S SCIENTIFIC SOCIETY Established 1872. Meetings first and third Thursdays in each month at St. John's Church Room, Lewisham High Road, S.E. Annual meeting, third Thursday in November. *President*, Malcolm Stodart; *Vice-Presidents*, W. J. Spratling, F.G.S., F. J. Tayler, M.B., J. Jenner Weir, F.L.S.; *Hon. Treasurer*, W. Dawson. *Hon. Secretary*, J. H. Sinclair, 25 Harcourt Road, Brockley, S.E.

BURNLEY PHOTOGRAPHIC SOCIETY Established 1885. Meetings, last Wednesday in each month, at 8 P.M., in the Society's Rooms, Bank Chambers, Hargreaves Street, Burnley. A dark room. *President*, John Butterworth, J.P.; *Vice-Presidents*, D. Drew, J.P., and J. C. Brumwell, M.D., J.P.; *Council*, W. Chadwick, A. Howarth, J. Holgate, William Lancaster, W. H. Hey, J. W. Houlden, W. Kippax, J. Pickles; *Treasurer*, J. L. Lee; *Secretary*. William Sutcliffe, 7 Bank Hall Terrace, Burnley.

BURTON-ON-TRENT NATURAL HISTORY AND ARCHAEOLOGICAL SOCIETY (Photographic Section) Established 1889. Meetings, first Wednesday in each month, at 46 High Street, Burton-on-Trent. *President*, R. Churchill; *Hon. Secretary* and *Treasurer*, J. E. Nowers, 282 Blackpool Street, Burton-on-Trent.

BURTON-ON-TRENT NATURAL HISTORY AND ARCHAEOLOGICAL SOCIETY (Photographic Section) Established 1889. Meetings, first Wednesday in each month, at 46 High Street, Burton-on-Trent. *President*, R. Churchill; *Hon. Secretary* and *Treasurer*, A. L. Stern, B.Sc., &c., 16 Alexandra Road, Burton-on-Trent.

BURY PHOTOGRAPHIC AND ARTS CLUB Established 1882. Ordinary meetings held every third Wednesday in the month at 7:30 P.M., at 13 Agar Street. Annual meeting, third Wednesday in October, at 7:30 P.M. *President*, William Booth; *Vice-Presidents*, Robt. Grundy, Jr. and E. W. Mellor; *Council*, J. M. Barbour, C. H. Openshaw, S. Litton, A. W. Dye and John Hoyle; *Hon. Treasurer*, J. R. Bertwistle; *Hon. Secretaries*, Roger Wood and Wm. Spencer, 11 Bolton Street, Bury, Lancashire.

CAMBERWELL CAMERA CLUB *President*, George Pike; *Secretary*, F. H. Atkins, 71 Paulet Road, S.E.

CAMBRIDGE CAMERA CLUB *President*, F. Morley; *Hon. Secretary*, F. E. Brown, 25 Sidney Street, Cambridge.

CAMBRIDGE UNIVERSITY PHOTOGRAPHIC SOCIETY Established 1881. Headquarters, 2 St. Mary's Passage. Meetings irregular. *President*, W. N. Shaw; *Vice-President*, Rev. G. B. Atkinson, M.A.; *Hon. Secretary* and *Treasurer*, W. Jackson, Pembroke College, Cambridge.

CAMERA CLUB Established 1885. The Camera Club is a social, scientific and artistic centre for amateur photographers and others interested in art and science. The Club is open on week days from 10 A.M. to midnight, and on Sundays from 10 A.M. to 11 P.M. It combines the ordinary advantages of a club with the appliances and conveniences of a photographic and scientific society. The Club premises include the following conveniences and advantages: A studio and an enlarging room, each with its own dark room attached; nine separate dark rooms available to members at all times; a laboratory for daylight operations; a workshop with fitted lathe and other scientific appliances; a billiard room, library, dining room, and large meeting room. An Annual Conference is organized under the auspices of the Club, and up to the present has been held at the Society of Arts. During the winter season, from October to May, meetings are held every Thursday for the reading of papers, for demonstrations, or lantern-slide exhibitions, and for the same season there is a concert on the first Monday in each month. Photographic exhibitions are held in the rooms from time to time, the members' annual show being arranged so as to commence at the date of the Annual Conference. A Club journal is published and sent free monthly to members. *President*, Captain W. de W. Abney, C.B., R.E., D.C.L., F.R.S; *Committee*, *Sir George Rendlesham Prescott, Bart., *Chairman*, *F. Machell Smith, *Vice-Chairman*, *Greensill Allen, W. Brooks, V. A. Corbouldi, *Francis Cobb, William Clarke, Lyonel Clark, *John France Collins, *G. Davison, Alfred Deed, E. J. Humphrey, *Enrico Ferrero, J. Gale, *William Asbury Greene, Richard Inwards, H. M. Elder, *A. Maskell, Duke of Newcastle, Andrew Pringle, *John Farquharson Roberts, B. Rous, F. Seyton Scott, *Ernest G. Spiers, the President and the Hon. Secretary (*ex-officio*); *Hon. Secretary*, *George Davison, Camera Club, Charing Cross Road. [*Directors of the Camera Club Company, Limited.]

CAMERA AND COMPANY Established 1891. A Postal Photographic Club for the circulation and criticism of prints entirely the work of members, and for a general interchange of ideas with a view to the mutual advancement in the science and art of photography. *Secretary* and *Treasurer*, N. Elliot, South Sea Cottage, Coldstream, N.B.

CARDIFF AMATEUR PHOTOGRAPHIC SOCIETY Established 1886. *President*, Charles F. Gooch; *Vice-Presidents*, Jonas Watson, J. P., Walter Insole, S. W. Allen, M.I.M.E., Alexander Kellar, T. Mansel Franklen; *Council*, E. Lewis, W. H. Kitchen, William Furlay, John Neale, John Weaver, Frederick Heitzman, E. H. Bruton, George Shepton, C. C. Perkins, A. McKinnon, C. H. Murrell, G. H. Wills, Jr., William Booth; *Treasurer*, W. Foster; *Hon. Secretaries*, G. H. Bedford and T. H. Faulks, 127 Bute Road.

CARLISLE AND COUNTY AMATEUR PHOTO-
GRAPHIC SOCIETY Established 1885. Meeting
first Tuesday in each month, in the Viaduct
Hotel, Carlisle. *President*, the Mayor of Carlisle;
Vice-Presidents, C. S. Hall, M.R.C.S., and H.
Y. Thompson, L.S.A.; *Committee*, J. Robson,
F. Ritson, J. H. Coward, J. Mackintosh, J. G.
Moffett; *Treasurer*, John Forsyth; *Secretary*,
John S. Atkinson, 55 South Pettril Street, Car-
lisle.

CHELTENHAM PHOTOGRAPHIC SOCIETY
Established 1865. Meetings on the second
Thursday in each month from October to May
inclusive. *President*, C. E. F. Nash, M.A.;
Committee, the officers and G. S. Penny, W. W.
Whittard, E. Wethered; *Treasurer*, J. Bull;
Secretary, W. C. Beetham, 22 Promenade Villas.

CHESTER SOCIETY OF NATURAL SCIENCE
AND LITERATURE (Photographic Section) Established 1887. Annual meeting in Grosvenor
Museum, last Friday in March, at 8 P.M. *Chairman of Section*, Dr. Stolterforth, M.A.; *Committee*, Mrs. T. H. Hignett, A. G. Ayrton, E.
G. Ballard, A.R.S.M., A. H. Hignett, George
Frater, J. M. Frost, F. Evans, C. W. Townshend; *Secretary* and *Treasurer*, J. H. Spencer,
36 Bridge Street, Chester.

CHISWICK CAMERA CLUB *Chairman*, R.
W. Watson; *Hon. Secretary* and *Treasurer*, H.
Harding Miller, Parkia, Chiswick.

THE CHORLEY POLYTECHNIC PHOTO-
GRAPHIC SOCIETY Established 1892. Head-
quarters, Fellery Street. *President*, J. T. Brierly;
Vice-Presidents, H. R. Dorning, R. Berry and
William Dornan; *Treasurer*, R. Gill; *Secre-
taries*, Jas. G. Welch and William Waring.

CITY OF BELFAST YOUNG MEN'S CHRISTIAN
ASSOCIATION CAMERA CLUB Established
1889. Meet on the first Monday in each month.
President, William Swanston, F.G.S.; *Vice-
Presidents*, William Strain, Robert McCann,
S. B. Coates, M.D., B. D. Wise, C.E.; *Com-
mittee*, John E. Pim, T. F. Bell, James A. Pol-
lock, Hamilton McCleery, T. B. Scott, William
Pollock; *Secretary*, James McCleery, 14 Wel-
lington Place; *Treasurer*, James H. Hamilton.

CLEVELAND CAMERA CLUB Established
1888. Meetings are held on the last Tuesday
of each month, at 8 P.M., at the Cleveland Literary and Philosophical Society's Hall, Middles-
brough. General meeting in January. *President*,

J. E. Stead. *Vice-Presidents*, G. Bainbridge and
Baker Hudson. *Council*, A. H. Atkinson, Dr.
W. W. Stainthorpe, Dr. William Knott, Dr.
Hopgood. *Secretary* and *Treasurer*, Joseph J.
Hallam, 11 Amber Street, Saltburn-by-the-sea.

CLYDESDALE CAMERA CLUB Established
1889. *President*, Henry Erskine Gordon. *Secretary* and *Treasurer*, Miss Burns, Castle
Wemyss, Wemyss Bay, N.B.

COLCHESTER CAMERA CLUB *President*,
Rev. C. L. Acland, M.A. *Hon. Secretary*, H.
Wright, 18 Head Street, Colchester.

CORNISH CAMERA CLUB Established 1889.
Meetings at Science Schools, Penzance, first and
last Tuesdays in each month. *President*, W. E.
Baily, F.L.S.; *Vice-President*, B. Vivian, M.R.-
C.S.; *Council*, Barnes Richards, N. H. Symons,
J. Bramwell, Jr.; *Hon. Treasurer*, W. Herbert
Percy; *Hon. Secretary*, H. Tonkin, 22 Market
Place, Penzance, Cornwall.

COVENTRY AND MIDLAND PHOTOGRAPHIC
SOCIETY Established 1883. Meetings held at
the Technical Institute on Wednesdays, fortnightly. Annual meeting, first Wednesday in
November, at 8 P.M. *President*, Councillor Andrews; *Vice-Presidents*, C. H. Waters, F. J.
Harker, H. Sturmey, E. J. Walker; *Council*,
H. W. Jones, Rev. H. S. Mercer, H. Hawley,
C. Browett; *Treasurer*, W. L. J. Orton; *Secretary*, Thomas W. Owen, The Terrace, Earls-
don, Coventry.

CREWE AMATEUR PHOTOGRAPHIC SOCIETY
Established 1889. *President*, Rev. W. G. Rams-
ford, M.A.; *Vice-Presidents*, J. Knott, J.P.,
W. Dishart, W. Eardley, E. Booth; *Council*,
W. W. Gibson and R. H. Dutton; *Treasurer*,
John Cherrey; *Secretary*, Thomas Gorrell, 106
Edleston Road.

CREWE SCIENTIFIC SOCIETY (Photographic
Section) Established 1891. Headquarters, Me-
chanics' Institution. Meetings, first Wednesday
in each month. *President*, A. H. Hignett; *Hon.
Treasurer*, J. Kendrick; *Hon. Secretaries*, W.
Bispham, 60 Samuel Street, and Jos. Laing,
Victoria Street.

CROMWELL PHOTOGRAPHIC CLUB Estab-
lished 1891. Headquarters, Cromwell Hotel,
Hall Quay, Great Yarmouth. Meetings, second
Monday of every month. *President*, R. H. Inglis
Palgrave, F.R.S.; *Vice-Presidents*, Miss V. Bux-
ton, John Bately, M.D.; *Hon. Treasurer*, T. W.

Swindell; *Hon. Secretary*, Chas. Rambold, Jr., 4 Dene Side, Great Yarmouth.

CROYDON CAMERA CLUB Meetings in the Public Hall, Croydon. *President*, Hector Maclean, F.G.S., *Vice-President*, Dr. H. J. Strong, J.P.; *Council*, W. J. Bishop, L. C. Brookes, A. E. Isaacs, L. Maxey, H. E. Neeves, C. F. Oakley, E. P. Overton, E. F. Smither; *Hon. Treasurer*, A. J. Sargeant; *Hon. Secretary*, George R. White, 55 Albert Road, Croydon; *Hon. Assistant Secretary*, E. F. Blow, 48 Clyde Road, Croydon.

CROYDON MICROSCOPICAL AND NATURAL HISTORY CLUB (Photographic Section) Established 1870. Ordinary meetings, first Friday in each month. Annual meeting held on the second Wednesday in January of each year, at the Public Hall, George Street, Croydon. *President*, Edward Lovett; *Vice-President*, H. G. Thompson, M.D.; *Committee*, D. Waller, Jr., John Weir Brown, I. A. Carter, B.A., W. Low Sarjeant; *Treasurer*, Edward B. Sturge; *Secretary*, Harry Douglas Gower, 16 Wandle Road, Croydon.

CYCLISTS' PHOTOGRAPHIC PORTFOLIO CLUB Established 1886, for mutual criticism of members' prints, which are circulated in four albums. Membership limited to 30. *Hon. Secretary*, W. L. J. Orton, 7 Bishop Street, Coventry.

DARLINGTON PHOTOGRAPHIC SOCIETY Established 1887. Meetings held on the second Monday in each month, at the Trevelyan Hotel, at 8 P.M. Annual meeting, first Monday in November. *President*, H. W. Hollis; *Vice-President*, E. Ensor, B.A.; *Council*, Messrs. Luck, Davis, Valentine, Cooper, Howlett, Secretary, President, Vice-President; *Treasurer*, P. J. Cooper, 68 North Road, Darlington; *Secretary*, P. W. Forster, Elmbank, Darlington.

DARTMOUTH AMATEUR PHOTOGRAPHIC SOCIETY *President*, Roger Mostyn; *Committee*, E. Anwyl, E. Bearcroft, B. Michelmore, C. Sims, J. H. Spanton, William Simpson, G. R. Whitaker, R. Whitaker; *Hon. Secretary* and *Treasurer*, George Barnston.

DERBY PHOTOGRAPHIC SOCIETY Established 1884. Ordinary monthly meetings, second Tuesday in each month, at 7:30 P.M. Annual meeting, second Tuesday in October. All held at Smith's Restaurant, Victoria Street, Derby. *President*, Captain W. de W. Abney, R.E., C.B., F.R.S.; *Vice-President*, Richard Keene; *Committee*, A H. Bennett, C. Bôurdin, G. Walker, C. B. Keene, Thomas Scotton, R. Woods; *Treasurer*, A. B. Hamilton; *Secretary*, Thomas A. Scotton, 9 Church Street, Derby.

DEVON AND CORNWALL CAMERA CLUB Established 1888. Club rooms, The Athenæum, Plymouth. Ordinary meetings on alternate Mondays, at 7:30 P.M. Annual meeting in September. *President*, Robert Burnard; *Vice-Presidents*, W. Gage Tweedy and Major R. Barrington Baker; *Council*, Dr. Aldridge, M.D., J. S. Hawker, E. H. Micklewood, David Roy, A. R. Norrington, W. Square, F.R.C.S., Captain Waye, R.N., Colonel Stewart, R.E.; *Hon. Auditor*, W. Luxon; *Hon. Treasurer*, A. A. Carnel; *Hon. Secretary*, J. Hansford Worth, 42 George Street, Plymouth.

DEVON AND CORNWALL CAMERA CLUB (Postal Branch) Two photographs are contributed four times per annum, making eight in all. Medals and the album itself are given as prizes on each occasion. *Hon. Critic* and *Judge*, Andrew Pringle, F.R.M.S. *Hon. Secretary*, J. D. Pode, Slade, Ivybridge, South Devon.

DEVONPORT CAMERA CLUB Established 1891. Headquarters, Temperance Hall. Meetings, alternate Monday evenings. *President*, J. B. Huddy; *Vice-Presidents*, E. Aslat, Dr. W. J. Gard; *Hon. Treasurer*, J. Crook, 14 Portland Road; *Hon. Secretary*, Charles R. Rowe, 5 Keppel Place.

DEWSBURY AMATEUR PHOTOGRAPHIC SOCIETY Established 1888. Ordinary meetings on the second Thursday in each month, at the Library, Dewsbury and District Technical School, at 7:30 P.M. Annual meeting in January. *President*, A. S. Marriott; *Vice-President*, Charles Naylor; *Committee*, J. Taylor, E. Scargill, S. Mitchell; *Secretary* and *Treasurer*, George Kilburn, 51 Eastfield, Batley Carr, Dewsbury.

DONCASTER MICROSCOPICAL AND GENERAL SCIENTIFIC SOCIETY Established 1880. The meetings of the Society, unless otherwise specified, will be held in the Robing room, Guildhall, at 8 P.M. *President*, H. H. Corbett, M.R.C.S., *Vice-Presidents*, J. M. Kirk, W. E. Atkinson, G. Winter, J. G. Walker, C.E.; *Committee*, T. Lovell Atkinson, M.A.L.L.B., Rev. W. R. Waston, W. Roberts, J. Shotton, J. B. Prosser,

Rev. Canon Tebbutt, M.A.; *Hon. Secretary* and *Treasurer*. M. H. Stiles, 2 French Gate, Doncaster.

DORSET AMATEUR PHOTOGRAPHIC ASSOCIATION Established 1886. Annual meeting held in December, at Dorchester. No regular ordinary meetings. Frequent meetings for outdoor work in different parts of the county are held in the summer. *President*, Rev. W. Miles Barnes, M.A.; *Committee*, Rev. E. J. Pope, C. C. H. D'Aeth, W. J. Skene; *Secretary* and *Treasurer*, Rev. T. Perkins, M.A., F.R.A.S., Grammar School, Shaftesbury.

DOUGLAS AND ISLE OF MAN PHOTOGRAPHIC SOCIETY Established 1890. Meeting every Tuesday at 7 P.M. Demonstrations, etc., last Tuesday in month. The Society meets at St. Thomas' Church Guild Rooms, Britannia House, Loch Parade, Douglas, Isle of Man. *President*, J. M. Nicholson; *Committee*, Messrs. Thomson, Ralphe, Johnson, Lomas; *Treasurer*, W. Harrison; *Secretary*, S. McIsaac, Lawn Villa, Douglas, Isle of Man.

DOVER AMATEUR PHOTOGRAPHIC SOCIETY *President*, M. Bradley; *Secretary*, W. Wyles, New Bridge, Dover.

DUBLIN Y. M. C. A. CAMERA CLUB Established 1891. *President*, T. C. Tichborne, LL.D.; *Committee*, Messrs. Binka, Cochrane, Grainger, Riky, Stewart, Reed; *Secretary*, L. Davidson, 32 Manor Street, Dublin.

DUKINFIELD PHOTOGRAPHIC SOCIETY Established 1888. Monthly meetings held on the fourth Tuesday in each month. The Society's Room, on the first floor of the Co-operative Hall, is open every Wednesday evening from 7 till 10 for demonstrations, general conversation, reading, discussions, etc. Annual meeting fourth Tuesday in April. *President*, J. T. Lees; *Vice-Presidents*, S. T. Ainsworth, W. Jenkinson, S. Woolley; *Council*, T. Borsey, H. Broadbent, R. Deakin, J. W. Hadfield, J. Leech, J. H. Snowdon; *Treasurer*, J. Winterbottom, Alderdale Terrace, Chapel Street, Dukinfield; *Secretary*, William H. Shirley, Commercial Buildings, King Street, Dukinfield.

DUNDEE AMATEUR PHOTOGRAPHIC ASSOCIATION Established 1890. Meetings held in the Association's Studio, Nethergate, Dundee, every Monday at 8 P.M. Excursions at intervals during the season. *President*, William Young;

Vice-President, J. R. Stewart; *Council*, D. Prophet, G. McKenzie, A. Robb; *Hon. Treasurer*, D. Ovens; *Hon. Secretary*, James Rogers, 22 Barrack Street, Dundee.

DUNDEE AND EAST OF SCOTLAND PHOTOGRAPHIC ASSOCIATION Established 1879. *Patron*, The Right Hon. the Earl of Strathmore. *President*, J. D. Cox; *Vice-Presidents*, G. G. Maclaren and W. Salmond; *Council*, W. Baxter, P. Feathers, D. Ireland, Dr. McGillivray, and the other names as above, J. W. Munro, A. Stewart, J. R. Stewart, J. R. Wilson, W. Bertie, W. F. Hill, Dr. J. K. Tulloch, H. Valentine; *Secretary* and *Treasurer*, V. C. Baird, Broughty Ferry, N.B.

DUNEDIN AMATEUR PHOTOGRAPHIC SOCIETY Meetings once a month in Union Chambers. *President*, W. Livingston; *Secretary*, R. A. Ewing, Elm Row.

DURHAM CITY CAMERA CLUB Established 1892. Headquarters, Shakespeare Hall. Meetings second Wednesday in each month, except June, July and August. *President*, Rev. H. C. Fox, M.A.; *Vice-Presidents*, Dr. Barron and Councillor E. White; *Hon. Secretary*, Robert Hauxwell, The Avenue, Durham.

EALING PHOTOGRAPHIC SOCIETY Established 1890. Meetings first and third Thursdays from October to April inclusive, at the Public Buildings, Ealing, at 8 P.M. *President*, H. W. Peal; *Vice-Presidents*, Dr. Common, F.R.S., Charles Jones, W. T. White, F. H. Williams; *Council*, A. Belt, Clifford Gibbons, F. Wakefield, C. Whiting; *Treasurer*, A. F. Taylor; *Secretary*, T. Simpson, Fennymere, Ealing.

EAST LONDON PHOTOGRAPHIC SOCIETY Established 1891. Headquarters, Shoreditch Town Hall, Old Street, E.C. Meetings second and fourth Tuesdays in each month. *President*, G. S. Pasco; *Vice-Presidents*, E. Stone, C. Tylee, F. Uffindell; *Hon. Secretary* and *Treasurer*, M. A. Wilkinson, 28 Shacklewell Lane, Kingsland, N.E.

EDINBURGH PHOTOGRAPHIC CLUB Established 1881. Meetings on the third Wednesday of each month, from October to June, at 5 St. Andrew Square, at 8 P.M. Annual meeting in November. *Board of Management*, John Stewart Smith (*Contener*), Thomas Wardale (*Treasurer*), G. G. Mitchell (*Secretary*), 139 Dalkeith Road.

EDINBURGH PHOTOGRAPHIC SOCIETY Established 1861. Society meets at 8 P.M. on the first Wednesday in each month, from October to June inclusive, in the Society's Hall, 38 Castle Street, Edinburgh. *President*, Hippolyte J. Blanc, F.S.A. (Scot.); *Vice-Presidents*, Dr. Drinkwater and W. T. Bashford; *Council*, Messrs. Crighton, Stewart-Smith, Jameson Turnbull, Auld, Balmain, Inglis, Roddick, Ayton, Brown, Oliphant, Patrick; *Treasurer*, James McGlashan; *Secretary*, Thomas Barclay, 180 Dalkeith Road, Edinburgh.

ELIZABETHAN PHOTOGRAPHIC SOCIETY (BARNET) Established 1887. Annual meeting, February. Meetings are held in the Art and Science Rooms every Monday, and Lantern Nights every month on Thursday (last Thursday in the month). *President*, Rev. J. Bond Lee, M.A.; *Vice-Presidents*, T. Samuels, L. Matthews, H. Milne; *Council*, W. Baddeby and H. E. Kingsford; *Treasurer*, G. W. N. Harrison, M.A.; *Secretary*, J. Brittain, Eastcote Lodge, Richmond Road, New Barnet, Herts.

EPPING FOREST PHOTOGRAPHIC SOCIETY (Photographic Section of the Fillebrook Athenæum) Established 1889. Ordinary meetings as may be arranged. Annual meeting in September. Meetings at Fillebrook Lecture Hall. *President*, G. A. Hutchinson; *Committee*, Rev. J. Bradford, H. Kind, J. W. Spurgeon; *Secretary* and *Treasurer*, J. W. Spurgeon, 1 Drayton Villas, Leytonstone, Essex.

EXETER AMATEUR PHOTOGRAPHIC SOCIETY Established 1860. Meetings are held the first Tuesday in each month from April to September, and on the first and third Tuesdays from October to March. Excursions are held the Saturday following the Ordinary Meetings, from April to September. The Annual General Meeting is on the first Tuesday in January. Headquarters, the College Hall, South Street. *President*, Dr. James Cheese; *Vice-President*, W. Price Wall; *Committee*, Messrs. Drake, Holden, Dudley, Berrie, Cole; *Treasurer*, J. Hinton Lake; *Secretary*, Rev. John Sparshatt, Fairfield House, Alphington Road, Exeter.

EXETER HALL CAMERA CLUB (In connection with the Young Men's Christian Association) *Hon. Secretary*, G. J. Ingram, 127 Manor Street, Clapham.

FAIRFIELD CAMERA CLUB Established 1891. Headquarters, "The High School," Fairfield, Liverpool. Meetings held monthly during summer, and fortnightly in winter on Tuesdays. *President*, J. L. Mackrell; *Vice-President*, H. J. Mallabar; *Council*, J. H. Welch, H. C. Hatton, J. Samuel, W. J. Sutherland, W. Pollard, H. Holt; *Excursion Committee*, W. Pollard, J. H. Welch, T. E. C. Wilson; *Hon. Secretary*, H. Holt; *Hon. Auditor*, T. E. C. Wilson; *Hon. Treasurer*, W. T. Sutton; *Hon. Secretary*, S. H. I. Smith, 17 Bentley Road, Liverpool.

FALKIRK AMATEUR PHOTOGRAPHIC ASSOCIATION Headquarters, Newmarket Street. *President*, Geo. Sheriff, Esq.; *Vice-President*, Jas. H. Aitken, Jr., Esq.; *Committee*, Messrs. Kirk, Johnston, Drummond, Beeby, and Captain Jarrett; *Treasurer*, James Cowan; *Secretary*, John Walls; *Assistant Secretary*, John Higgins.

FAVERSHAM INSTITUTE PHOTOGRAPHIC SOCIETY Established 1890. The ordinary meetings are held on the third Tuesday in every month, at the Faversham Institute, at 8:15 P.M. Annual meeting in April. *President*, The Right Hon. Viscount Throwley; *Vice-Presidents*, Dr. C. J. Evers, Captain Hooper, W. C. Stunt; *Committee*, C. Cremer, F. Crosoer, A. N. Filmer, F. C. Jackman, M. Laxon, H. C. Sernark; *Secretary* and *Treasurer*, Percy Dan, 44 East Street, Faversham, Kent.

CITY AND GUILDS OF LONDON INSTITUTE TECHNICAL COLLEGE FINSBURY PHOTOGRAPHIC SOCIETY *President*, Prof. R. Meldola, F.R.S.; *Hon. Secretary*, E. E. Gardner.

FOREST HILL SCIENTIFIC AND MICROSCOPICAL SOCIETY (Photographic Section) *Hon. Secretary*, J. L. M. Porter, 15 Wood Vale, Forest Hill, S.E.

FORMBY CAMERA CLUB Established 1888. Meetings on alternate Mondays at 8 P.M., in Congregational Church Schools, during winter. Meetings discontinued in summer; replaced by outdoor excursions. *President*, Rev. Walter Elstub; *Vice-President*, W. Mason; *Secretary* and *Treasurer*, S. R. Hunt, Grange Cottage, Formby.

FRIENDS' PHOTOGRAPHIC SOCIETY Established 1888. A private society, meeting at members' houses once a month regularly, with occasional extra meetings. *Secretary* and *Treas-*

urer, A. J. Ransome, Bush Hill Park, Enfield, London, N.

FRIENDS' PHOTOGRAPHIC SOCIETY Established 1888. A private society, meeting at members' houses once a month regularly, with occasional extra meetings. *Secretary* and *Treasurer*, William Beck. Jr., 3 Glebe Place, Stoke Newington, London, N.

FROME AND DISTRICT PHOTOGRAPHIC CLUB Established 1891. *President*, Rev. H. B. Hare; *Vice-President*, W. Fussell; *Secretary* and *Treasurer*, A. W. Dalby, Butts Hill, Frome.

GATESHEAD INSTITUTE CAMERA CLUB *Hon. Secretary*, G. R. Johnston, 1 Park Terrace, Gateshead.

GLASGOW AND WEST OF SCOTLAND AMATEUR PHOTOGRAPHIC ASSOCIATION Established 1883. Meetings, third Monday of each month from October to April. Conversation meetings every Monday throughout the year. Hour of meeting, 8 P.M. *President*, John Morison, Jr.; *Vice-President*, Thomas Taylor; *Council*, R. H. Elder, Archibald Watson, William Miller, Dr. McCorkindale, W. J. B. Halley, And. Brown; *Auditors*, John Parker and Andrew Lithgow; *Treasurer*, Hugh Reid; *Secretaries*, William Goodwin, 3 Lynedoch Street, and J. C. Oliver, 247 Bath Street. Rooms, 180 West Regent Street, Glasgow.

GLASGOW PHOTOGRAPHIC ASSOCIATION Established 1861. Meetings are held on the first Thursday of the month, during the winter, in the Philosophical Society's Rooms, 207 Bath Street. *President*, William Lang, Jr.; *Vice-Presidents*, J. Craig Annan and Archdeacon Watson; *Council*, John Annan, Robert Gardner, William J. McIlwrick, Andrew Mactear, George Mason, John Morrison; *Treasurer*, George Bell; *Secretary*, Frederick Mackenzie, 122 Wellington Street, Glasgow.

GLENALMOND PHOTOGRAPHIC CLUB Meetings fortnightly, on alternate Saturdays. *President*, A. S. Reid, M. A., F.G.S.; *Librarian*, W. H. Maxwell; *Keeper of Album*, Mr. Kitto; *Treasurer*, L. H. Maxwell; *Secretary*, C. Cunningham Craig.

GLOUCESTERSHIRE POTOGRAPHIC SOCIETY Reconstructed 1887. Ordinary meetings, fourth Monday in each month. Annual meeting in April. *President*, Rev. Mowbray Trotter; *Vice-President*, Mr. F. H. Burr; *Treasurer*, Dr.

Hodges; *Committee*, Messrs. W. C. Beetham, W. Crump, G. Embrey, A. H. Pitcher, T. G. Smith; *Hon. Secretary*, W. Walwin.

GRAPHIC SOCIETY Established 1885. Ordinary meetings are held once a fortnight, with short intervals, except in April and October. Annual meeting in middle of January. Winter and indoor meetings at the Athenæum, Plymouth. *Council*, the Chairman, Treasurer, Secretary, H. R. Baab, —— Foster, Miss Gidley, Miss Stoyle; *Treasurer*, G. F. Watson; *Secretary*, I. S. Hawker, Mutley House, Plymouth.

GREAT YARMOUTH CAMERA CLUB Established 1890. *President*, F. Danby Palmer, D.L.; *Council*, Henry Dudley Arnott, John J. Owles, Colonel Shuttleworth, R.A.; *Treasurer*, John Taylor, National Provincial Bank; *Secretary*, H. Harvey George, The Tower, Gorleston, Great Yarmouth.

GREENOCK CAMERA CLUB Established 1888. Ordinary meetings held on third Thursday of each month, at 7:30 P.M., from September to April inclusive, in Museum Committee Room, Kelly Street, Greenock. Annual meeting, April, same place. *Council*, H. W. Walker, John Maclean, James Wright; *President*, James Graham; *Vice-President*, Wm. U. Park; *Treasurer*, Duncan Nicol; *Secretary*, William Blair, 40 Brisbane Street, Greenock.

GUILDFORD PHOTOGRAPHIC SOCIETY Established 1890. Headquarters, Chapel Street. Meetings, second Tuesday in each month. *President*, G. J. Jacobs, F.R.A.S.; *Vice-President*, J. Russell; *Hon. Treasurer*, J. H. Nunn; *Hon. Secretaries*, A. W. Bullen and J. H. Nunn, 115 High Street, Guildford.

HACKNEY PHOTOGRAPHIC SOCIETY Established 1889. Ordinary meetings every Tuesday, at 206 Mare Street, Hackney, at 8 P.M. Annual meeting on the second Tuesday in May, each year. *President*, Herbert Robinson; *Council*, W. L. Barker, F Houghton, R. Beckett, W. P. Dando, F. W. Gosling, Dr. Roland Smith; *Treasurer*, I. O. Grant; *Curator*, A. Dean; *Hon. Secretary*, W. Fenton Jones, 12 King Edward Road, Hackney, N.E.

HALIFAX CAMERA CLUB Established 1891. Ordinary meetings, first Monday in each month, at 8 P.M. Annual meeting in June. *President*, Edward J. Smith; *Vice-President*, Thomas Illingworth; *Committee*, W. Wainhouse, Dr.

Leech, E. Finlinson, E. J. Walker, W. H. Ostler; *Hon. Treasurer*, J. I. Learoyd; *Hon. Secretary*, Thomas Kershaw, 15 Queen's Road, Halifax.

HALIFAX PHOTOGRAPHIC CLUB Established 1881. Meets the last Thursday in each month in the Mechanics' Hall, at 7:30 P.M. *President*, B. Rowley; *Vice-Presidents*, T. Illingworth and E. J. Smith; *Council*, B. B. Bingley, Major Holroyde, H. Mossman, Councillor S. Smith, Joseph Whiteley, together with the Officers; *Auditor*, S. Goodman; *Treasurer*, E. H. Child; *Hon. Secretary*, W. Clement Williams, 13 Aked's Road, Halifax.

HALTWHISTLE AND DISTRICT PHOTOGRAPHIC SOCIETY Established 1890. Meetings are held at the bank at irregular times. *President*, Dr. W. R. Speirs; *Vice-President*, George Clark; *Secretary* and *Treasurer*, David Macadam, Carlisle City and District Bank, Limited, Haltwhistle.

HAMPSTEAD PHOTOGRAPHIC CLUB Established 1887. Meetings held at members' houses on alternate Monday evenings. Members limited to twenty. *Treasurer*, C. A. Watkins. *Secretary*, Bertram W. Wild, Gladesmore, Willesden Lane, Brondesbury, N.W.

HARLESDEN AND WILLESDEN PHOTOGRAPHIC SOCIETY Established 1890. Meetings held on the second Tuesdays in the month, at the Court House, at 8:30 P.M. *President*, John Naylor; *Council*, J. Seed, T. Clapton, G. Pay, C. Winterbon, W. Hocking; *Treasurer*, L. R. Price; *Secretary*, Isaac Cohen, 26 Wendover Road, Harlesden, N.W.

HASTINGS AND ST. LEONARDS PHOTOGRAPHIC SOCIETY Established 1888. Meetings, third Monday in each month, at 8 P.M. *President*, Wilson Noble, M.P.; *Vice-Presidents*, Lord Brassey, K.C.B., J. H. Blomfield, S. W. Bultz, Rev. A. M. Macdona, J. H. Mayor, A. C. Routh, M.D., W. Shuter, W. Stubbs, M. Sullivan, Macer Wright; *Council*, Rev. A. M. Macdona, J. H. Mayor, M. Sullivan, H. J. Godbold, J. H. Gibson; *Hon. Treasurer*, Rev. A. B. Cotton; *Hon. Secretary*, A. Brooker, Memorial Buildings, Hastings.

HELIOS POSTAL PHOTOGRAPHIC CLUB Formed in 1887 for the examination and criticism of the work of members. An album circulates each month, containing the photographs,

and also a notebook for questions, discussions, etc. Number of members limited. *Hon. Secretary*, W. Cooper, 18 High Street, Marlborough, Wilts.

HEREFORDSHIRE PHOTOGRAPHIC SOCIETY Established 1889. Evening meetings, first Tuesday in each month. Annual meeting, first Tuesday in October. Field days, first Thursday in each month. Meetings held at Mansion House, which is headquarters. *President*, Alderman Blake; *Vice-Presidents*, Alfred Watkins, T. J. Salwey, J. Parker; *Council*, W. C. Gethen, E. Pilley, R. Clark, E. W. H. Chave, C. H. Woodhouse, H. J. Wilson, B. C Kinsey, A. C. Edwards, Jr.; *Hon. Treasurer*, W. E. Haines, High Town; *Hon. Secretaries*, J. Parker, C.E., and E. G. Davies, Mansion House, Hereford.

HOLBORN CAMERA CLUB Established 1889. *President*, A. Horsley Hinton; *Vice-Presidents*, Fred Brocas, S. T. Chang, T. O. Dear, D. R. Lowe; *Committee*, J. Avery, E. H. Bayston, A. J. Golding, A. Hodges, F. Knights, J. Stevens, A. T. Elsworth; *Treasurer*, Albert Bell; *Secretary*, Frederick J. Cobb, 3 Albion Grove, Barnsbury, N.

HOLMFIRTH AMATEUR PHOTOGRAPHIC ASSOCIATION Established 1885. The society meets on the last Friday of each month, at each member's house, and there are outings during the summer months. *President*, Arthur Preston; *Secretary* and *Treasurer*, David Bilson, Berchin House, Holmfirth.

HOVE CAMERA CLUB Established 1892. Headquarters, Hove Town Hall. Meetings, second Tuesday in each month. *President*, G. B. Woodruff; *Vice-Presidents*, A. Hollis, M.D., H. H. Taylor, F.R.C.S., R. Dawson, M.D., and C. Job; *Hon. Secretary* and *Treasurer*, James Williamson, 144 Church Road, Hove.

HUDDERSFIELD PHOTOGRAPHIC SOCIETY Established 1888. Meetings on alternate Thursdays, at Y.M.C.A., King Street, at 7:30. Annual meeting on first Thursday in November. *President*, Surgeon-Major Foster; *Vice-Presidents*, Alfred Armitage and T. K. Mellor; *Committee*, W. H. Charlesworth, A. Clarke, B. Crook, T. H. Fitton, Herbert Haigh, F. W. Mills, H. T. Young, Hamor Oldfield, Rev. G. C. B. Madden, *Secretary* and *Treasurer*, H. G. Brierley, Glen View, Gledholt, Huddersfield.

HULL PHOTOGRAPHIC SOCIETY Established 1884. Headquarters, Prospect Street. Meetings every Thursday evening. *President*, C. D. Holmes; *Vice-President*, J. Pybus; *Treasurer*, D. W. Sissons; *Lanternist*, Dr. J. Walker; *Librarian*, B. M. Stoakes; *Council*, J. H. Allcott, Adams, C. F. Amos, G. J. Boville, Rev. Coleman, Rev. W. Hay, F.E.A., Croshaw, E. H. Howlett, F.R.C.S., A. N. Jameson, T. Rose, Dr. Stothard, Dr. Hollingsworth; *Hon. Secretaries*, A. H. White, 141 Westbourne Avenue, Hull, E. E. Cohen, 127 Beverley Road, Hull.

ILKESTON PHOTOGRAPHIC SOCIETY Established 1891. Annual meeting in March, and other meetings as required. *President*, Joseph Carroll, M.B., D.P.H.; *Committee*, Officers, and Messrs. P. Sudbury, C. Sudbury, Higton, Kelly; *Treasurer*, George W. Woolliscroft; *Secretary*, William Shakespeare, Bath Street, Ilkeston.

IPSWICH PHOTOGRAPHIC SOCIETY Established 1888. Meetings are held at the Art Gallery, Ipswich, on the second Wednesday in each month at 8 P.M., except May, June, July, August and September. In these months excursions are held as arranged. *President*, J. Dixon Piper; *Vice-Presidents*, F. Mason and E. H. Myddelton-Garey; *Committee*, R. Cash, A. C. Churchman, J. E. Curtis, A. F. Penraven, J. C. Wiggin, F. Woolnough; *Secretary* and *Treasurer*, Leonard Hill, Ashdown, Foxhall Road, Ipswich.

ISLE OF THANET PHOTOGRAPHIC SOCIETY Established 1888. Meetings held on first and third Wednesdays in each month, excepting July, August and September, at St. George's Church Club House. *President*, Rev. H. Bartram, M.A.; *Vice-Presidents*, R. Hicks, W. Saunders, Rev. C. E. Eastgate, M.A.; *Committee*, E. Deacon, H. Holloway, Jr., J. Roe, A. Vigar, E. E. Wastall and G. Wellden; *Hon. Secretaries*, E. Baily, 9 Queen Street, G. F. Blower, Memel Villa, Ramsgate.

JERSEY AMATEUR PHOTOGRAPHIC SOCIETY Established 1890. Meetings are held at 21 Grove Place, Jersey, first Wednesday of month. Annual meeting, first Wednesday in April. *President*, Captain T. Lamb, South Lancashire Regiment; *Vice-President*, Lieutenant-Colonel Jackson; *Committee*, A. Messervy, J.P., J. Andrews; *Treasurer*, G. L. Maistre Gruchy; *Secretary*, F.

Woodland Toms, F.I.C., F.C.S., 21 Grove Place, Jersey.

KEIGHLEY AND DISTRICT PHOTOGRAPHIC ASSOCIATION Established 1889. Meetings held on first and third Tuesdays in each month, October to March, at Mechanics' Institute, North Street, Keighley. Annual meeting, February. *President*. J. W. Laycock; *Vice-Presidents*, Saml. Bairstow and Thos. Heaps; *Committee*, W. H. Bailey, A. N. Kershaw, E. Myers, C. E. Smith, Robt. Smith, Rev. T. Mellodey, Alex. Keighley and J. Waters; *Treasurer*, Walter Mitchell; *Secretary*, John Gill, 27 Highfield Lane, Keighley.

KENDALL LITERARY AND SCIENTIFIC INSTITUTION (Photographic Section) Established 1886. Meetings held in the Museum Library on the second Wednesday in each month, at 7:30 P.M. Annual meeting in September. Field meetings during summer months at times convenient to members. *Chairman*, Isaac Braithwaite; *Committee*, Frank Wilson, Samuel Rhodes, Chairman, Secretary, Treasurer of Section, Secretary of the Institution (*ex officio*); *Treasurer*, F. P. Heath; *Secretary*, Charles E. Greenall, Thorny Hills, Kendall.

KENSINGTON AND BAYSWATER PHOTOGRAPHIC SOCIETY Established 1892. Headquarters, Horbury Rooms, Kensington Park Road, W. Meetings, second and fourth Mondays in each month. *President*, Hon. L. M. Sinclair; *Hon. Treasurer*, F. S. Haber, 3 Landsdowne Crescent, Notting Hill, London, W.; *Hon. Secretary*, Charles W. Brainwell, 7 Lower Terrace, Notting Hill, London, W.

KILMARNOCK AMATEUR PHOTOGRAPHIC SOCIETY *President*, Alexander Millar; *Vice-President*, Thomas Ferguson; *Treasurer*, J. W. Wallace; *Secretary*, James Thomson, 82 Hill Street, Kilmarnock.

KIMBERLEY CAMERA CLUB Established 1890. *President*, Rev. Father Ogle; *Vice-President*, F. Skead, B.A.; *Committee*, C. A. Chappell, John Henry, G. D. Pieser, F. Titmas; *Hon. Secretary* and *Treasurer*, Malcolm Macfarlane.

KINGS LYNN Y. M. C. A. PHOTOGRAPHIC CLUB Established 1891. Headquarters, Y.M.-C.A. Rooms, St. James Street. Meetings, second Tuesday in each month. *President*, J. M. Bridges; *Vice-President*, Rev. G. Wrigglesworth; *Hon. Secretary* and *Treasurer*, W. Winch, St. James Street, Kings Lynn.

LANCASTER PHOTOGRAPHIC SOCIETY Established 1889. Meetings held on last Tuesday in each month at the Springfield Barracks. Annual meeting, last Tuesday in March. *President*, H. I. Storey; *Vice-Presidents*, J. W. Pickard and H. J. J. Thompson; *Committee*, S. Fawcett, W. O. Roper, A. R. D. MacDonald and R. W. Wearing; *Treasurer*, A. B. S. Welch; *Secretary*, W. Briggs, 21 Cheapside, Lancaster.

LANTERN SLIDE EXCHANGE CLUB Established 1889. Limited to eighteen members. Box of slides circulated monthly. *Hon. Critic*, A. R. Dresser; *Secretary* and *Treasurer*, W. T. Tucker, 12 Herrick Road, Loughborough.

LANTERN SOCIETY Established 1890. Meetings held at 20 Hanover Square, at 8 P.M., on the second and fourth Mondays from October to April inclusive. Annual meetings, second Monday in November. *President*, The Hon. Slingsby Bethell, C.B.; *Vice-President*, T. H. Holding; *Council*, G. G. Baker-Cresswell, E. K. Hall, W. H. Maw, E. M. Nelson (Chairman), A. R. Sheppee, E. R. Shipton; *Secretary*, Commander C. E. Gladstone, R.N., 6 Bolton Street, W.

LEAMINGTON AMATEUR PHOTOGRAPHIC SOCIETY Established 1887. Meetings on the first and third Fridays in the month, at 5:30 P.M., at the Trinity Church Room, Morton Street. *President*, Surgeon-General Ranking; *Council*, Messrs. Champion, Maze-Gregory, Gowan, Green, Magrath, Ranking, Stanley, Caleb, Williams; *Hon. Treasurer*, W. B. Magrath; *Hon. Secretaries*, R. Aspa, Priory House, Leamington, and B. Magrath, 39 Clarendon Square, Leamington.

LEEDS PHOTOGRAPHIC SOCIETY Founded 1852, re-established 1881. Ordinary meetings, first Thursday in each month. Technical Evenings, third Monday in the month, at the Mechanics' Institute, Leeds. *President*, E. H. Jacob, M.A., M.D.; *Vice-Presidents*, Godfrey Bingley, S. A. Warburton; *Committee*, Godfrey Bingley, W. A. M. Brown, Herbert Denison, E. H. Jacob, M.A., M.D., A. E. Nichols, Rev. E. S. Palmer, Robert Steele, T. W. Thornton, J. H. Walker, S. A. Warburton; *Hon. Treasurer*, T. W. Thornton; *Hon. Secretaries*,

Herbert Denison, Robert Steele, 12 East Parade, Leeds; *Hon. Lanternist*, J. H. Walker; *Hon. Librarian*, W. A. M. Brown.

LEEDS Y. M. C. A. PHOTOGRAPHIC CLUB Established 1888. Meetings are held at the rooms of the Y. M. C. A., 13 South Parade, Leeds, on the Monday before the first Tuesday in each month at 8 P.M. Annual meeting, fourth Friday in March. *President*, Godfrey Bingley; *Treasurer* and *Secretary*, F. W. Fisher, 9 Meanwood Terrace, Servia Grove, Camp Road, Leeds.

LEICESTER AND LEICESTERSHIRE PHOTOGRAPHIC SOCIETY Established 1885. Meetings held in the Mayor's Parlor, Old Town Hall, at 8 P.M., on the second Wednesday in each month. Indoor meetings from October to April; outdoor from May to September. *President*, F. G. Pierpoint; *Vice-President*, J. Porritt; *Committee*, Messrs. Bankart, Partridge, Joliffe, Squire and Weatherhead; *Treasurer*, A. W. Wilson; *Secretary*, H. Pickering, High Cross Street, Leicester.

LEIGH PHOTOGRAPHIC SOCIETY Established 1892. Headquarters, Old Grammar School. Meetings, alternate Thursdays. *President*, J. H. Stephen; *Vice-President*, James Ward, B.A.; *Hon. Treasurer*, E. A. Williams; *Hon. Secretary*, W. Rose Moore, 56 Bradshawgate, Leigh.

LEITH AMATEUR PHOTOGRAPHIC ASSOCIATION Established 1888. Meetings held on the last Tuesday of every month at 8 P.M. Annual General Meeting, last Tuesday of January. *President*, William Dougall; *Vice-President*, Thomas W. Dewar; *Council*, Messrs. Smith, Ewart, Lormier, Hunter, McCreadie, Chapman, Swanston, Campbell, Wilson; *Hon. Treasurer*, John Pourie; *Hon. Secretary*, Alexander Pitkethly, 8 Wilkie Place, Leith.

LEITH PHOTOGRAPHIC LANTERN CLUB Established 1889. The Club meets weekly for practical work from October to May, and is restricted to membership. *Hon. President*, John Sanderson; *President*, John Tait Guthrie; *Treasurer*, John Walker; *Secretary*, James Reid, 29 Woodville Terrace, Leith.

LEWES PHOTOGRAPHIC SOCIETY Established 1888. Ordinary meetings are held on the first Tuesday in each month at the Fitzroy Library, High Street, at 8 P.M. *President*, J. Tunks; *Vice-President*, G. J. Wightman; *Com-*

mittee, E. J. Bedford, W. Carpenter, H. Curtis, W. B. Funnell and W. J. Young; *Hon. Secretary* and *Treasurer*, H. B. Constable, 5 East Street, Lewes.

LEWISHAM HIGH ROAD CAMERA CLUB Established 1890. Meetings held on first and third Friday in each month throughout the year. *President*, Rev. J. Morley Wright; *Vice-President*, Alfred H. Miles; *Committee*, M. Stodart, E. Eastwood, Prof. Lambert, M.A., B. Davidson; *Secretary* and *Treasurer*, R. W. James, 35 Tyrwhitt Road, St. Johns, S.E.; *Asst. Secretary*, H. Sprunt, 192 New Cross Road, S.E.

LINCOLN CAMERA CLUB Established 1892. Headquarters, School of Science. Meetings, twice monthly. *President*, Rev. G. Stall, LL.D.; *Vice-President*, H. Mantle; *Hon. Treasurer*, J. M. Warnener; *Secretaries*, W. R. Lilly, Riseholme Road, J. W. Horton, Brayford Wharf.

LIGHT AND COMPANY Limited to thirty amateur photographers. Objects: The circulation and criticism of photographs (in a monthly portfolio), entirely the work of members, and for a general interchange of ideas with a view to the mutual advancement in the science and art of photography. *Hon. Secretary*, Wallace G. Thomson, 12 Laurel Bank, Halifax.

LIGHT AND TRUTH POSTAL PHOTOGRAPHIC CLUB Portfolios of prints circulated monthly, with book for criticisms, discussions, etc. *Hon. Secretary*, Henry E. Trew, A.P.S., 107 Old Town Street, Plymouth.

LITERARY PHOTOGRAPHIC CLUB Established 1887. Founded for the circulation and exchange, among the members, of photographs of literary or historical interest. *Hon. Secretary*, R. A. R. Bennett, Walton Manor Lodge, Oxford.

LIVERPOOL AMATEUR PHOTOGRAPHIC ASSOCIATION Established 1863. *President* Wm. Tomkinson; *Vice-Presidents*, Jos. Earp, A. Tyrer; *Treasurer*, P. H. Phillips; *Hon. Secretary House Committee*, J. H. Welch; *Council*, A. J. Cleaver, W. P. Christian, W. Hughes, H. J. Houghton, A. F. Stanistreet, Henry Lupton, B. Boothroyd, G. A. Kenyon, H. B. Millar, F. Anyon, F. K. Glazebrook, P. Lange; *Librarian*, J. Woolfall; *Auditor*, A. Bradbury; *Hon. Secretary*, F. B. Illingworth, 2 Melville Place, Liverpool; Club rooms, Percy Buildings, Eberle Street, Liverpool.

LIVERPOOL CAMERA CLUB Established 1891. Ordinary meetings, second and fourth Wednesday in each month, in the rooms, 128A Mount Pleasant, at 7:30 P.M. Annual meeting in February. Field days from April to September, and Lantern evenings from October to March. *President*, Cecil F. Webb, B.A., D.D.S.; *Vice-Presidents*, James Hawkins and James Smith, Jr.; *Council*, William A. Stuart, J. Herbert Jones, Charles H. Freeman, Alexander C. Yule, W. Anderson Brown, Harry Handley, Ross C. Robbins, William Haywood and Thomas Edwards; *Hon. Secretary* and *Treasurer*, William Tansley, 14 Wentworth Street, Everton, Liverpool; *Club Motto*, "Each for all and all for each."

LIVERPOOL PHYSICAL SOCIETY (Photographic Section) Established 1890. Headquarters, University College, Liverpool. *President*, Dr. F. Hurter; *Hon. Secretary*, Dr. Charles A. Kohn, University College, Liverpool.

LIVERPOOL CENTRAL Y. M. C. A. CAMERA CLUB Established 1889. Meetings held every Wednesday, from 7 to 10 P.M. *President*, William Prior Christian; *Vice-Presidents*, T. Jameson and I. Shone; *Secretary* and *Treasurer*, John C. Lee, 56 Garrick Street, Liverpool; *Assistant Secretary*, H. Hannah, 104 Moss Grove, Liverpool.

LIVERPOOL UNIVERSITY COLLEGE PHOTOGRAPHIC SOCIETY *President*, Dr. C. A. Kohn; *Hon. Secretary*, James T. Conroy, B.Sc., The Hollies, Montpelier Crescent, New Brighton, Cheshire.

LONDON AND PROVINCIAL PHOTOGRAPHIC ASSOCIATION Established 1882. The meetings are held every Thursday evening, at 8 o'clock, at the Champion Hotel, 15 Aldersgate Street, close to G.P.O. *President*, J. Traill Taylor; *Trustees*, Capt. de W. Abney, F.R.S., and W. S. Bird; *Committee*, H. D. Atkinson, F. H. Berry, W. Bedford, R. P. Drage, G. T. Harris, T. C. Hepworth, F. W. Hindley, H. R. Hume, A. Mackie, E. W. Parfitt, J. S. Rolph, W. J. Tabrum and T. E. Freshwater; *Librarian*, F. W. Pask; *Hon. Secretary*, H. Snowden Ward, Memorial Hall, E.C.; *Hon. Treasurer*, John Spiller.

LONDON SOCIAL CAMERA CLUB Established 1887. Headquarters, Carr's Restaurant, 265 Strand. *President*, Wilson Barrett; *Vice-*

President, R. W. Thomas; *Committee*, G. Wheeler, Jr., H. Beckford, W. H. Cornell; *Treasurer*, G. Wheeler, 25 Culford Road, Kingsland; *Secretary*, Herbert E. Smith, 41 Alkham Road, Stamford Hill, N.

LOUGHBOROUGH LITERARY AND SCIENTIFIC SOCIETY (Photographic Section) Established 1888. Meetings held on the second Wednesday in each month. *President*, J. B. Colgrove, M.A.; *Vice-President*, Alderman W. C. Burder; *Committee*, John W. Taylor, Charles Coltman, and the Office Holders; *Secretary* and *Treasurer*, W. T. Tucker, 12 Herrick Road, Loughborough.

LOUTH AND DISTRICT PHOTOGRAPHIC SOCIETY *President*, Captain Smyth; *Hon. Secretary*, S. Francis Clarke, L.D.S., Upgate, Louth, Lincs.

THE LOWESTOFT AND DISTRICT PHOTOGRAPHIC SOCIETY *President*, Capt. R. Horman Fisher; *Chairman*, W. Stringfield; *Committee*, Mrs. A. Young, F. Mayhem, Rev. A. Wells, F. Smith, F. W. Emuss, Jas. Rose; *Hon. Treasurer*, W. J. Roberts; *Hon. Secretary*, Miss A. Lee, Stringfield.

LUTON AND DISTRICT PHOTOGRAPHIC SOCIETY Established 1890. Meetings held at the Coffee Tavern, Cheapside, on alternate Mondays, at 8 P.M. *President*, Cyril Flower, M.P.; *Vice-Presidents*, A. Carruthers, F. E. Percival, W. Wardill; *Council*, A. V. Spratley, T. Dawson, W. Morrison, J. Davis, W. Roberts, G. W. Bindloss; *Treasurer*, W. Boutwood; *Secretary*, George Bunyan, Elizabeth Street, Luton.

MAIDSTONE AMATEUR PHOTOGRAPHIC CLUB Established 1888. Meetings held every Friday evening, at "The Palace." Annual meeting in February. *President*, J. E. Austin; *Committee*, H. Bear, P. Adams, F.R.C.S., H. A. Potvine, C. E. Wright, W. Day, F. Laurence, H. Sandland, H. W. Morfett, L. Green, F.C.S.; *Hon. Treasurer*, R. P. Grant; *Hon. Secretary*, L. Stansell, F.C.S., Bydews, Holland Road, Maidstone.

MANCHESTER AMATEUR PHOTOGRAPHIC SOCIETY Established 1885. Ordinary meetings, second Tuesday in each month, in Lecture Hall, Athenæum. Annual meeting, last Tuesday in January. *President*, J. W. Wade; *Vice-Presidents*, J. Davenport, J. G. Jones, Rev. H. J. Palmer, M.A., H. Smith; *General Committee*, E. Ashman, J. Bathe, T. M. Brook, J. Drinkwater, T. Glazebrook, Dr. Hamilton, F. W. Parrott, E. F. Prince, W. H. Shirley, H. Sykes; *Librarian*, C. C. Bowker; *Editor of Magazine*, Geo. Wheeler; *Hon. Treasurer*, C. Dawson, 66 Peter Street; *Hon. Secretary*, Randolph Gilmore, 1B Cooper Street.

MANCHESTER CAMERA CLUB Established 1885. Ordinary meetings held at the Victoria Hotel, Manchester, on the third Wednesday of the month, at 7:30 P.M. *Treasurer*, J. Davenport; *Committee*, J. Davenport, J. Drinkwater, J. T. Foster, W. Hepburn, J. W. Wade; *Hon. Secretary*, Chas. Dawson, 66 Peter Street, Manchester.

MANCHESTER PHOTOGRAPHIC SOCIETY Established 1855. Ordinary meetings are held on the second Thursday in each month, at the rooms, 36 George Street. Lantern meetings are held on the fourth Wednesday, from October to March inclusive. Annual meeting is held in October. *President*, Abel Heywood, Jr.; *Vice-Presidents*, A. Brothers, F.R.A.S., T. R. Cobley, S. Okell, F.R.A.S., J. Schofield, H. M. Whitefield; *Council*, D. E. Benson, F. W. Burt, T. Chilton, C. H. Coote, F. Edwards, J. T. Hughes, J. Macnamara, M. W. Thompstone, J. Wood, H. Woolley; *Lantern Section Committee*, M. W. Thompstone, H. M. Whitefield, J. Wood, H. Woolley. *Treasurer*, W. G. Coote; *Hon. Secretary*, W. H. Farrow, 36 George Street, Manchester.

MANCHESTER Y. M. C. A. PHOTOGRAPHIC CLUB Established 1890. Headquarters, 56 Peter Street. Meetings, first Thursday in each month. *President*, J. A. Beith; *Vice-President*, W. H. Newell; *Hon. Treasurer*, G. T. White; *Hon. Secretary*, John Irvine, 55 Peter Street, Manchester.

MARGATE PHOTOGRAPHIC SOCIETY Established 1892. Headquarters, 24 Cecil Square. Meetings, monthly, on Thursdays. *President*, Dr. Elliotte; *Hon. Secretary* and *Treasurer*, A. King, B.Q., 24 Cecil Square, Margate.

MIDLAND CAMERA CLUB *President*, Hall-Edwards, L.R.C.P.; *Vice-President*, Rev. J. Henry, F.R.G.S.; *Committee*, H. R. Leech, M.R.C.S., W. W. J. Nicol, D.Sc., Edw. Morton, Dr. Ratcliffe, Rowland White; *Hon. Treasurer*, S. G. Mason; *Hon. Secretary*, Walter D. Welford.

MIDLOTHIAN CAMERA CLUB *President*, Sidney J. G. Williams; *Vice-President*, W. A. Scott-Wallace; *Treasurer*, G. M. Denholm; *Hon. Secretary*, A. D. Guthrie, Bonnington, Edinburgh.

MONTROSE PHOTOGRAPHIC ASSOCIATION *President*, D. Ferrier, F.C.S.; *Secretary*, F. Japp, 8 Union Place, Montrose.

MORLEY AND DISTRICT AMATEUR PHOTOGRAPHIC SOCIETY Established 1888. Meet first Tuesday in each month. *President*, Samuel Atkinson; *Vice-President*, J. Richardson; *Treasurer*, Sol. Tomlinson; *Secretary*, Harold E. Spafford, 12 Parliament Street, Morley, Leeds.

MUNSTER CAMERA CLUB Established 1891. Ordinary meetings held on second Wednesday in each month, at 8 P.M. Annual meeting in October. Temporary rooms, Crawford Municipal School of Art, Nelson Place, Cork. *President*, Major J. Douglas Lysaght, A.P.D.; *Vice-Presidents*, Ringrose Atkins, M.A., M.D., Denny Lane, M.A., H. S. Noblett; *Committee*, D. Franklin, J. Bennet, J. Bradshaw, J. Day, R. Foley, P. Halliman, W. Harrington, H. Lund, G. Percival, K. B. Williams; *Treasurer*, William R. Atkins, F.C.A.; *Secretary*, Denham Franklin, J. P., 74 South Mall, Cork.

MUTUAL IMPROVEMENT POSTAL PHOTOGRAPHIC SOCIETY Established 1892. *President*, F. E. Goater; *Hon. Secretary* and *Treasurer*, Albert B. Moss, 64 Wood Lane, Uxbridge Road, London, W.

NELSON CAMERA CLUB Meetings are held on the third Wednesday of each month. Visitors are invited and will receive notice of meetings on application to the Secretary. *Patron*, His Excellency the Right Hon. the Earl of Onslow; *President*, Charles Y. Fell; *Hon. Secretary*, F. W. MacLean, A.M., Inst., C.E.

NEWCASTLE-ON-TYNE AND NORTHERN COUNTIES' PHOTOGRAPHIC ASSOCIATION Established 1881. Meetings are held in the Association's rooms, Central Exhange Art Gallery, Granger Street, at 7:30 P.M., on the second and fourth Tuesdays in each month, except May, June, July, August and September. During the preceding months outdoor meetings are held. Annual meeting, second Tuesday in January. *President*, A. S. Stevenson, J.P.; *Vice-Presidents*, J. P. Gibson and H. G. Ridgeway; *Council*, M. Auty, W. P. Brewis, T. O. Mawson, W. E. Cowan, W. Parry, G. L. Snowball, J. H. Robinson, J. Watson, L. Williamson; *Treasurer*, J. W. Robson; *Secretary*, Edgar G. Lee, 11 Beverley Terrace, Cullercoats, near Newcastle-on-Tyne.

NEWCASTLE (STAFFORDSHIRE) AND DISTRICT AMATEUR PHOTOGRAPHIC SOCIETY Established 1889. Meetings held every alternate Wednesday in Newcastle at 8 P.M. *President*, Colonel Dutton; *Local Vice-Presidents*, Thomas Stanway (Hanley), H. E. Whytehead (Stoke-on-Trent), W. E. Leek (Newcastle); *Council*, Wilberforce Beach, H. Broomfield, F. C. Carter, J. D. Illidge, S. Illidge, A. Stockton; *Hon. Secretaries*, W. W. Beach, West Brampton, Newcastle, Staffordshire, and J. D. Illidge, Earl Street, Newcastle, Staffordshire.

NEWPORT CAMERA CLUB Established 1891. Headquarters, Albert Hall. Meetings, fourth Monday in each month. *President*, Edmund H. Watts, Jr., F.R., G.S.; *Vice-Presidents*, Archdeacon Bruce, M.A., and Alderman George H. Llewellyn; *Hon. Treasurer*, E. J. Smith; *Hon. Secretaries*, F. Parsons, F.S., Sc., and H. E. Lewis, 60 High Street, Newport, Mon.; *Curator*, J. W. Atkins.

NEWPORT SKETCHING AND PHOTOGRAPHIC SOCIETY Established 1888. Headquarters, Town Hall. Meetings first Monday in each month. *President*, Alfred Swash, M.S.A.; *Vice-President*, J. S. Kerslake; *Hon. Treasurer*, Ernest Banks; *Hon. Secretary*, John J. Swalwell, The Lea, Gold Tops, Newport, Mon.

NORFOLK AND NORWICH CAMERA CLUB Established 1884. Meetings take place at the Bell Hotel, Norwich, at 8 P.M., on the second Monday of every month, except during the summer, when special excursions are made. *President*, W. T. Bensly, LL.D.; *Vice-Presidents*, Messrs. Algar and Harvey George; *Committee*, Messrs. Lathorn, Day, Fison and Dr. Thomson; *Hon. Secretary* and *Treasurer*, Colonel H. Wood, C.B., 95 Thorpe Road, Norwich.

NORTHAMPTONSHIRE NATURAL HISTORY SOCIETY AND FIELD CLUB (Photographic Section) Established 1876. *President of Section*, H. Manfield; *Hon. Secretary*, Jos. J. Wetherell, Billings Road, Northampton.

NORTH KENT AMATEUR PHOTOGRAPHIC SOCIETY Established 1887. Meetings are held on the second Thursday in each month at 8

P.M. Excursions during the summer are arranged. *President*, I. C. Johnson, J.P.; *Vice-President*, E. J. Wall; *Council*, J. K. Barlow, P. J. Boorman, J. Caddel, J. S. Dismorr, E. W. Field, F. Hammerton, S. Hodsoll, A.C.A., S. R. Macartney, J. H. Morris, T. Nettleingham, T. Pilkington, C. A. Rotherham, H. Sandford; *Secretary* and *Treasurer*, G. W. Cobham, 3 Edwin Street, Gravesend.

NORTH LONDON PHOTOGRAPHIC SOCIETY Established 1885. Meetings are held on the first and third Tuesdays in each month at Wellington Hall, Upper Street, Islington, N. *President*, J. Traill Taylor; *Council*, G. J. Clarke, J. Douglas, W. Few, C. R. Griffiths, B. J. Grover, Rev. E. Healy, A. Mackie, J. Oakley, E. W. Parfitt, R. Tanner; *Curator*, W. T. Coventon; *Hon. Secretary*, W. Bishop, 69 Oakfield Road, Stroud Green, N.

NORTH MIDDELSEX PHOTOGRAPHIC SOCIETY Established 1888. Meetings held at Jubilee Hall, Hornsey Road, on second and fourth Mondays in each month at 8 P.M. sharp. *President*, J. W. Marchant; *Vice-Presidents*, H. Walker, F. L. Pither; *Council*, C. Beadle, F. Cherry, C. C. Gill, C. O. Gregory, T. C. Lathbridge, J. C. S. Mummery, J. Saville, H. Smith, J. Steuart, W. Taylor, J. L. Treadway, S. E. Wall; *Treasurer*, F. W. Cox; *Hon. Secretary*, J. McIntosh, 14 Lowman Road, Holloway; *Asst. Hon. Secretary* and *Curator*, F. M. Ainsley, 6 Dagmar Road, Stroud Green.

NORTH STAFFORDSHIRE NATURALISTS' FIELD CLUB AND ARCHAEOLOGICAL SOCIETY (Photographic Section) *President*, H. E. Whytehead.

NORTH SURREY PHOTOGRAPHIC SOCIETY Established 1887. Meets every alternate Tuesday at the West Norwood Constitutional Club, Norwood Road, S.E. *President*, J. Morrish; *Vice-President*, L. Wolff; *Secretary* and *Treasurer*, Robt. W. Wilson, 42 Norwood Road, S.E.

NORTH WALES AMATEUR PHOTOGRAPHIC SOCIETY Established 1892. Headquarters, News Room and Library, 44 Mostyn Street, Llandudno. Meetings, first and third Thursdays in each month. *President*, W. Bevan; *Hon. Treasurer*, Elias Jones; *Hon. Secretary*, Rev. George E. Catlin, Christ Church, Llandudno.

NOTTINGHAMSHIRE AMATEUR PHOTOGRAPHIC ASSOCIATION Established 1884.

Meetings, alternate Monday evenings at 8 o'clock. Annual meeting, first Monday in October. Dark room, Library. *President*, H. Blandy, L.D.S. Edin.; *Vice-Presidents*, Prof. Heaton and C. B. Wright; *Committee*, R. S. Armitage, T. S. Piggin, H. A. A. Wigley, G. E. Williamson, Rev. A. C. Beckman, Thomas Hodgson, M. Tuquet, J. D. Pearson, T. Hammond, Dr. Howitt; *Treasurer*, S. Wells, Lindenholme, Carendon Road, Nottingham; *Hon. Secretary*, P. E. Knight, Java Villa, Mythe Street, Mapperley, Nottingham.

NOTTS CAMERA CLUB *Hon. Secretary*, H. Blandy, 1 Posters Street, Nottingham.

OXFORDSHIRE NATURAL HISTORY SOCIETY AND FIELD CLUB Re-established 1887. The meetings are held on alternate Thursdays at 8 P.M. in the Museum. The annual meeting held in January. *President*, Prof. A. H. Green, M.A., F.R.S.; *President of Photographic Section*, E. Ryman-Hall; *Treasurer*, G. C. Druce, 118 High Street, Oxford; *Secretary*, Mrs. F. H. Peters, St. Margaret's Road, Oxford.

OLDHAM PHOTOGRAPHIC SOCIETY Established 1867. All meetings are held at the Lyceum, Union Street, Oldham. Monthly meetings on the last Thursday in each month, in the Club room at 7:45 P.M. Weekly meetings every Thursday evening in the Society's room from 8 to 10. The Annual meeting is held on the last Thursday in October. *President*, Wallace Thompson; *Vice-President*, J. Chadwick. *Committee*, J. H. Ashton, J. Brooks, J. S. Dronsfield, J. Greaves, Jr., T. Heywood, W. Jackson; *Librarian*, L. Tetow; *Treasurer*, W. Schofield; *Hon. Secretary*, T. Widdop, 16 Burnaby Street, Oldham; *Asst. Secretary*, W. A. Nash.

"OUR CAMERA CLUB" (LEYTONSTONE) Established 1891. *President*, Dr. W. Pickett Turner; *Committee*, the Officers of the Society; *Curator*, H. H. Summers, Chalcot, Leytonstone; *Treasurer*, Tom Symmons; *Secretaries*, R. Overton and F. F. Sanderson.

OXFORD PHOTOGRAPHIC SOCIETY Established 1887. Meetings held on the first and third Tuesdays in each month at 8 P.M. usually in the Society's rooms, 136 High Street. The annual meeting is held on the first Tuesday in October. The rooms are open from 10 A.M. to 10 P.M. on week days. *President*, E. A. Ryman-Hall; *Vice-Presidents*, C. C. Cole, W. W. Fisher,

M.A., A. F. Kerry, M.A. (Exeter College), Councillor J. H. Salter; *Committee*, the Officers, W. J. King, G. W. Norton, T. E. Food, H. Jenkins, A. Robinson, G. A Smith; *Hon. Treasurer*, R. A. R. Bennett, M.A.; *Hon. Secretaries*, F. A. Bellamy, F.R.Met.Soc. 4 St. John's Road, Oxford, and J. H. H. Minn, 105 Walton Street, Oxford. Official address, Hon. Secretaries, 136 High Street, Oxford.

OXFORD UNIVERSITY PHOTOGRAPHIC CLUB Established 1891. Meetings held at 8 P.M. every other Thursday or Friday during Term in the Club rooms. *President*, H. W. Case (Queen's College); *Committee*, R. G. Barnes (B.N.C.) and O. V. Darbisher (Balliol); *Hon. Treasurer*, James Walker, M.A. (Christ Church); *Hon. Secretary*, A. J. Clay, New College, Oxford.

PAISLEY PHOTOGRAPHIC SOCIETY Established 1857, re-organized 1885. Meets on the second Tuesday of each month from October till April. Fortnightly excursions on the Saturdays during the summer months. *Hon. Presidents*, H. H. Smiley and Stewart Clark; *Hon. Vice-Presidents*, Robert Harris, James Donald, Jr. and James Barr; *President*, Matthew Morrison; *Council*, Robert Ferrier, Alex. Kilpatrick, Alex. Gardiner, Jr., A. F. M'Callum, Thos. H. Taylor; (*Lantern Section*) A. Kilpatrick, T. H. Taylor, Thomas Rastall, 4 Douglas Terrace, Inchuman Road (*Secretary*); *Treasurer*, Robert D. Caldwell; *Secretary*, David B. Jack, Glencairn, Blackhall.

PEOPLE'S PALACE PHOTOGRAPHIC CLUB Established 1887. The Club meets on the first and third Fridays in the month in the new Technical Schools of the People's Palace. Persons eligible for membership are students of any subject, either at the People's Palace or any other institution. Entrance fee, 1s.; annual subscription, 2s. 6d. *President*, Sir Edmund Hay Currie; *Vice-Presidents*, E. Howard Farmer, C. W. Hastings, R. Mitchell; *Committee*, Alexander Albu, Robert Beckett, W. J. Downing, C. W. Gamble, John Hawkins, Thos. Lawday, H. Marriott; *Treasurer* and *Secretary*, William Barrett, 16 Clare Road, Forest Gate, E.

PERTSHIRE SOCIETY OF NATURAL SCIENCE (Photographic Section) Established 1889. *President*, Andrew Thomson, D.Sc., M.A., F.R.S.E.; *Committee*, A. Hodge, R. C. Ferguson, James Stewart, Dr. Ferrier; *Secretary*, William Ellison, 2 Dalhousie Street, Perth.

PETERBOROUGH PHOTOGRAPHIC SOCIETY Established 1887. Meetings at the Museum, Minster Precincts, at 8 P.M., on the first Monday in each month. *President*, Dr. G. Kirkwood; *Vice-Presidents*, Dr. T. J. Walker, J.P.; J. H. Hetley, H. M. Townsend, E. Worthington, G. W. Leigh; *Committee*, W. H. Marsh, J. F. Perkins, W. H. Pentney, A. C. Taylor, B. R. Ward; *Hon. Treasurer*, W. Atkinson, Albion Terrace, Lincoln Road; *Hon. Secretary*, A. W. Nicholls, 11 Cromwell Road.

PHOTOGRAPHERS' BENEVOLENT ASSOCIATION Established 1873. Meetings as required, held by kind permission of the Photographic Society of Great Britain in their rooms, 50 Great Russell Street, Bloomsbury, London, W.

PHOTOGRAPHIC CLUB Established 1879. Meetings, every Wednesday evening, at 8 P.M., at Anderton's Hotel, Fleet Street, L.C. Annual meeting, first Wednesday in November. *Trustees*, W. Bedford, Frank Haes; *Committee*, F. P. Cembrano, Jr., Edgar Clifton, R. P. Drage, E. W. Foxlee, J. Guardia, H. M. Hastings, J. Nesbit, J. B. B. Wellington; *Curator*, H. R. Hume; *Recorder*, Thomas Bedding; *Librarian*, E. A. Newell; *Hon. Secretary* and *Treasurer*, F. A. Bridge, East Lodge, Dalston Lane, London, N.E.

PHOTOGRAPHIC CONVENTION OF THE UNITED KINGDOM Established 1886. Meets at various towns. *President-Elect*, G. Mason; *Council*, James Ewing, F. Barclay, W. Bedford, H. J. Blane, C. H. Bothamley, F. A. Bridge, J. J. Briginshaw, A. A. Cornell, A. Cowan, R. P. Drage, G. Davison, F. Evans, J. P. Gibson, M. J. Harding, H. M. Hastings, A. S. Henderson, T. C. Hepworth, R. Keene, J. Austin King, Paul Lange, Wm. Lang, Jr., A. Levy, C. Phipps Lucas, A. Mackie, W. W. Naunton, J. Porritt; A. Pringle, J. B. Sayce, A. Seaman, H. M. Smith, H. Sturmey, J. Stuart, T. Traill Taylor, A. Tate, J. M. Turnbull, L. Warnecke, G. W. Webster, J. B. B. Wellington, A. Werner, R. Hansford Worth; *Hon. Secretary*, F. P. Cembrano, Jr., 10 Cambridge Gardens, Richmond Hill, Surrey.

PHOTOGRAPHIC SOCIETY OF GREAT BRITAIN Established 1851. The ordinary meetings are held at the Society's Rooms, 50 Great Russell Street, Bloomsbury, W.C., at 8 P.M., on the second Tuesday of each month from November to June inclusive. Annual general meeting on the second Tuesday in February. Extra meetings, called 'Technical Meetings,' are held on the fourth Tuesday in each month. *Patrons*, Her Majesty the Queen and H.R.H. the Prince of Wales; *President*, Capt. W. de W. Abney, C.B., R.E., D.C.L., F.R.S., F.C.S.; *Vice-Presidents*, T. Sebastian Davis, F.C.S.; J. Glaisher, F.R.S., F.R.A.S.; J. Spiller, F.I.C., F.C.S.; Sir H. Trueman Wood, M.A.; *Treasurer*, G. Scamell; *Council*, W. Ackland, G. L. Addenbrooke, W. Bedford, W. S. Bird, F. P. Cembrano, Jr., A. Cowan, T. R. Dallmeyer, W. E. Debenham, W. England, Col. J. Gale, F. Hollyer, F. Ince, G. Lindsay Johnson, M.A., M.D., A. Mackie, Capt. A. M. Mantell, R.E., A. Pringle, J. W. Swan, M.A., F.I.C., F.C.S., J. Traill Taylor, Prof. J. M. Thomson, F.I.C., F.C.S., Leon Warnerke, Silverhowe; *Hon. Secretary*, H. Chapman Jones, F.I.C., F.C.S., 11 Eaton Rise, Ealing, W.; *Ass't. Secretary*, R. Child Bayley, 50 Great Russell Street, Bloomsbury, W.C.

PHOTOGRAPHIC SOCIETY OF IRELAND Established 1854, Re-established 1879. Rooms, 15 Dawson Street, Dublin. Meetings second Friday and fourth Thursday in each month. Annual meeting, second Friday in February. *President*, George Massfield, J.P.; *Vice-Presidents*, Sir Howard Grubb, F.R.S., J. A. Scott, M.B.; *Council*, M. Hedley, F.R.C.V.S., E. McD. Cosgrave, M.D., J. A. C. Ruthven, A.M.T.C.E., R. M. Inglis, J. Carson, C.E., A. M. Geddis, A. Werner, J. White, J. H. Woodworth, I. R. Strangways, M.A.; *Treasurer*, W. Bewley; *Secretary*, J. H. Hargrave, B.A., A.M.I.C.E., 3 Newtownsmith, Kingstown, Ca., Dublin.

POLYTECHNIC PHOTOGRAPHIC SOCIETY Established October, 1891. Headquarters, Polytechnic, 309 Regent Street, W. Meetings, first and third Fridays in each month. *President*, Quintin Hogg; *Vice-Presidents*, W. E. Debenham and Robert Mitchell; *Hon. Treasurer*, Fred. W. Jackson; *Hon. Secretary*, Fred. R. Tissington, 102 Shaftesbury Road, Crouch Hill, N.

PORTSMOUTH AMATEUR CAMERA CLUB Established 1888. Meetings are held in the Young Men's Christian Association Buildings, Edinburgh Road, Landport, on the first and third Wednesdays in each month. *President*, C. Nicholas, *Vice-Presidents*, H. Hickey and R. Carrick; *Committee*, R. Carrick, L. Cooper, W. H. Cooke, F. Hooper, C. Jurd, E. H. Martlew, C. Nicholas, &c.; *Hon. Treasurer*, H. Nicholas; *Hon. Secretary*, G. Knight, 12 Middle Street, Southsea.

POSTAL PHOTOGRAPHIC CLUB Established 1886. For the circulation, criticism and exchange of prints taken by members, and discussions on various topics by means of a note-book; *Secretary*, R. A. R. Bennett, Walton Manor Lodge, Oxford.

POSTAL PHOTOGRAPHIC CLUB Established 1890. *Secretary* and *Treasurer*, George D. Nickels, 1 South Town Cottages, Upton Road, Torquay.

POSTAL PHOTOGRAPHIC SOCIETY Established 1882. Committee meetings are held every three months, and the annual meeting in June, at the Vestry House. *President*, Dr. Horace Day; *Committee*, Rev. W. Miles Barnes, Robert Tindall, H. N. Malan, Walter Withall.

PRESTON CAMERA CLUB Established 1891. Ordinary meetings, second Thursday in the month at 8 P.M., in the Club Chambers, Hill Place. Annual meeting in March. *President*, Colonel Oliver; *Vice-President*, I. Simpson; *Committee*, H. Jackson, W. I. T. Jackson, A. E. Lewty, B. Simpson, O. Simpson; *Treasurer*, Oswald Simpson; *Secretary*, W. J. T. Jackson, 55 Fishergate.

PUDSEY DISTRICT PHOTOGRAPHIC SOCIETY Established February, 1891. Meetings, Mechanic's Institute, Pudsey, every alternate Tuesday from October to April, and first Tuesday in each month from April to October, open to both amateur and professional. *President*, Dr. W. L. Hunter; *Vice-Presidents*, Messrs. J. Barrow and H. Crossley; *Committee*, H. Clapham, W. S. Prowther, T. Marshall, H. E. Vickers, W. Goodall; *Hon. Treasurer*, J. Goodman; *Hon. Secretary*, W. H. Hinings, Manor House Street, Pudsey, Yorkshire.

PUTNEY PHOTOGRAPHIC SOCIETY Established 1890. Meetings held on the second Wednesday and last Saturday in each month from October to April, and first Wednesday in the month from May to September, at 8:30 P.M.

Annual meeting, May. Headquarters, High Street, Putney. *President*, Hon. Baron Pollock; *Vice-Presidents*, Rev. L. Macdona and Dr. W. J. Sheppard; *Council*, Dr. J. F. Farrar, H. Faulkner, Jr., T. Gilbert, W. F. Gorin, L. S. Zachariasen, William Martin, Jr., Charles Ballard; *Treasurer*, William Martin, Jr.; *Joint Hon. Secretaries*, L. S. Zachariasen, Alfred Villa, Putney Bridge Road, S.W., and W. F. Gorin, 3 Montserrat Road, Putney, S.W.

READING AMATEUR PHOTOGRAPHIC SOCIETY Established 1889. Ordinary meetings, second Wednesday in each month at 7:30 P.M. Annual general meeting, last Wednesday in January. *President*, W. Berkeley Monck; *Vice-Presidents*, Colonel Hawkes, C.B., Walter Palmer, Charles Stephens; *Committee*, B. J. Austin, A. Harrison, J. Long, J. G. Wyly, J. T. Strange, W. Moore, Dr. Richardson, F. Wheeler; *Secretary* and *Treasurer*, J. Phillips, 10 Abbot's Walk.

REDCAR AND COATHAM AMATEUR PHOTOGRAPHIC ASSOCIATION *Hon. Secretary*, E. H. Saniter, 176 High Street, Redcar.

RICHMOND CAMERA CLUB Established 1890. Meetings every Monday at 8:30 P.M., at the Greyhound Hotel, Richmond, Surrey. *President*, F. P. Cembrano, Jr.; *Committee*, J. H. Alabaston (Lanternist), G. Ardaseer, (Librarian), C. H. Davis, A. C. Hunter, F. Neville and G. W. Ramsay; *Secretary*, P. Ennis, 28 Halford Road, Richmond, Surrey.

ROYAL COLLEGE OF SCIENCE PHOTOGRAPHIC SOCIETY Established 1888. Headquarters, Royal College of Science. Meetings Tuesdays, fortnightly. *President*, Capt. Abney; *Vice-Presidents*, Dr. H. H. Hoffert and Chapman Jones; *Hon. Secretary*, J. K. Snelus, Royal College of Science, South Kensington, London.

R. N. E. COLLEGE PHOTOGRAPHIC CLUB Established 1891. *President*, W. S. Hill, R.N.; *Committee*, H. M. Wall, R.N., J. S. Constable, R.N., F. J. Charlton, R.N., and W. B. Hall, R.N., with President and Secretary; *Hon. Secretary* and *Treasurer*, G. N. Leslie, R.N., R. N. E. College, Devonport.

ROCHDALE AND DISTRICT PHOTOGRAPHIC SOCIETY Established 1890. Meetings, second Tuesday and fourth Monday in each month. *President*, John Albert Bright, M.P.; *Hon. Treasurer*, J. H. Hoyle; *Hon. Secretaries*, Wm.

Ingham, Saml. Ingham, 30 Freehold Street, Rochdale.

ROCHESTER NATURALISTS' CLUB (Photographic Section) Established 1891. Headquarters at the Mathematical School. Meetings every alternate Saturday. *Hon. Secretary*, E. Siddons Wilson, 1 Hillside Villas, Western Road, Strood, Rochester.

ROSSENDALE PHOTOGRAPHIC ASSOCIATION Established 1889. Ordinary meetings held on the last Monday in each month, at 8 P.M. Annual meeting in September. Place of meeting, Townsend Chambers, Rawtenstall. *President*, Joseph Ashworth; *Vice-Presidents*, John Taylor and James H. Hargreaves; *Council*, J. Booth, A. Heap, M. H. Coates, G. A. Duerr; *Financial Secretary*, John Riley; *Secretary*, F. G. Killingbeck, 62 Rank Street, Rawtenstall.

ROTHERHAM PHOTOGRAPHIC SOCIETY Established 1889. Ordinary meetings first Tuesday in each month. Annual meeting, first Tuesday in October. *President*, Dr. F. B. J. Baldwin; *Vice-Presidents*, E. I. Hubbard, W. H. Haywood, G. T. M. Rackstraw; *Council*, J. Wright, W. Shepherd, W. Mason, J. W. Whittington, T. W. Mosby; *Treasurer*, James Leadbeater; *Secretary*, Henry C. Hemmingway, 6 Stanley Street, Rotherham.

SCIENCE SCHOOLS (SOUTH KENSINGTON) PHOTOGRAPHIC SOCIETY *President*, Captain Abney; *Hon. Secretary*, P. C. Coultes, Normal School of Science, South Kensington, London.

SELBY CAMERA CLUB Established 1891. Headquarters, Park Street. Meetings every Thursday during the winter months. *President*, Rev. A. G. Tweedee, M.A.; *Vice-Presidents*, Wm. Rawling and J. C. Thompson; *Hon. Librarian*, W. J. Allison; *Hon. Secretary* and *Treasurer*, W. N. Cheesman, The Crescent, Selby.

SELBY PHOTOGRAPHIC SOCIETY Established 1887. Meetings are held during the winter months once a month, or oftener if necessary; and during the summer months excursions as may be arranged. Present meeting place, St. James' Schools. *Secretary* and *Treasurer*, J. T. Atkinson, F.G.S., Hill Field House, Selby.

SHAFTESBURY PHOTOGRAPHIC SOCIAL Established 1888. Meetings held every Friday evening at 8:30, at the Craven Lecture Hall, Foubert's Place, Regent Street, London, W.

President, G. Davison; *Vice-Presidents*, A. Ibbetson and O. J. Holder; *Committee*, R. Aitken, G. A. E. Robinson, D. T. Rintoul, H. Miles, N. Baker, E. Bull; *Treasurer*, T. T. Samora; *Hon. Secretary*, John B. Rintoul, 31 Brewer Street, Regent Street, W.

SHAW CHURCH INSTITUTE PHOTOGRAPHIC AND ART SOCIETY Monthly meetings, first Friday in each month. *President*, E. Brooks; *Vice-President*, Rev. E. E. Goodacre, B.A.; *Committee*, J. H. Ashton, J. Waddington, J. Broadbelt, A. Clegg; *Secretary*, John Maiden, 91 Rochdale Road, Shaw.

SHEFFIELD BRANCH OF THE N. A. P. P. Established 1891. Meeting, first Tuesday in each month, held at the Talbot Hotel, Sheffield. *President*, J. Crosby; *Vice-President*, W. Dakin; *Committee*, A. Seaman, J. H. Ainley, T. N. Langton, J. E. Eddison, F. M. Whaley, G. V. Yates; *Treasurer*, G. T. Y. Dickinson; *Secretary*, A. E. Yates, Fargate, Sheffield.

SHEFFIELD CAMERA CLUB Established 1888. Headquarters, New Surrey Street. Meetings held on the fourth Wednesday in each month, at 7:30 P.M. Annual meeting, January. *President*, G. E. Maleham; *Vice-Presidents*, T. H. Morton, M.D., J. H. Rawson; *Treasurer*, B. W. Winder, F.C.S., F.R.M.S.; *Hon. Secretary*, W. Gilley, Jr., Kenwood Park Road; *Council*, G. T. W. Newsholme, Prof. Arnold, A. Copley, Dr. Edward Skinner, W. H. Strangeways, Geo. Ellinor.

SHEFFIELD OPTICAL LANTERN SOCIETY Established 1890. *President*, E. G. Draper; *Vice-Presidents*, J. T. Frith and J. Clowes; *Committee*, H. Staniforth, J. Maclaurin, T. G. Allen, W. Platts, T. Baker, I. W. Whittington, J. Simpson and J. Temperton; *Treasurer*, E. Copley; *Secretary*, J. S. Stephens, 6 Sheaf Gardens Terrace, Sheffield.

SHEFFIELD PHOTOGRAPHIC SOCIETY Established 1876. Ordinary meetings, first Tuesday in the month, at 7:30 P.M., in the Masonic Hall, Surrey Street. Annual meeting, October. *President*, B. J. Taylor; *Vice-Presidents*, George Bromley and Thomas Firth; *Council*, W. T. Furness, W. Vickers Davy, G. Sampson, Jr., Joseph Smith, T. G. Hibbert; *Reporter*, E. H. Pearce; *Treasurer*, Bradley Nowill; *Secretary*, Ernest Beck, Fairmont, Shoreham Street, Sheffield.

SHROPSHIRE CAMERA CLUB Established 1886. Ordinary meetings held second Wednesday in each month during winter session. Annual meeting held in January. *President*, M. J. Harding; *Vice-Presidents*, W. S. Buddicom, J.P., G. Bidlaks, I. R. Greatorex; *Council*, W. Alltree, W. Bowdler, W. Burson, Dr. Cureton, W. Heath, R. I. Irwin, J. L. Della Porta, F. W. Williams; *Treasurer*, M. J. Harding; *Hon. Secretary*, Walter W. Naunton, 9 The Square, Shrewsbury.

SIMPSON MEMORIAL PHOTOGRAPHIC SOCIETY (MOSTON, MANCHESTER) Established 1891. Meet on the first Wednesday in the month, at 8 P.M. *President*, James Wood; *Vice-President*, T. R. Cobley; *Council*, W. H. Tyas, J. Edwards, J. Price, J. B. Stockwell, W. Coulthurst; *Treasurer*, J. G. Sankey; *Secretary*, J. A. Dearden, Ashley Mount, Ashley Lane, Harpurhey, Manchester.

SOUTH HORNSEY PHOTOGRAPHIC SOCIETY Established 1891. Meetings every third week. *Chairman*, P. A. Legge; *Vice-Chairman*, D. B. Harrower; *Hon. Secretary* and *Treasurer*, Harold A. Rutt, 2 Alexandra Road, Finsbury Park, London, N.

SOUTH LONDON PHOTOGRAPHIC SOCIETY Established 1889. Ordinary meetings, first and third Mondays in month, at 8 P.M. Annual meeting, first Monday in April. Place of meeting, Hanover Hall, Hanover Park, Rye Lane, Peckham, S.E. *President*, F. W. Edwards; *Vice-Presidents*, Maurice Howell, Dr. T. G. Munyard, W. Rice, H. G. Banks; *Committee*, M. Boxall, C. Eldridge, A. Fellows, J. F. Fitness, W. Groves, H. R. Herbert, B. Lyon, J. Miller, F. W. Webb; *Hon. Treasurer*, E. A. Whitby; *Curator*, G. H. Moss; *Hon. Secretary*, Chas. H. Oakden, 51 Melbourne Grove, East Dulwich, S.E.

SOUTH MANCHESTER PHOTOGRAPHIC AND LANTERN SOCIETY Established 1892. Headquarters, Longford Lecture Hall. Meetings, last Monday in each month. *Chairman*, W. I. Chadwick; *Vice-Chairman*, W. Liemell; *Hon. Treasurer*, E. M. Bowden; *Hon. Secretary*, M. W. Thompstone, Beaufort House, Brooklands near Manchester.

SOUTHPORT PHOTOGRAPHIC SOCIETY Established 1888. Meetings on the third Tuesday in each month, at 7:45 P.M., at Shaftesbury

Buildings, Eastbank Street, Southport. *President*, Edward Clough; *Vice-Presidents*, Dr. Hawksley and J. S. Dickin; *Council*, Messrs. Harper, A. Quayle, A. Boothroyd, Cave; *Hon. Treasurer*, H. Heaton; *Hon. Secretaries*, Messrs. Marsden, Ardour Street, and Wallis, 46 Talbot Street.

SOUTHPORT SOCIAL PHOTOGRAPHIC CLUB Established 1890. Headquarters, The Studio, Cambridge Arcade, Southport. Meetings every Wednesday. *President*, Robt. J. Parks; *Vice-Presidents*, A. Dunmore, A. Quayle; *Council*, Miss Dunmore, Miss Unsworth, C. F. Depree, G. Cross, J. C. Smith, W. P. Brown; *Librarian*, M. G. Cross; *Hon. Secretary* and *Treasurer*, J. R. Cave, 52 Nevill St., Southport.

SOUTHSEA AMATEUR PHOTOGRAPHIC SOCIETY Established 1888. Meetings are held on the first and third Wednesday in the month, at 9 P.M. Annual meeting, second Wednesday in January. *President*, J. J. Thornton; *Vice-President*, Dr. F. Lord; *Council*, A. Fisher, A.S.A., C. H. Grant, A. H. Wood, A. J. Hammond and J. Sawyer; *Treasurer*, J. J. Thornton; *Hon. Secretary*, Major Bruno, H.M., Gun Wharf; *Assistant Hon. Secretary*, G. Whitefield, King's Road, Southsea.

SPEN VALLEY PHOTOGRAPHIC SOCIETY Established 1890. *President*, Dr. F. Farrow; *Vice-Presidents*, Wm. Bell, Dr. J. A. Sutherland, B. H. Goldthorp, S. Mortimer, Dr. John Sykes, F. Law; *Council*, E. Hirst, J. Burnhill, Metcalf, Markland, A. H. Knowles, J. C. Phelon, George Potts, R. Smith, W. H. Wright; *Treasurer*, E. Smith; *Hon. Secretary*, J. H. Jackson, Cleckheaton.

STAFFORDSHIRE POTTERIES AMATEUR PHOTOGRAPHIC SOCIETY Established 1890. Meetings, first Tuesday in the month, in the Town Hall, Burslem, at 8 P.M. *President*, Edward B. Wain; *Vice-Presidents*, R. S. Burgess, T. Blackshaw, F. Bettany and W. Burgess, U. S. Consul; *Committee*, W. Slater, J. Porter, F. Tryner, W. H. Whalley, E. J. Stonier, J. W. Myatt; *Treasurer*, S. Crosse; *Secretaries*, J. F. Hewitt, 35 Market Place, Burslem, and F. C. Powell, Swan Square, Burslem.

ST. BARTHOLOMEW'S HOSPITAL PHOTOGRAPHIC SOCIETY Established 1889. The Society is for the study of the application of Photography to medicine. Meetings are held at St.

Bartholomew's Hospital at no particular stated dates. *President*, Dr. W. J. Russell, F.R.S.; *Vice-Presidents*, Dr. V. D. Harris and Lewis Jones; *Committee*, the Officers, D. M. Eccles, H. A. Eccles, J. A. Crump; *Treasurer*, Dr. James Andrew; *Secretaries*, D. H. Armitage and R. J. Hillier, St. Bartholomew's Hospital, London, E.C.

ST. BRIDE'S MUTUAL PHOTOGRAPHIC SOCIETY Established 1887, under the name of "The Teachers' Photographic Society." Meet for outings the first Saturday, and for discussions the third Wednesday in each month. Place of meeting varies. Annual general meeting for election of officers in April. *President*, W. Rice; *Patrons*, Captain W. de W. Abney, R.E., F.R.S., etc., and the Rev. A. Johnson, M.A., F.L.S.; *Council*, J. Colman, A. Gill, D. R. Lowe, A. Nunn; *Treasurer*, G. A. Freeman, B.Sc., F.G.S.; *Secretary*, Fred. Brocas, 86 Fleet Street, E.C.

STEREOSCOPIC CLUB Established 1891. Meetings at the Brooklands Hotel, Brooklands, near Manchester, first Monday in the month. *President*, J. Whitelegg; *Council*, W. J. Cunliffe, J. Vos, W. I. Chadwick; *Treasurer*, J. Vos; *Secretary*, W. I. Chadwick, Brooklands, near Manchester.

STOCKPORT PHOTOGRAPHIC SOCIETY Established 1890. Meetings on the second Wednesday of each month, at the Mechanics' Institute. *President*, Thomas Kay, Esq., J.P.; *Vice-Presidents*, Col. Turner, J.P., Walter Hyde, W. B. Leigh; *Treasurer*, T. Bedford; *Hon. Secretary*, B. S. Harlow, Buckan House, Heaton Norris, Stockport; *Assistant Secretary*, H. J. Robinson; *Committee*, A. M. Gourley, H. J. Heginbotham, G. H. Broome, F. G. Brooke, H. N. Cooper, Oliver Coppock, H. D. F. Dobson, Samuel Kay, G. Hidderley.

STOCKTON PHOTOGRAPHIC SOCIETY Established 1886. Meetings held on second Tuesday in each month, in the Society's own rooms, Masonic Court, High Street, at 8 P.M. Annual meeting in December. *President*, H. Macdonnell; *Vice-Presidents*, J. H. Jackson and W. Downs; *Treasurer*, J. H. Rhodes; *Council*, H. Bradley, A. H. Byers, W. S. Fothergill, W. Hodgson, W. Moult, W. W. Stainthorpe, M.D.; *Hon. Secretary*, J. E. Ellam, Yarm.

SUNDERLAND PHOTOGRAPHIC ASSOCIATION Established 1888. *President*, W. Pinkney; *Vice-President*, A. Stafford; *Council*, W. Bartram, J. W. Broderick, J. Lynn, W. Milburn, A. Peddie, W. J. Pope, W. Pratt, R. Stafford; *Treasurer*, T. Walton; *Secretary*, C. E. Cowper, Thornhill Gardens, Sunderland.

SUN & COMPANY Established 1886. A Postal Photographic Society, limited to forty amateurs, for the monthly circulation and criticism of photographs, entirely the work of members, and for a general interchange of ideas, with a view to mutual advancement in the science and art of photography. *Committee*, A. D. Guthrie, A. Pitkethly, F. W. Williams, and the Hon. Secretary. Application for vacancies should be made to the Hon. Secretary, Martin J. Harding, 4 Lexden Gardens, Shrewsbury.

SURBITON AMATEUR PHOTOGRAPHIC SOCIETY Established 1888. Annual meeting held early in February. All meetings held at the Oscillators Tricycle Club room, King Charles Road, Surbiton. *President*, W. Montague Robertson; *Vice-President*, A. D. Doughty; *Committee*, W. Whitfield, F. J. Barclay, E. H. Hancock, C. Simpson, R. E. Plaistow; *Secretary* and *Treasurer*, Arthur E. Lane, The Ferns, King Charles Road, Surbiton.

SUTTON (SURREY) SCIENTIFIC AND LITERARY SOCIETY (Photographic Club) Established 1886. Meetings, first Tuesday in the month, in the Society's rooms. *President*, E. de Clifford; *Secretary* and *Recorder*, Mrs. Emily Culverhouse, Heathfield, Wallington near Sutton, Surrey.

SYDENHAM CAMERA CLUB Established 1890. Headquarters, Greyhound Hotel. Meetings, alternate Tuesdays. *President*, T. C. Cole; *Vice-President*, G. Austin; *Hon. Secretary* and *Treasurer*, H. H. Gray, 9 Thicket Road, Auerley, S.E.

SWANSEA AMATEUR PHOTOGRAPHIC ASSOCIATION Established 1888. Meetings held at Tenby Hotel, the last Friday in every month, at 7:30. Annual meeting in October. *President*, B. H. Morgan; *Vice-Presidents*, W. E. Brown and C. W. Slater; *Treasurer*, Henry Hoskins; *Secretary*, E. Ernest Morgan, BrynNant, Swansea.

TALBOT CIRCULATING PHOTOGRAPHIC ALBUM CLUB Established 1886. *Secretary*, Frederick H. Davies, 7 Temple Row, Birmingham.

TOOTING CAMERA CLUB Inaugurated 1890. Meetings held at the schools, Church Lane, Tooting Graveney, S.W., every three weeks, on Tuesday evening, at 8:15 P.M. General meeting held on the last Tuesday in March, at 8 P.M. *President*, A. H. Anderson; *Vice-President*, J. H. Beckett; *Committee*, W. Irwin, J. F. Child, H. Berger; *Treasurer*, C. D'E. Stowell; *Hon. Secretary*, G. H. Dollery, 'Glion,' Lucien Road, Tooting Common, S.W.

TORQUAY PHOTOGRAPHIC ASSOCIATION Established 1890. Ordinary meetings on the second Tuesday in each month, at 8 P.M. from October to March, inclusively. Annual meeting on the first ordinary meeting in October. *President*, E. Vivian, J.P., M.A., F.R.G.S.; *Vice-President*, A. R. Hunt, M.A., F.G.S., *Treasurer*, H. C. Howell; *Secretary*, George Edwards, Walnut Lodge, Chelston, Torquay.

TUNBRIDGE WELLS AMATEUR PHOTOGRAPHIC ASSOCIATION Established 1887. Ordinary meetings, first Thursday in the month, at the Mechanics' Institute, at 8 P.M. Excursions during the summer. Annual meeting in January. Exhibition in November. Members of recognized clubs and societies are at liberty to attend the ordinary meetings as visitors upon giving notice in writing to the Hon. Secretary. *Patron*, Sir David Salomens Bart. *President*, Francis G. Smart, M.A.; *Vice-Presidents*, Rev. A. T. Scott, J. G. Calway, Rev. J. E. Rogers; *Committee*, J. W. Morgan, A. W. Pierson, E. Catchpole; *Hon Auditor*, W. E. Brampton; *Hon. Treasurer*, B. Whitrow; *Hon. Secretary*, Joseph Chamberlain, 14 Calverley Park Gardens.

TOYNBEE CAMERA CLUB Established 1890. Meetings on Tuesday at 7:30 P.M., at Toynbee Hall, 28 Commercial Street, Whitechapel. *President*, Rev. K. Jameson, M.A.; *Vice-Presidents*, F. E. Bartholomew and A. Price; *Committee*, T. W. Hull, W. H. Jennings, H. T. Malby, G. West; *Treasurer*, J. E. Monk; *Secretaries*, Thomas W. Glare, 37 Brunner Road, Walthamstow; A. E. Birch, 35 Heathland Road, Stoke, Newington.

TYNESIDE CAMERA CLUB Established 1891. Private club meetings held every alternate Monday throughout the year, at Clarence Street

Schools, Newcastle-on-Tyne. Dark room open to members from 6 A.M. till 10 P.M. all the year round. *President*, J. F. McKie, Esq.; *Vice-President*, A. D. Rothwell; *Treasurer*, Thos. Simpson; *Secretary*, Thos. Ord-Birkett, Clarence Street Schools; *Council*, Messrs. Bell, Angus, Elliot and Lawson.

ULSTER AMATEUR PHOTOGRAPHIC SOCIETY Established 1886. *President*, Alexander Tate, C.E.; *Vice-Presidents*, William Swanson, F.G.S., and John Brown; *Committee*, J. J. Andrew, S. B. Coates, M.D., James Leslie, J. M'Cleery, James Stelfox, William Gray, E. Braddell, R. J. Evans; *Treasurer*, R. E. Workman; *Secretary*, Dr. Cecil Shaw, 14 College Square East, Belfast.

UNIVERSITY COLLEGE PHOTOGRAPHIC SOCIETY Established 1889. Ordinary meetings, alternate Tuesdays during the session, at 5 P.M. Annual meeting, first fortnight in June, at University College. *Committee*, E. S. Worrall, R. W. Boyce, H. W. Woodall; *Treasurer*, Dr. R. T. Plimpton; *Secretary*, John C. Chorley, University College, Gower Street, W.C.

UPPER HOLLOWAY CYCLING CLUB (Camera Division) *Hon. Secretary*, F. W. Timms.

UTTOXETER PHOTOGRAPHIC SOCIETY Established 1890. Meetings held at Carter Street, Uttoxeter. *President*, Lord Parker; *Vice-President*, Rev. C. F. Lowry Barnwell; *Committee*, Messrs. Hardy, Bamford, Walker, Udall, Parker; *Treasurer*, R. T. A. Hardy; *Secretary*, A. Parker, High Street, Uttoxeter, Staffordshire.

VIEWFINDERS CLUB Established 1890. Meeting, first Monday of each month at 8 P.M., at 31 Chambers Street. Annual meeting, October. *Convener*, F. Dundas Todd, 29 Panmure Place, Edinburgh.

WAKEFIELD AND DISTRICT PHOTOGRAPHIC SOCIETY Established 1890. Annual general meeting, October 9. Ordinary meetings fortnightly, on a Friday evening, at 8 P.M., at the Technical and Art School and the Mechanics' Institution alternately. *President*, A. W. Stanfield, J.P.; *Vice-Presidents*, Isaac Briggs, J.P., and Captain Norwood; *Committee*, H. A. Halliwell, G. F. Firth, H. Crutchley, J. H. Chaplin, G. Campbell, G. Parkin, *Treasurer*, C. W. Richardson; *Secretary*, W. Townend, 21 King Street, Wakefield.

WALLASEY PHOTOGRAPHIC ASSOCIATION Established 1885. Ordinary meetings, first Wednesday in each month, at 8 P.M., at the Egremont Institute, Egremont, Cheshire. Annual meeting, first Wednesday in December, as above. *President*, Colonel E. T. D. Cotton-Jodrell, M.P.; *Vice-Presidents*, C. B. Reader and James Gill; *Council*, H. B. Sharp, H. Wilkinson, A. E. Varcoe, J. Bardsley, W. Priestley, J. W. Gregg; *Auditor*, C. W. Bullock; *Treasurer*, J. Fullerton; *Secretary*, Geo. G. Breading, Church Street, Egremont, Cheshire.

WALTON PHOTOGRAPHIC SOCIETY Established 1889. Monthly meetings in the Class Room, Arnot Street Schools, County Road. *President*, Jno. Kennedy; *Council*, Jno. Parke, Henry Sharrock, Henry E. Burn, F. Murphy, W. B. Beaton, Geo. Latimer; *Secretary* and *Treasurer*, W. A. Brown, 20 Richmond Terrace, Brack Road, Liverpool.

WARRINGTON AMATEUR PHOTOGRAPHIC SOCIETY Established 1886. Meetings are held at the Museum, Bold Street, on the last Tuesday in each month, at 8 P.M. Annual meeting, last Tuesday in January. *Council*, Thomas J. Down (*President*), H. N. Houghton and William Pierpont (*Vice-Presidents*); *Committee*, Messrs. H. Bond, J. Harding (Eustace Street), J. Harding (Liverpool Road), J. Hallows, G. Kirby, Thos. Welsby, C. Aylward; *Treasurer*, P. Dalton; *Librarian*, J. Skelton; *Auditor*, J. Fairhurst; *Hon. Secretary*, H. Pritchard, 162 Orford Lane, Warrington.

WEST KENT AMATEUR PHOTOGRAPHIC SOCIETY Established 1888. Meetings fortnightly. *President*, Andrew Pringle; *Vice-President*, A. R. Dresser; *Council*, Messrs. Jones, Court, Nash, Hastings, Starnes, Crowe, Reeves, Mourdant; *Secretary* and *Treasurer*, Edward Hawkins, Manor Estate, Sidcup.

WEST LONDON PHOTOGRAPHIC SOCIETY Established 1888. Meetings held on the second and fourth Fridays in each month, at the Lecture Hall, Broadway, Hammersmith, at 8 P.M. *President*, J. A. Hodges, *Vice-Presidents*, C. Bilton, B.A., W. L. Colls, W. A. Brown, C. Whiting; *Council*, J. J. Adam, J. Desiré England, R. Horton, George Lamley, H. Selby, R. W. Watson, A. W. Scanlan, G. E. Varden, J. Wilson, C. Winter; *Hon. Auditors*, T. Turner and J. Stein; *Hon. Lanternist*, R. Horton; *Hon. Librarian*, J. Wilson; *Hon. Treasurer*, W. H. Whitear; *Hon. Secretary*, L. C. Bennett; *Assistant Hon. Secretary*, W. S. Rogers.

WEST SURREY PHOTOGRAPHIC SOCIETY Established 1887. Meetings held on first and third Wednesdays in each month at St. Mark's Schools, Battersea Rise, S.W. *President*, J. Gale; *Vice-Presidents*, G. Davison, W. Winsford, J. L. Lyell; *Committee*, A. Borley, W. Graham, G. Hellyer, G. H. James, P. A. Martin, G. H. Seward, A. Robertson; *Hon. Librarian*, E. Swingler; *Secretary* and *Treasurer*, F. H. Smith, 107 Falcon Road, London, S.W.

WIGAN PHOTOGRAPHIC SOCIETY *President*, Mr. J. A. E. Lowe; *Vice-Presidents*, Rev. J. S. Barnes, M.A., Mr. G. R. Newman, Mr. R. Wardman; *Council*, Messrs. W. Heaton, J. H. Atherton, J. Smith, B. B. Hartley, S. Richardson, H. Hill, Percy Clark, and the Officers; *Hon. Treasurer* and *Secretary*, Mr. Fred. Betley, 11 Swinley Road, Wigan.

WINDSOR AND ETON PHOTOGRAPHIC SOCIETY *Hon. Secretary*, W. Oldham, 100 Eton.

WOLVERHAMPTON AMATEUR PHOTOGRAPHIC SOCIETY *President*, H. Holcroft, M.A., F.C.S.; *Vice-President*, Lyons Wright, Esq.; *Committee*, T. Ironmonger, Esq., J.P., J. Stokes, E. A. White, S. R. Rhodes, W. Ratcliffe, J. M. Taylor, W. E. Oakley, W. German; *Hon. Treasurer*, F. J. Gibson; *Hon. Secretaries*, J. W. Evans, J. Gale, 52 Darlington Street; *Hon. Secretary Survey Committee*, S. R. Rhodes, 53 Queen Street, Wolverhampton.

WOOLWICH POLYTECHNIC PHOTOGRAPHIC SOCIETY Established April, 1892. *President*, A. R. Dresser, Esq.; *Vice-Presidents*, Alan R. Young, Esq., F. Didden, Esq.; *Hon. Secretary*, W. Dawes, 145 Chestnut Road, Plumstead.

WORCESTER AMATEUR PHOTOGRAPHIC SOCIETY Founded March, 1890. Headquarters, Guildhall, Worcester. *President*, W. R. Higgs; *Vice-President*, A. Webb; *Hon. Secretary*, J. J. Thomasson, Silver Street, Worcester.

WORCESTERSHIRE CAMERA CLUB Established 1888. Meetings held in the School of Science, Kidderminster, and are variable in date. We issue a programme of fixtures. *President*, Michael Tomkinson; *Vice-Presidents*, Albert Cowell and Arthur Comber; *Committee*, Miss C. Badland, Miss E. Cowell, C. J. Carter, J. S. Hussey, R. Varney, C. Walker; *Treasurer*, Benjamin Hepworth; *Secretary*, William Ray, F.C.S., F.I.C., School of Science, Kidderminster.

WORCESTER TRICYCLE CLUB (Camera Section) Founded April 7, 1892. Headquarters, Bell Hotel. Meetings every Thursday. *President*, A. Gyngell; *Council*, J. Cam, W. Cam, F. E. Hill, S. Hill, T. James, J. F. Santonna, and the Treasurer; *Hon. Treasurer*, F. E. Hill; *Hon. Secretary*, Thos. J. Hobson, Laurel Villa, Boughton Street, St. John's, Worcester.

WYLDE GREEN CAMERA CLUB Established 1889. Ordinary meetings, last Friday in every month, at 8 P.M., at the Town Hall, Sutton Coldfield. Annual meeting, last Friday in November. *President*, The Mayor of Sutton Coldfield, Alderman A. H. Evans, J.P.; *Vice-Presidents*, J. B. Stone, J.P., Alderman H. H. Plante, J.P., G. H. Dugard; *Council*, W. Betts and C. J. Fowler; *Hon. Treasurer*, T. S. Hooper; *Hon. Secretary*, C. Harold Harcourt, The Sycamores, Sutton Coldfield, near Birmingham.

YORK PHOTOGRAPHIC SOCIETY Established 1887. Meetings first Tuesday in the month, at the Victoria Hall. *President*, F. Vincent; *Vice-President*, H. C. Swailes; *Council*, G. Pawson, A. C. Hick, A. J. T. Ogden, R. Redpath; *Treasurer*, R. Bainbridge; *Secretary*, F. G. Benson, 50 Scott Street, York.

YORKSHIRE COLLEGE PHOTOGRAPHIC CLUB Established 1881. Meetings are held on the last Thursday in each month throughout the College session at 7:30 P.M. Annual meeting in June. *President*, Professor Jacob, M.D.; *Committee*, C. H. Bothamley, F.I.C., F.C.S., A. E. Nichols, J. Kitchen; *Secretary* and *Treasurer*, Harry B. Hall, 20 Regent Terrace, Edwin Road, Leeds.

YORKSHIRE PHILOSOPHICAL SOCIETY (Photographic Section) Established 1888. *President*, Tempest Anderson, M.D., B.Sc., &c.; *Vice-Presidents*, W. Monkhouse and J. N. Kitching; *Committee*, J. T. Atkinson, H. D. Taylor, Dr. Bateman, B. Wales; *Secretary* and *Treasurer*, Henry R. Moiser, F.G.S., Heworth Grange, York.

Societies in India, Australia, New Zealand, China, and Japan (1892)

AUCKLAND CAMERA CLUB *President*, Mr. Sturtevant; *Secretary*, Robert B. Walrond, St. Stephen's Avenue, Parnell, Auckland.

AUCKLAND PHOTOGRAPHIC CLUB General meetings, the second Friday in each month. Annual meeting in October. Club rooms, Australian Mutual Provident Society's Buildings, Queen Street, Auckland. *President*, Dr. J. Logan Campbell; *Vice-Presidents*, Josiah Martin and J. R. Hanna; *Committee*, R. L. Caldwell, W. C. Frazer, T. Humphries, A. J. Hunter; *Hon. Treasurer*, R. Indson; *Hon. Secretary*, G. R. Boulton, Bank near Southwalls, Queen Street.

FOOCHOW (CHINA) CAMERA CLUB *President*, G. Siemssen; *Vice-President*, F. J. Rentzsch; *Hon. Treasurer*, H. W. Churchill; *Hon. Secretary*, J. Mencarini.

INDIA, PHOTOGRAPHIC SOCIETY OF Established 1886. Ordinary meetings are held every Thursday evening at 6:30 P.M., at the Club Room, 57 Park Street, Calcutta. Annual meeting takes place in May. *President*, Sir Comer Petheram, Bart., Q.C.; *Vice-Presidents*, J. G. Apcar and J. S. Gladstone; *Committee*, P. Donaldson, N. Giannacopulo, A. Tocher, J. H. Lane, A. L. H. Palmer, T. H. Wilson, W. H. Jobbins, E. M. Showers, Colonel M. W. Rogers, R.E.; *Treasurer*, George Ewing; *Secretary*, T. Archdale Pope, 57 Park Street, Calcutta, India.

JAPAN, PHOTOGRAPHIC SOCIETY OF Established June, 1889. *President*, Viscount Enomoto, *Vice-Presidents*, Professor D. Kikuchi, M.A. (Cantab.), Dr. E. Divers, F.R.S., Count U. Toda; Viscount N. Okabe, Prof. C. D. West, M.A.; *Treasurers*, A. T. Hare and Y. Isawa; *Secretaries*, Professor I. Ishikaua and Professor W. K. Burton.

MADRAS, AMATEUR PHOTOGRAPHIC SOCIETY OF Meetings last Tuesday in each month at 6 P.M. *Patrons*, H. E. The Right Hon. Lord Connemara, G.C.I.E., Governor of Madras, and H. E. Lieut.-General Sir Charles G. Arbuthnot, K.C.B., R.A., Commander-in-Chief, Madras. *President*, F. Dunsterville; *Vice-Presidents*, G. Oppert, Ph.D., and C. V. Sundaram Sastri; *Committee*, R. H. Cama, I.M.D., T. M.

Horsfall, C.S., D. E. W. Leighton, C. Michie Smith, B.Sc., F. H. Trevithick, The Zemindar of Challypully; *Secretary* and *Treasurer*, T. Wake, Egmore, Madras.

NORTHERN TASMANIAN CAMERA CLUB Meetings on the second Friday in each month at 7:30 P.M. *President*, William Aikenhead; *Vice-President*, H. A. Roome, M.B.; *Committee*, J. Bosner, R. L. Parker, J. Lay; *Secretary*, *Treasurer* and *Librarian*, F. Styant-Browne.

QUEENSLAND AMATEUR PHOTOGRAPHIC SOCIETY Club rooms and dark room at Hunter's Treasury Buildings, George Street, Brisbane. Ordinary meetings held on the first Friday in each month. *President*, J. W. Sutton; *Vice-Presidents*, J. Thomson, M.B., F. R. Hall, D. T. Lyons; *Committee*, N. G. Chancellor, H. J. Cottell, T. Bertinshaw; *Curator*, W. S. A. Hunter; *Treasurer*, J. Campbell; *Hon. Secretary*, A. R. L. Wright, Permanent Building Society Chambers, Adelaide Street, Brisbane.

QUEENSLAND PHOTOGRAPHIC SOCIETY Established 1884. Ordinary meetings held on the 15th of each month. *President*, Hon. A. C. Gregory, M.L.C., F.R.G.S.; *Vice-Presidents*, Professor J. H. Pepper, J. W. Sutton, W. C. Hume; *Committee*, D. T. Lyons, T. Mirfin, H. W. Fox; *Librarian*, F. R. Hall; *Treasurer*, C. A. Gilder; *Hon. Secretary*, C. M. Allen, Diocesan Registry, George Street, Brisbane.

SOUTH AUSTRALIAN AMATEUR PHOTOGRAPHIC SOCIETY Meetings held at the Chamber of Manufacturers on the second Thursday in each month, at 8 P.M. *President*, His Excellency the Right Hon. the Earl of Kintore, G.C.M.G.; *Vice-Presidents*, Dr. Cockburn, Professor Bragg, Dr. Rennie; *Chairman*, S. J. Dailey; *Vice-Chairman*, G. Stace; *Committee*, J. Robertson and A. Kirchner; *Treasurer*, R. B. Adamson; *Hon. Secretary*, F. C. Krichauff, Office of the Superintendent of Public Buildings.

SYDNEY AMATEUR PHOTOGRAPHIC SOCIETY Meetings on the second Thursday in each month. *President*, E. L. Monteflore; *Vice-Presidents*, H. Paterson and J. H. Simpson; *Hon. Secretary*, Henry Chapman, 143 King Street, Sydney.

TASMANIAN PHOTOGRAPHIC AND ART ASSOCIATION Established 1887. Meetings at the Royal Society's Museum, on the second Friday in each month. A dark room is available for visitors. *Patron*, His Excellency Sir Robert G. C. Hamilton, K.C.B.; *Vice-Patrons*, His Honor Sir Lambert Dobson and Hon. Dr. Agnew; *President*, Curzon Allport; *Vice-Presidents*, Russell Young, R. Henry, E. Scott, A. Morton, J. F. Echlin. *Committee*, A. L. Butler, E. R. Ash, W. J. Beattie, H. Downing, R. McGuffie, W. R. Morris, R. Shepherd; *Treasurer*, F. J. Paterson; *Secretary*, Nathaniel Oldham, 92 Argyle Street, Hobart.

VICTORIA, AMATEUR PHOTOGRAPHIC ASSOCIATION OF, MELBOURNE The Association meets on the second Tuesday in each month at the Royal Society's Hall, Victoria Street, Melbourne. Visitors from British, American or Continental societies will be made welcome at any of the meetings. *President*, E. C. Bell; *Vice-Presidents*, F. A. Kernot and John Lang; *Committee*, J. H. Mulvany, H. C. Ward, J. McEwan, A. M. Henderson, E. J. Hughes; *Hon. Librarian*, E. A. Walker; *Scientific Custodian*, R. W. Harvie; *Hon. Treasurer*, J. J. Fenton; *Hon. Secretary*, J. H. Harvey, 278 Victoria Parade, East Melbourne.

VICTORIA CAMERA CLUB Established 1887. Meetings on the first Monday in each month. Field meetings every three weeks in summer. *President*, Hon. F. S. Dobson, LL.D.; *Vice-President*, A. M. Henderson; *Committee*, James Pettigrew, A. Harper, H. B. Clutten; *Secretary* and *Treasurer*, Alfred Henry Farmer, 54 Elizabeth Street, Melbourne.

Appendix

CATALOG OF LOST DAGUERREOTYPE VIEWS OF THE AMERICAN WEST

Before he became San Francisco's leading photographer in the 1850s, Robert Vance completed one of the first photographic documentaries of the American West—over 300 daguerreotype views (in whole-plate size, 6½ x 8½ inches) of California during 1849–50. Vance was apparently an Easterner who went to California in the gold rush with a camera instead of a pick and shovel. He took views of people and activities in the mines, and of California scenery, creating a collection of considerable note which he placed on exhibit in New York City in 1851. But the photographs did not sell, and Vance returned to California in 1852, leaving them behind for a second offering in 1853. Today the views are not known to exist, and it has been speculated that they were lost in Ohio or in the San Francisco earthquake and fire in 1906. Still others believe they will someday be found. Following is a catalog of the principal views in the collection published in an 1853 photographic journal:

1. Panoramic view of San Francisco, from the top of Union Hotel in Portsmouth Square. Showing the whole surrounding country, bay, and islands.
2. Views of San Francisco, before and after the May fire, taken from the top of Russia Hill, north of the City.
3. View of Clay street, before and after the fire, taken from Dupont street.
4. Views of Central street, before and after the fire, taken from Kearney street.
5. View of California street, between Montgomery and Sanson streets.
6. Panoramic view of San Francisco, from the corner of Montgomery and Broadway streets, before the May fire, showing the shipping, and Mission lands in the distance.
7. View of the burnt district, from the corner of Montgomery and Broadway streets; four days after the May fire.
8. View of the burnt district, from the corner of Montgomery and Broadway; after the June fire.
9. View of the west side of Montgomery street, from Clay Street, before the May fire.
10. View of the same after the fire.
11. Panoramic view of Stockton, from the top of the Stockton House, showing the whole surrounding country.
12. View of Stockton House.
13. Panoramic view of San Francisco, from Powell street.
14. Ruins of the city next day after the May fire, from the head of California street.
15. Ruins of the burnt district, from Powell street; after the June fire.
16. View of Telegraph Hill, from Union Hotel.
17. Views of Jackson street; before and after the May fire.
18. Views of Sacramento street; before and after the fire.
19. East side of Portsmouth square; before and after the fire.
20. End of central Wharf, and shipping.
21. Belle Union—Sociedad and Louisiana gambling houses, on the north side of Portsmouth square.
22. View of Dupont street, from Clay-st.
23. Merchants street, and east side of Portsmouth square; before the fire.
24. Merchants street; after the fire.
25. Views of Sanson street; before and after the fire.
26. Views of California street; before and after the fire.
27. Montgomery street; before and after the fire.
28. View of the end of Pacific Wharf.
29. View of Oriental Hotel.
30. Part of Central Wharf, from Whitehall Hotel—east view.
31. West view of Central Wharf, from same place.

32. West side of Portsmouth square; before fire. West side of Portsmouth square; after fire.

33. South side of Portsmouth square.

34. Cunningham's Wharf and Yerba Buena Island, in the bay.

35. Stockton street, from Clay Street.

36. Broadway, from Powell street.

37. Washington street, from Dupont street.

38. Kearney street, from Broadway; on election day.

39. Panoramic view of San Francisco, from the top of Telegraph Hill; showing the entrance to the bay, from the ocean, the opposite coast of Sancelita, Angel Island, and entrance to San Pablo bay.

40. View of Telegraph Hill, from Clay street.

41. View of Pacific street.

42. Mining scene in a street of Placerville.

43. Panoramic view of Placerville, from a Hill east of City; this being the first place of arrival for those crossing the Plains.

44. View of Coloma, from a Hill north of the place on the west side of the river.

45. Coloma; showing river and surrounding country.

46. View of Capt. Sutter's saw-Mill and dam across the American river.

47. Rear view of the saw-mill race, where the gold was first discovered by Capt. Sutter.

48. View of Main street, Coloma, from the court House.

49. Panoramic view of Coloma, from the east side of the river.

50. View of Coloma, from the west side of the river.

51. Panoramic view of Sonora.

52. Holden's Garden at Sonora, from which the largest lump of gold ever found, was taken, weighing twenty-eight pounds.

53. View of Yuba city, on Feather river, mouth of the Yuba river.

54. View of Main street, Makelame.

55. Panoramic view of Makelame, with ball mountain in the background.

56. Indian hut near Yuba city.

57. View of Indians on the Stanislaus river, dressed for a war dance.

58. Valley of Stanislaus river at Knight's ferry.

59. View of Malones, on Carson's creek, foot of gold mountain, in which is the richest quartz vein in the world, one company alone taking out $25,000 per week!

60. Evening view at Knight's ferry on the Stanislaus river.

61. Residence of Capt. Webber, at Stockton.

62. View of Indian commissioners, Dr. Wozencraft, Col. Johnson, Indian agent, and clerks, in treaty with the Indians.

63. View of Hangtown.

64. Scenery of Yuba river near Marysville.

65. View of Indian village on Capt. Sutter's plantation.

66. Indian village near Yuba city.

67. View of four Indian chiefs, and wife and sister of the celebrated chief Kasuse.

68. A group of Indian chiefs on the Feather river.

69. Indian village on the Stanislaus river.

70. Indians, cooking.

71. View of Indians dressed for a dance.

72. Indian, dancing.

73. Miners at work on little deer creek, at Nevada.

74. View of gold run.

75. View of Mission church, three miles from San Francisco. This Mission, Dolores, now time-worn and crumbling to ruins, was a proud and influential religious establishment, of the days of the Jesuits, founded more than a century ago, and even up to the time of the deposition of the late government, was considered one of the most interesting Spanish missions in the whole of California.

76. Part of the Mission church changed to a Hotel, with Green and Bowen's omnibuses in front.

77. Spanish house near the mission, with omnibus in front.

78. Panoramic view of the mission and surrounding country.

79. View of the mission, taken from the hill south of the church, showing the country between it and San Francisco.

80. View of miners at work near Nevada; showing the manner of washing gold with the Long Tom.

81. Miners at work on deer creek; showing the manner of sluice washing.
82. View of gold run, a mining district near Nevada.
83. Mining scene at Placerville.
84. and 85. Views—front and back of a saw-mill, near Nevada, worked by mule power.
86. Panoramic view of gold run; so called from the rich gold diggings, it being one of the first places where gold was discovered; the gold lying at a depth of thirty feet from the surface.
87. Miners at work at Gold run.
88. Mining scene at Sonora.
89. View of Central street, from a height south of the city.
90. Main street, Nevada.
91. View of Central street, Nevada.
92. Panoramic view of Nevada city, with the surrounding forest; giving the enormous size to which the trees attain in this region, some three hundred feet in height, and twenty-seven feet in circumference.
93. Panoramic view of Benicia, showing the Straits of Oarquines, on the opposite coast, Martinez village, with the surrounding country, also the U. S. Barracks, Pacific Steam Navigation Company's works, &c:; this place is a port of entry, and destined to be a place of first importance as a commercial city.
94. View of steamer Senator at the wharf.
95. View of steamer Confidence.
96. Jay street, Sacramento City, from the levee.
97. View of Hock farm, the residence of Capt. Sutter, on Feather river.
98. Hock farm, from the east side of the river.
99. View of Hock farm, from the top of the house, and the celebrated Bute mountains, sixteen miles distant.
100. Residence of Capt. Sutter; group in front, of the Captain, his daughter and son-in-law.
101. View of levee at Marysville, and steamers.
102. View of Hangtown.
103. Panoramic view of Acupulco, from a hill back of the city, showing the city, Fort, Harbor, with the steamers, Panama and Sea Bird, and others, lying at anchor.
104. Acupulco, from the bay, showing a front view of the city and mountains in the background.
105. Panoramic view of Panama, taken from the cathedral, showing the surrounding country, Island of Bogota, and others in the Pacific, ruins of various churches and monasteries.
106. View of the cathedral.
107. View of the Islands opposite Panama.
108. View of the cathedral at Cuzco, Peru.
109. View of a portion of Valparaiso, S.A.
110. Panoramic view of Marysville, California, from the top of the United States Hotel, giving a beautiful view of the surrounding country, with its forests of oak.
111. Ferry at Marysville, on the Yuba river.
112. View of Main-st., do.
113. A California theatre, at Marysville.
114. U. S. Hotel.
115. View of west side of the square.
116. View of south side of the square.
117. View of north side of the square.
118. Knight's ferry (Stanislaus river).
119. A view.
120. Washington, from the levee, at Sacramento.
121. View of the levee at Sacramento, taken from the south end.
122. Levee and river, from Washington, opposite.
123. Jay street, Sacramento, from top of the hotel in 2d street.
124. Panoramic view of Sacramento, with surrounding country, giving a view of Washington, opposite, separated by the Sacramento river.
125. Hotel, cor. of second and Jay street.
126. East and south view of Sutter's fort.
127. North and east view of Sutter's fort.
128. Part of first street and levee.
129. Portrait of Capt. Sutter.
130. English Admiral's house, Valparaiso, S.A.
131. View of Valparaiso, from the American counsel's residence, showing fort and barracks in the distance.

PUBLISHERS' ALBUMS, PORTFOLIOS AND BOOKS ILLUSTRATED WITH ORIGINAL PHOTOGRAPHS

(Examples of Nineteenth-Cenutry Items Occasonally To Be Found at Auctions, Photography Galleries, or Old Book Stores)

ANDERSEN, HANS CHRISTIAN *The Improvisators: or Life in Italy* (London, circa 1873), illustrated with 60 albumen photographs depicting views of Rome, portraits of Romans, etc.

ANNAN, THOMAS Limited edition of a portfolio of 40 photographs of the Glasgow slums prepared for the Glasgow City Improvement Trust (Glasglow, 1878). Annan was considered the leading Scottish portrait photographer of his day. He introduced the carbon photographic process in Scotland in 1866.

———— *The Old Country Houses of the Old Glasgow Gentry* (Glasgow, 1878), illustrated with 100 Woodburytypes. Second edition limited to 225 copies.

———— *Days at the Coast* (Glasgow, circa 1868), illustrated with 12 photographs.

AUCHINCLOSS, WILLIAM S. *Ninety Days in the Tropics, or Letters from Brazil* (Wilmington, Del., 1874), illustrated with 9 photographs of the harbor of Rio de Janeiro, native inhabitants, Bahia, St. Thomas, etc.

BALDWIN LOCOMOTIVE WORKS *Baldwin Locomotive Works* (Philadelphia, 1881), a 101-page catalog with 18 colotypes of Baldwin locomotives and other line drawings.

BEDFORD, FRANCIS *North Wales* (circa late 1870s). Album of 20 4 x 6½-inch albumen photographs.

BEECHER, H. C. *A Trip To Mexico* (Toronto, 1880), illustrated with 6 photographs.

BLACK, C. C. *Michael Angelo Buonarroti* (London, 1875), a biography of the sculptor, painter, and architect illustrated with 20 carbon prints.

BLANQUART-EVRARD, L. D. *Album Photographie de L'Artiste et de L'Amateur* (Lille, 1851).

BOOTE AND NIVEN *Album Vistas de Buenos Aires* (Buenos Aires, 1880), illustrated with 29 albumen photographs of city views, Indians, etc. Prints vary in size from 2½ x 3½ to 7½ x 10 inches.

BOURNE, SAMUEL *Views in Kashmir* (1865), a portfolio of 25 mounted photographs taken by Bourne on his second Himalayan expedition in 1864. Fine copy from collection of the Duke of Argyle sold for $625 at a 1972 New York auction.

BURTON, W. K. *Japanese Earthquake at Ai-Gi* (Tokyo, 1891). Text by Prof. Milne illustrated with 29 large photographs taken mostly by W. K. Burton, secretary of the Photographic Society of Japan, and reproduced in "permanent" form by K. Ogawa, the noted Japanese photographer who visited and studied with various U.S. photographers in 1883–84. Eleven mounted photographs of the October 28, 1891, earthquake (probably from a copy of this portfolio) sold for $90 at a 1972 New York auction. The lot was not identified at the auction.

BYRNES, THOMAS *Professional Criminals of America* (New York, 1886), illustrated with 36 heliotypes, 34 consisting of 6 mug shots each.

CLIFFORD, CHARLES *Vistas del Capricho* (1856). Album containing 50 views of the palace of the Duke del Infantado at Guadalajara.

———— *Voyage en Espagne* (1858), illustrated with 400 photographs, some calotypes and some albumen prints, depicting the decaying grandeur of Spanish palaces of the fourteenth to sixteenth century, views of cathedrals, monuments, and scenery around major Spanish cities.

COOPER, THOMPSON (editor). *Men of Mark* (London, 1876–83). Five volumes with biographical notes by Cooper, and containing a total of 254 Woodburytype photographs of British royalty, statesmen, and literary figures. Photographs by Mayall, Downey, Adam-Salomon, and Carjat. A set of these volumes assembled from different sets (some with detached bindings; others with leaves disbound) sold for $350 at a 1972 New York auction.

CURTIS, EDWARD S. *The North American Indian* (New York, 1906–30), a limited edition of 500 sets, each set consisting of 20 books illustrated with photogravures and 20 portfolios, each containing 36 folio-size photogravures. The 36 photogravures from Portfolio 15 from one set of the limited edition, sold as a single lot (in mint condition) at a February 1972 New York auction, brought $2,585; whereas the same group of 36 photogravures from another set of the limited edition, sold individually, brought a total of only $620 at the same auction house four months later.

DARWIN, CHARLES *The Expression of the Emotions in Man and Animals* (1872), the first book illustrated with heliotypes from negatives by Oscar Rejlander (1813–75).

DELAMOTTE, PHILIP HENRY *Progress of the Crystal Palace at Sydenham* (London, 1885), a documentation of the re-erection of the palace with 160 photographs.

DOWNEY, W. AND D. *The Cabinet Portrait Gallery* (London, 1890; first series), an album containing 36 Woodburytype and carbon prints of British royalty and other celebrities.

DRAKE, SAMUEL ADAMS *Historic Fields and Mansions of Middlesex* (Boston, 1874), illustrated with 20 collotypes, eighteen from negatives by Boston area photographers.

DUCAMP, MAXIME *Egypt, Nubia, Palestine and Syria* (Paris, 1852; London, 1852), illustrated with 125 photographs prepared at the Blanquart-Evrard printing establishment at Lille.

DYER, THOMAS H. *The Ruins of Pompeii* (London, 1867), illustrated with 18 albumen photographs.

ELIOT, GEORGE *Romola* (London, 1888), illustrated with 20 size 5½ x 4-inch albumen photographs, mostly views of Florence.

EMERSON, PETER H. *Life and Landscapes of the Norfolk Broads* (London, 1886), a portfolio edition with 40 platinum prints and text by T. F. Goodall. Other illustrated works by Emerson include: *Pictures From Life in Field and Fen* (London, 1887); *Pictures of East Anglian Life* (London, 1888); *The Compleat Angler* (London, 1888); *Wild Life on a Tidal Water* (London, 1890); *On English Lagoons* (London, 1893); and *Marsh Leaves* (London, 1895).

ENGLAND, WILLIAM *Panoramic Views of Switzerland, Savoy and Italy* (circa 1864), an album of 77 photographs.

FARDON, GEORGE F. *San Francisco Album* (Herre and Bauer, circa 1856), an album said by its publishers to contain the earliest collection of views of an American city. Because of the gold rush, San Francisco became one of the most photographed of U.S. cities in the period 1849–55.

FLAGG, WILSON *The Woods and By-ways of New England* (Boston, 1872), illustrated with 22 heliotypes of New England landscapes.

FRITH, FRANCIS *Egypt, Nubia and Ethiopia Illustrated* (London, 1862), containing 100 mounted stereographs and explanatory text. Copy with minor foxing, and some leaves detached, brought $150 at a New York auction in 1971.

————— *Lower Egypt and Ethiopia* (London, circa 1862), containing 37 folio-size mounted photographs with explanatory text. Copy with some foxing, outer joints and corners worn, brought $300 at a New York auction in 1971.

————— *Upper Egypt and Ethiopia* (London, circa 1862), containing 37 folio-size mounted photographs with explanatory text. Copy with some foxing, outer joints and corners worn, brought $500 at a New York auction in 1971.

GARDNER, ALEXANDER *Photographic Sketch Book of the Civil War* (Washington, D.C., 1866, 2 vols.). Contains 100 mounted photographs by A. and J. Gardner, Timothy O'Sullivan, Pywell, Reekie, W. M. Smith, Knox, Woodbury, Wood and Gibson, and Barnard and Gibson. Copy lacking title pages sold for $2,500 at a 1972 auction in New York.

GEORGE, H. B. *The Oberland and Its Glaciers* (1866), a book illustrated with 28 photographs by Ernest Edwards.

GRUNDY, WILLIAM MORRIS *Sunshine in the Country* (1861), an anthology of poetry with 20 photographs by Grundy published posthumously in 1859.

GUILBERT, EDMUND *The Home of Washington Irving* (New York, 1867), a portfolio with text and 7 mounted photographs by George G. Rockwood.

HALL, MR. AND MRS. S. C. *The Book of the Thames* (London, 1867), illustrated with 15 albumen photographs and 140 line cuts.

HARRINGTON, JOHN *The Abbey and Palace of Westminster* (London, 1869), illustrated with 25 albumen photographs of the abbey and 15 of the palace, all by Harrington, who served as architectural photographer of Brighton.

HAYDEN, F. V. *Sun Pictures of Rocky Mountain Scenery* (New York, 1870), illustrated with 30 large photographs by Capt. A. J. Russell. Edition limited to 500.

HITTEL, JOHN S. *Yosemite: Its Wonders and Its Beauties* (San Francisco, H. H. Bancroft, 1868), illustrated with 20 photographs by "Helias," pseudonym at the time for Eadweard Muybridge.

Homes of American Statesmen (New York, 1854), by various authors, with a frontispiece photograph by John A. Whipple of the John Hancock House in Boston. Although considered the first book published in the United States with an original, tipped-in photograph, copies have sold at New York auctions for as little as $50 to $100.

HOWITT, WILLIAM AND MARY *Ruined Abbeys and Castles of Great Britain* (London, 1862). Book contains 27 photographs by William Bedford, G. W. Wilson, Roger Fenton, and others. Copy sold for 42 pounds ($97.44) at a 1972 London auction.

IRVING, WASHINGTON *A Legend of the Katskill Mountains* (New York, 1870), illustrated with 4 carbon prints by Napoleon Sarony of actor Joseph Jefferson in role of Rip van Winkle.

JACKSON, W. H. *Photographs of the Yellowstone National Park and Views in Montana and Wyoming Territories* (Government Printing Office, 1873), an album of 41 foliosize photographs taken by the F. V. Hayden western survey. Copy with some wearing of plates brought $5,750 at a 1971 New York auction.

JENNINGS, PAYNE *The English Lakes* (circa 1875), a portfolio with 18 mounted photographs, each accompanied by a page of text.

JEPHSON, JOHN MOUNTENEY *Narrative of a Walking Tour in Brittany* (London, 1859), illustrated with a stereograph frontispiece by Taylor. Book was issued with a box of 90 card stereographs of Brittany views.

————— *Shakespeare: His Birthplace, Home and Grave* (London, 1864), illustrated with 15 albumen photographs by Ernest Edwards.

KEBLE, JOHN *The Christian Year, Thoughts in Verse for the Sundays and Holidays Throughout the Year* (London, 1878), illustrated with 12 carbon prints from negatives by Fr. Overbeck.

KING, MOSES *Harvard and Its Surroundings* (Cambridge, 1882; 4th edition), illustrated with 40 Albertypes and numerous engravings.

KING, THOMAS STARR *The White Hills: Their Legends, Landscape and Poetry* (New York, 1870), illustrated with 4 original photographs and 60 additional illustrations.

KNEELAND, PROF. SAMUEL *The Wonders of Yosemite Valley, and of California* (Boston, 1871), illustrated with 10 mounted photographs by John P. Soule.

LEDGER, EDMUND *The Sun: Its Planets and Their Satellites* (London, 1882), illustrated with 3 Woodburytypes, one from a negative by the New York astrophysicist L. M. Rutherford.

LEMOINE, J. M. *Maple Leaves* (Quebec, 1865; 3rd series), illustrated with 21 albumen photographs.

LIECHTENSTEIN, PRINCESS MARIE *Holland House* (London, 1874, 2 vols.), illustrated with 37 Woodburytypes, principally from negatives by Philip H. Delamotte. Book also contains numerous engravings and lithographs.

LONGFELLOW, HENRY WADSWORTH *Hyperion: A Romance* (London, 1865), illustrated with 24 albumen photographs by Francis Frith.

LORCHERER, ALOIS *Photographisches Album der Zeitgenossen* (Munich, 1854), an album containing calotype portraits of celebrities.

MAUL AND POLYBLANK *Photographic Portraits of Living Celebrities* (London, 1856–59), a portfolio of portraits with biographical notices issued monthly as a single portrait with a page or two of letter press.

MAYHEW, HENRY *London Labour and the London Poor* (London, 1851), illustrated with engravings made from daguerreotypes by Richard Beard.

MCLEES AND BECK *Gallery of Photographic Portraits of Senators, Representatives and Delegates of 35th Congress* (Washington, circa 1856), containing 311 portraits which publishers stated were "in no instance a copy from a painting or engraving." Publishers also claimed book to be the "largest collection of perfectly authentic photographic portraits ever published."

MUYBRIDGE, EADWEARD *Animal Locomotion* (Philadelphia, 1887), 11 volumes and a series of portfolios containing 781 folio-size photographs printed by the Photogravure Company of New York.

NASMITH, JAMES, AND JAMES CARPENTER *The Moon: Considered as a Planet, a World and a Satellite* (London, 1874), illustrated with 24 photographs. Copy with minor foxing and binding shaken brought $110 at a New York auction in 1971.

NEWHALL, JAMES R. *Centennial Memorial of Lynn, Essex County, Massachusetts*, (Lynn, Mass., 1876), illustrated with 7 Albertypes depicting views of the city and its buildings.

PAYN, JAMES *The Lakes in Sunshine* (London, 1868), illustrated with 14 mounted photographs by Garnett and Sproat.

PERKINS, FRED B. *The Central Park* (New York, 1864), illustrated with 52 photographs by W. H. Guild, Jr.

PIOT, EUGÈNE *Italie Monumentale* (May 1851–?).

PONTI, CARLO *Ricordo di Venezia*, a series of albums published during the 1860s, each containing 20 large views (some by other photographers).

READ, WILLIAM J. *Sketches of a Summer Tour* (New York, 1866), privately printed with 11 albumen photographs of European scenes and personages.

REID, JOHN EATON *A History of the County of Bute* (1864), illustrated with 9 photographs by Thomas Annan.

RICHARDSON, CHARLES F. AND HENRY A. CLARK *The College Book* (Boston, 1878), a history of such institutions as Harvard, Yale, Cornell, William and Mary, Rutgers, etc., illustrated with numerous heliotypes.

RITCHIE, LADY *Alfred, Lord Tennyson and His Friends* (1893), illustrated with 26 photogravures by Julia Margaret Cameron and her son, Henry H. H. Cameron. Edition limited to 400.

SCOTT, SIR WALTER *Marmion* (1866), illustrated with photographs by Thomas Annan.

———— *The Poetical Works of Sir Walter Scott*, with a memoir of the author (London, Edinburgh, New York, 1864), illustrated with two albumen photographs of Loch Katrine.

———— *The Lord of the Isles* (London, 1871), illustrated with 9 mounted photographs by S. Thompson and Russell Sedgfield. Copy was sold for 12 pounds ($27.84) at a 1972 London auction.

SEDDON, JOHN P. *Rambles in the Rhine Provinces* (London, 1868), illustrated with 14 size 6 x 4½-inch albumen photographs of views near the Rhine and other illustrations.

SKEEN, W. L. H. AND CO. *Photographs of Ceylon* (Colombo, circa late 1880s), an album with 18 size 6 x 8-inch mounted albumen photographs depicting the architecture, antiquities, and inhabitants of Ceylon.

SMITH, THEOPHILUS *Sheffield and Its Neighborhood* (London, 1865), illustrated with 16 albumen photographs.

SMYTH, C. PIAZZI *Teneriffe, An Astronomer's Experiment* (London, 1858), illustrated with 19 albumen stereograph photographs. Although the first book published with stereograph illustrations, a copy brought only $65 at a 1971 auction in New York.

SOLEY, JAMES RUSSELL *Historical Sketch of the United States Naval Academy* (Washington, D.C., 1876), illustrated with 24 photographs of buildings, ships, grounds, students at work, etc.

STACKELBERG, BARONESS *The Life of Carmen Sylva* (London, 1890), a life of the Queen of Roumania translated from the German by Baroness Deichmann, illustrated with 5 Woodburytypes (one scene and 4 portraits).

STARK, JAMES H. *Stark's Illustrated Bermuda Guide* (Boston, 1884), illustrated with 16 collotypes, maps, and engravings.

STIEGLITZ, ALFRED *Picturesque Bits of New York and Other Studies* (New York, R. H. Russell, 1898) a portfolio with 12 phogravures on 14 x 17 paper.

STIRLING, WILLIAM *Annals of the Artists of Spain* (1847–48), illustrated with 66 calotypes printed at W. H. Fox Talbot's printing establishment. Book was first on art illustrated with photographs. Edition was limited to 25.

SWEETSER, M. F. *Views in the White Mountains* (Portland, Me., 1879), a portfolio containing 12 folio-size Albertypes, some of locomotives.

TALBOT, WILLIAM H. FOX *The Pencil of Nature* (London, 1844–46), issued in six parts, the set illustrated with 24 calotypes, each accompanied by a commentary. This was the world's first photographically illustrated book. A copy brought $6,500 at a 1971 auction in London.

————— *Sun Pictures in Scotland* (1845), a portfolio of 23 calotypes without accompanying text. Copy with faded prints brought $3,000 at a 1972 London auction.

TALLIS, JOHN *History and Description of the Crystal Palace* (London, 1851), illustrated with engravings made from daguerreotypes taken by Richard Beard.

TENNYSON, ALFRED *The Idylls of the King* (1874 and 1875), illustrated with 24 photographs by Julia Margaret Cameron.

THOMSON, JOHN *The Antiquities of Cambodia* (1867), illustrated with 16 size 8 x 10-inch photographs.

————— *Illustrations of China and Its People* (1873–74), four volumes illustrated with 200 photographs, many of them of street scenes and street traders.

————— *Through Cyprus With a Camera* (1879), two volumes illustrated with 60 photographs.

————— AND A. SMITH *Street Life in London* (1877), illustrated with 36 Woodburytypes.

WHEELER, J. TALBOYS *The History of the Imperial Assemblage at Delhi, January 1, 1877,* illustrated with 24 Woodburytypes by Samuel Bourne and other photographers.

WILLIAMS, JAMES LEON *The Home and Haunts of Shakespeare* (London, 1892), a limited edition of 300 numbered sets of five portfolios, containing 45 folio-size photogravures, 15 plates in watercolor, and 150 halftone illustrations with the text.

WILSON, GEORGE WASHINGTON *Scottish Scenery* (circa 1870s), an album with 10 photographs, several of Edinburgh.

————— *Photographs of English and Scottish Scenery: Gloucester Cathedral* (Aberdeen, 1866), illustrated with 12 photographs accompanied with text.

————— *Edinburgh and Scottish Scenery* (no date), an album of 30 photographs. Copy with 4 loose prints sold for 85 pounds ($197.20) at a 1972 auction in London.

WRIGHT, HENDRICK *Historical Sketches of Plymouth, Luzerne County, Pa.* (Philadelphia, 1873), illustrated with 23 mounted photographs.

Bibliography

BIBLIOGRAPHY

BONI, ALBERT *Photographic Literature: An International Bibliographical Guide to General and Specialized Literature*, New York, Morgan & Morgan, 1962.

BROTHERS, ALFRED *Photography: Its History, Processes, Apparatus & Materials*, London, Charles Griffin & Co., 1892.

DARRAH, WILLIAM CULP *Stereo Views, A History of Stereographs in America and Their Collection*, Times & News Publishing Co., Gettysburg, Pa., 1964.

EDER, JOSEF MARIA *The History of Photography*, translated by Edward Epstean, New York, Columbia University Press, 1945.

GERNSHEIM, HELMUT *Creative Photography*, Boston, Boston Book & Art Shop, 1962.

———— AND ALISON *The History of Photography*, London, Thames & Hudson, 1969, revised from an earlier (1955) edition.

HARRISON, W. JEROME *A History of Photography*, New York, 1887. Available in reprint from Arno Press, New York, N.Y.

JUDGE, ARTHUR W. *Stereoscopic Photography*, London, 1950.

EDITORS OF LIFE. *Caring for Photographs, Display, Storage, Restoration*, New York, Time, Inc., 1972.

LOTHROP, EATON S., JR. *A Century of Cameras*, Morgan & Morgan, Dobbs Ferry, N.Y., 1973.

MATHEWS, OLIVER *Early Photographs and Early Photographers*, New York, London, Toronto, Pitman Publishing Corp., 1973.

NEWHALL, BEAUMONT *The History of Photography from 1839 to the Present Day*, New York, 1964.

———— *On Photography. A Source Book on Photo History in Facsimile*, New York, 1956.

———— *The Daguerreotype in America*, New York, 1961.

———— AND NANCY *Masters of Photography*, New York, 1958.

RINHART, FLOYD AND MARION *American Daguerreian Art*, New York, Clarkson N. Potter, 1967.

———— *American Miniature Case Art*, New York, A. S. Barnes and Company; London, Thomas Yoseloff, Ltd., 1969.

ROOT, MARCUS A. *The Camera and The Pencil, or The Heliographic Art*, 1864. Available in reprint from Helios Press, Pawlet, Vt.

RYDER, JAMES F. *Voigtlander and I*, Cleveland, 1902. Available in reprint from Arno Press, New York, N.Y.

TAFT, ROBERT *Photography and The American Scene*, New York, Macmillan, 1938. Available in reprint from Dover Publications, New York, N.Y.

WERGE, JOHN *The Evolution of Photography*, London, 1890. Available in reprint from Arno Press, New York, N.Y.

Notes

NOTES

1. W. Jerome Harrison, Nov. 13, 1855, from a lecture on the progress of photography recorded in *Anthony's Photographic Bulletin*, vol. 18, Feb. 26, 1887, pp. 105–107.

2. *Photographica*, vol. 5, no. 9, Nov. 1973, p. 5, monthly journal of the Photographic Historical Society of New York, Inc.

3. *Image*, vol. 14, no. 5–6, Dec. 1971, journal of the International Museum of Photography at George Eastman House, Rochester, N.Y.

4. *The New York Times*, April 18, 1972.

5. *Yesterday's Cameras*, March 1974, a privately circulated newsletter and registry for antique and classic cameras, edited by George Gilbert, Riverdale, N.Y.

6. *The New Yorker*, May 1, 1971, "On and Off the Avenue," by Janet Malcolm.

7. *The Wall Street Journal*, Oct. 8, 1974, "Why the Photography Market Is Booming," by Manuela Hoelterhoff.

8. *American Heritage*, vol. 18, no. 5, Aug. 1967, "One Man's Gold Rush: A Klondike Album," with text by Murray Morgan.

9. *American Heritage*, vol. 25, no. 2, Feb. 1974, "The Splendid Indians of Edward S. Curtis," by Alvin M. Josephy, Jr., p. 96.

10. *Humphrey's Journal*, vol. 3–4, April 15, 1852, "Burning of the National Daguerreotype Miniature Gallery," pp. 12–13.

11. *The Evolution of Photography*, by John Werge, London, 1890, p. 87.

12. *Anthony's Photographic Bulletin*, vol. 17, Jan. 9, 1886, pp. 4–6.

13. *Philadelphia Photographer*, vol. 8, Dec. 1871, p. 398.

14. *Photographic Times*, vol. 28, March 1896, pp. 125–26.

15. *Philadelphia Photographer*, vol. 14, April 1877, pp. 97–98.

16. *Newsweek*, Oct. 21, 1974, p. 64.

17. *The New York Times*, March 23, 1975, an interview with Lee Witkin, by Gene Thornton, Arts and Leisure section, p. 32.

18. *Popular Photography*, February 1974, "Critical Focus," by Kenneth Poli, p. 14.

19. *The History of Photography*, by Helmut and Alison Gernsheim, Thames and Hudson, London, 1969, p. 119.

20. Ibid.

21. *The Photographic Art-Journal*, vol. 5, June 1853, "Photography in the United States," pp. 334–41.

22. *Daguerreian Journal*, vol. 2, July 1, 1851, p. 115.

23. *U.S. Letters Patent, 9,354*, Oct. 26, 1852, awarded to Charles L'Homdieu, of Charleston, S.C., also referenced in *American Daguerreian Art*, by Floyd and Marion Rinhart, New York, Clarkson N. Potter, Inc., note 5, p. 108.

24. *Photography and the American Scene*, by Robert Taft, New York, Dover Publications, Inc., 1964, p. 92.

25. *The American Annual of Photography*, vol. 63, 1949, "The Preservation of Daguerreotypes," by Frank R. Fraprie, p. 204.

26. *Treatise of Photography on Collodion*, by Charles Waldack and P. Neff, Cincinnati, 1858, from the Introduction.

27. *American Journal of Photography*, vol. 2, n.s., 1859, pp. 75–77.

28. *Humphrey's Journal*, vol. 7, May 1, 1855, pp. 9–11.

29. *The American Annual of Photography*, vol. 63, 1949, "The Preservation of Daguerreotypes," by Frank R. Fraprie, p. 204.

30. *Journal of the Franklin Institute*, vol. 10, Aug. 1845, p. 116.

31. *Anthony's Photographic Bulletin*, vol. 19, June 23, 1888, article by Henry Hunt Snelling, pp. 368–69.

32. *The Evolution of Photography*, by John Werge, London, 1890, p. 70.

33. These views are now at the International Museum of Photography at George Eastman House, Rochester, N.Y.

34. *The History of Photography*, by Helmut and Alison Gernsheim, p. 119.

35. *The Corsair*, Feb. 22, 1840, p. 794. This publication was a New York gazette of literature, art, dramatic criticism, fashion, and novelty, published 1839–40.

36. *Photographica*, vol. 4, no. 9, Nov. 1972, p. 3.

37. *The American Annual of Photography*, vol. 63, 1949, "The Preservation of Daguerreotypes," by Frank R. Fraprie, p. 200.

38. *American Miniature Case Art*, by Floyd and Marion Rinhart, A. S. Barnes and Co., New York; Thomas Yoseloff, London, 1969, p. 41.

39. Ibid.

40. *The American Annual of Photography*, vol. 63, 1949, "The Preservation of Daguerreotypes," by Frank R. Fraprie, p. 200.

41. *American Miniature Case Art*, by Floyd and Marion Rinhart, A. S. Barnes and Co., New York; Thomas Yoseloff, London, 1969, pp. 184–89.

42. *Photographica*, vol. 3, no. 6, Oct. 1971, "A Letter From Eastman House," by Melissa Reed, p. 6.

43. Method provided courtesy of John H. Lindenbusch, Executive Director, Missouri Historical Society.

44. *Collectors' Guide To American Photography*, by Louis Walton Sipley, American Museum of Photography, Philadelphia, 1957, p. 17. The American Museum of Photography is no longer in existence; its

contents were purchased by the 3M Company, St. Paul, Minn.

45. *The History of Photography*, by Helmut and Alison Gernsheim, p. 238.

46. *Stereo Views*, by William Culp Darrah, Gettysburg, Pa., 1964, p. 30.

47. Ibid.

48. Ibid. p. 8.

49. Ibid.

50. *The History of Photography*, by Helmut and Alison Gernsheim, p. 257.

51. *Stereo Views*, by William Culp Darrah, Gettysburg, Pa., 1964, pp. 50–57.

52. Ibid., pp. 39; 102–06.

53. Ibid., p. 123.

54. Ibid., pp. 117–24.

55. Ibid., p. 121.

56. Ibid., p. 22.

57. *Philadelphia Photographer*, vol. 7, Jan. 1870, pp. 15–17.

58. *The History of Photography*, by Helmut and Alison Gernsheim, p. 295.

59. *Photography and The American Scene*, by Robert Taft, New York, Dover Publications, Inc., 1964, p. 149.

60. *The Photographic News*, Aug. 5, 1864, p. 383.

61. Photo caption, p. 58. The information pertaining to Perrin comes from '*Dear Old Kit*,' by Harvey Lewis Carter, University of Oklahoma Press, Norman, Okla., 1968. Carter uses the same illustration in his book (p. 97); however, he concludes (p. 233) that the seated man with Kit Carson is not Perrin, but Col. John C. Frémont, for whom Kit Carson served as a guide on three western U.S. expeditions in the 1840s. Carter refers to the photograph reproduced in '*Dear Old Kit*' as made from a "daguerreotype" provided by the Denver Public Library. He also states that the "daguerreotype" contains a "penciled notation on the back" (identifying the man with Kit Carson as Frémont), and that "prints" were available "for several years' after the "daguerreotype" was taken, which Carter asserts was probably 1849. The photograph from which the reproduction on page 58 of this book was made is a carte de visite. While daguerreotypes were copied in carte de visite format after 1860, this specimen is an original carte de visite which can be dated at about the time Perrin joined Kit Carson's forces. If the Denver Library photograph is, indeed, a daguerreotype, the "penciled notation" would have to be on a label affixed to the daguerreotype case or to the back of the image metal plate. "Prints" of the photograph would not have been available in carte de visite form in the 1850s, since cartes de visite were not made prior to 1860. Persons familiar with photographs of Frémont may also question Carter's identification of the seated man with Kit Carson. In 1849, Carson would have been 40 and Frémont 36; in 1861, Carson was 52 and Frémont 48.

62. Photo caption, p. 58. Meissonier was particularly influential in gaining recognition on the Continent for Eadweard Muybridge's photographic revelations of human and animal locomotion. On November 26, 1881, Meissonier gave Muybridge a large reception at his Paris residence, which was a major topic of news at the time. Muybridge projected life-size images on a screen of a horse in motion, using a zoöpraxiscope. For the first time, eminent artists and scientists of Paris, who were present at the reception, learned of the true phases of a horse's gait. Muybridge later said of the event: "M. Meissonier exhibits the greatest interest in my work, and through his commanding influence I have obtained a recognition here which is extremely gratifying and advantageous."

63. *Photography and The American Scene*, by Robert Taft, New York, Dover Publications, Inc., 1964, p. 349.

64. *Collectors' Guide To American Photography*, by Louis Walton Sipley, American Museum of Photography, Philadelphia, 1957, pp. 22–23.

65. *Image*, vol. 17, no. 1, March 1974, "Dating Early Photographs by Card Mounts and Other External Evidence: Tentative Suggestions," by Arnold R. Pilling, p. 12.

66. *The History of Photography*, by Helmut and Alison Gernsheim, p. 300.

67. *Humphrey's Journal*, vol. 6, July 1, 1854, "On The Production of Waxed Paper Negatives," by James How, pp. 90–95.

68. *Eye To Eye*, Sept. 1953, article on Missouri Historical Society photograph collection by Charles van Ravenswaay.

69. "Victor Prevost, Photographer, Artist, Chemist," an illustrated lecture by W. I. Scandlin, delivered before the Photographers Association of America, 21st annual convention, Detroit, Aug. 6, 1901.

70. *Humphrey's Journal*, vol. 14, June 15, 1862, article by Capt. De Champlouis, translated from the *Bulletin de la Société Française de Photographie*, p. 1.

71. *A History of Photography*, by W. Jerome Harrison, New York, 1887, p. 82.

72. *American Journal of Photography*, vol. 9, March 1888.

73. *Wilson's Photographic Magazine*, vol. 29, April 2, 1892, "The Various Kinds of Photographic Prints," by D. Bachrach, Jr., pp. 196–200.

74. *Image*, April 1955, "60,000 Eggs A Day," by Beaumont Newhall.

75. Ibid.

76. *Wilson's Photographic Magazine*, vol. 29, April 16, 1892, "The Various Kinds of Silver Prints," by D. Bachrach, Jr., pp. 231–34.

77. *Photography: Its History, Processes, Apparatus and Materials*, by Alfred Brothers, London, 1892, p. 245.

78. *The History of Photography*, by Helmut and Alison Gernsheim, p. 281.

79. *Philadelphia Photographer*, vol. 16, 1879, "On The Fading of Silver Photographs," by F. A. Wenderoth, pp. 130–33.

80. Ibid.

81. *The History of Photography*, by Helmut and Alison Gernsheim, p. 400.

82. Ibid., p. 402.

83. Ibid., pp. 399–400.

84. *Anthony's Photographic Bulletin*, vol. 18, April 23, 1887, article by W. E. Partridge, pp. 242–45.

85. *Wilson's Photographic Magazine*, vol. 29, April 16, 1892, "The Various Kinds of Silver Prints," by D. Bachrach, Jr., pp. 231–34.

86. Ibid.

87. *Wilson's Photographic Magazine*, vol. 34, Oct. 1897, "Printing Methods," by D. Bachrach, Jr., pp. 459–63.

88. *Creative Photography*, by Helmut Gernsheim, Boston, 1962, p. 249.

89. *Humphrey's Journal*, vol. 19, Jan. 1, 1868, pp. 259–60.

90. *A History of Photography*, by W. Jerome Harrison, New York, 1887, pp. 100–103.

91. Ibid., p. 105.

92. *Philadelphia Photographer*, vol. 10, July 1873, "Photo-Mechanical Printing," pp. 241–44; *Image*, Sept. 1957, "The Woodburytype," by J. S. Mertle, pp. 165–70.

93. *Image*, Sept. 1957, "The Woodburytype," by J. S. Mertle, pp. 165–70.

94. *The History of Photography*, by Helmut and Alison Gernsheim, pp. 548–49.

95. *Journal of the Society of Arts*, article by Ernest Edwards, April 28, 1871.

96. *The History of Photography*, by Helmut and Alison Gernsheim, p. 544.

97. *The American Journal of Photography*, vol. 10, May 1889, "The Limits of Photogravure," by A. Dawson, pp. 175–82.

98. Ibid.

99. *The History of Photography*, by Helmut and Alison Gernsheim, p. 244.

100. *Anthony's Photographic Bulletin*, vol. 25, Jan. 1, 1894, "The New Movement in England," by H. P. Robinson, pp. 8–11.

101. *Creative Photography*, by Helmut Gernsheim, Boston, 1962, p. 119.

102. Ibid., pp. 122–30.

103. *Anthony's Photographic Bulletin*, vol. 25, Jan. 1, 1894, "The New Movement in England," by H. P. Robinson, pp. 8–11.

104. *The New York Times*, Oct. 20, 1952.

105. *Anthony's Photographic Bulletin*, vol. 6, June, 1875, p. 192.

106. *The History of Photography*, by Helmut and Alison Gernsheim, p. 453.

107. *Photo Era*, vol. 2, Dec. 1898, p. 172.

108. *The History of Photography*, by Helmut and Alison Gernsheim, p. 447.

109. *American Heritage*, vol. 21, June 1970, "Take A Kodak With You—George Eastman Did," by Carla Davidson.

110. *Latent Image*, by Beaumont Newhall, New York, 1967, p. 62.

111. *Anthony's Photographic Bulletin*, vol. 1, Feb. 1870, p. 6.

112. *Anthony's Photographic Bulletin*, vol. 14, Feb. 1883, p. 62.

113. *Photographic Times*, vol. 6, July 1876, p. 49.

114. *Aperture*, vol. 15, Spring 1970, "French Primitive Photography," pp. 7–8.

115. *Harper's*, Aug. 1889.

116. *Photographic Times*, vol. 3, June 1873, p. 84.

117. *Photographic Times*, vol. 2, Dec. 1872, p. 182.

118. *Harper's*, Aug. 1889.

119. *Wilson's Photographic Magazine*, vol. 36, Feb. 1889, p. 93.

120. *Photographica*, vol. 6, June–July 1974, p. 3.

121. *William H. Fox Talbot*, by Andre Jammes, New York, Macmillan Publishing Co., 1972, p. 12.

122. *Philadelphia Photographer*, vol. 3, Jan. 1886.

123. *The History of Photography*, by Helmut and Alison Gernsheim, pp. 286–87.

124. *Popular Photography*, April 1973, "Photographic Portfolios: They're In, But Will They Sell?", by Jacob Deschin, p. 93.

125. *Philadelphia Photographer*, vol. 5, Feb. 1868.

126. *Photographic Times*, vol. 3, April 1873, pp. 66–67.

127. *Collectors' Guide To American Photography*, by Louis Walton Sipley, American Museum of Photography, Philadelphia, 1957, pp. 30–33.

128. *The First American Museum of the Photo-Graphic Arts*, American Museum of Photography, Philadelphia, 1956, p. 10.

129. *Anthony's Photographic Bulletin*, vol. 22, Feb. 14, 1891, pp. 73–75.

130. *The History of Photography*, by Helmut and Alison Gernsheim, p. 344.

131. Ibid., p. 342.

132. Ibid., p. 343.

133. *American Artisan*, vol. 1, Nov. 9, 1864, p. 215.

134. *The History of Photography*, by Helmut and Alison Gernsheim, pp. 318–19.

135. *Anthony's Photographic Bulletin*, vol. 2, June 1871, p. 226.

136. Regional U.S. photographer listing. The names in this list have been compiled from a number of sources, principally from listings in the *Daguerreian Journal*, Nov. 1, 1850, and Dec. 15, 1851; *The Daguerreotype in America*, by Beaumont Newhall (New York Graphic Society, N.Y., 1961); *American Daguerreian Art*, by Floyd and Marion Rinhart (New York, Clarkson N. Potter, 1967); *Picture Gallery Pioneers 1850 to 1875*, by Ralph W. Andrews (New York, Bonanza Books, 1964); reports on early photographer meetings in the August, September and October, 1851, and February 1853, issues of the *Photographic Art Journal*; articles by R. Bruce Duncan in the October 1971 and July 1972 issues of *Graphic Antiquarian*; and from numerous isolated references in other principal nineteenth-century photographic journals.

137. Turn-of-the-century "art" photographer listings. The information in these listings was compiled from several sources, including *Creative Photography*, by Helmut Gernsheim (Boston Book and Art Shop, Boston, 1962); *The Painterly Photograph*, an exhibi-

tion catalog prepared by Weston Naef and Suzanne Boorsch, The Metropolitan Museum of Art, New York, January 8, 1973; *Sun Artists*, a portfolio of monographic booklets issued between October 1889 and July 1891, edited by W. Arthur Boord; *Early Photographs and Early Photographers* by Oliver Mathews (Pitman, N.Y., Toronto, London, 1973); and isolated references in several turn-of-the-century American photographic journals.

138. *American Heritage*, Aug. 1968.

139. *Photography Collection, Humanities Research Center, The University of Texas*, a leaflet prepared by the center.

140. *Image*, vol. 14, Dec. 1971.

141. *Graphic Antiquarian*, July 1972, "The History of Photography at the Smithsonian Institution," by David Haberstich.

142. *The First American Museum of the Photographic Arts*, pamphlet prepared by the American Museum of Photography, Philadelphia, Pa., 1956.

143. *Picturescope*, vol. 19, no. 4, 1971.

144. *American Heritage*, Aug. 1972, "Local History Makes Good—Sometimes," by Walter Muir Whitehill.

145. *Old New York In Early Photographs*, by Mary Black, New York, Dover Publications, Inc., 1973.

146. *Chicago History*, vol. 4, no. 1, Fall 1964.

147. *Eye To Eye*, Sept. 1953, article by Charles van Ravenswaay.

148. *Picturescope*, vol. 24, no. 4, 1973.

Indexes

INDEX TO TEXT

INDEX TO ILLUSTRATIONS

Sumner, Charles, 66, 82